The World's Best Typography®

The 40th Annual of the
Type Directors Club

a — Zangezi Sans Black by Daria Petrova
b — TwoBit D, Extra Bold. TwoBit A, Black by MuirMcNeil

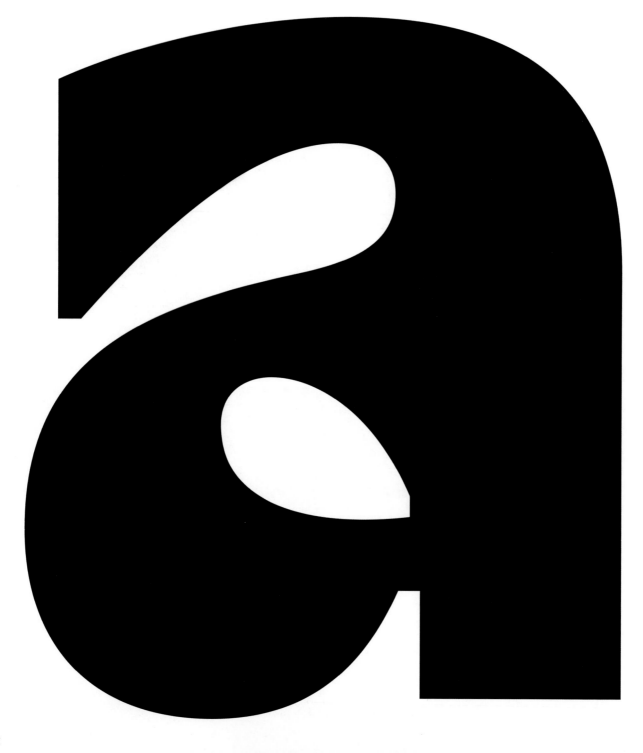

TDC Medal 2018
Fiona Ross

Linotype Bengali Extra Bold trial character by
Ananda Bazar Patrika designed under guidance
from Fiona Ross. (Non-Latin Type Collection,
University of Reading).

Fiona Ross photographed at
the University of Reading, 2019
by Andrew G. Hobbs

This year the Type Directors Club presented the TDC medal to Dr. Fiona Ross, in recognition of a forty-year career of working on typefaces seen and used by millions, alongside helping new generations of designers learn to address some of the most complex issues of supporting the world's languages typographically.

Fiona will not often describe herself as a typeface designer. Despite deep expertise, she will also not describe herself as an expert, but rather as a typographic specialist—a careful distinction typical of her deep respect for the complexity of writing systems beyond those with roots in the Latin alphabet. What she undeniably has is an incredibly sophisticated eye for understanding not just how these forms come together to represent languages, but also how they can perform well typographically. It has been through her evolving role as a type director for type development projects, guiding their forms as well as their fitness for purpose, that she has made such a significant impact on publishers and readers worldwide.

Fiona's involvement with type design and typography arose from her post-graduate studies in Sanskrit and Indian paleography. In 1978 she joined Linotype-Paul Limited in the United Kingdom as a research assistant, a specialist in languages and scripts with no clear career path forward. In time she succeeded Walter Tracy as manager of their department, becoming the company's first female manager. Fiona's small team—primarily staffed by women—was responsible for the design of Linotype's non-Latin fonts and typesetting schemes, notably those using Arabic, Indian, and Thai scripts. Their work served publishers in areas of the world that had typographic needs as pressing as anyone else's but whose writing systems are complex and historically compromised by Latin-centric type technologies. It was Fiona and this team at Linotype who made the effort not only to adapt typefaces for new technologies but also to properly research how those scripts ought to behave, in order to elevate them to the possibilities that were afforded by the developments in typesetting and type production. Over the years, it was the care and diligence and the collaboration with designers and local specialists that really made these typefaces dominate the areas of the world where they were used.

The work that came out of Linotype took on a life of its own because of its influence in the publishing sphere in India, the Middle East, and other related countries using some of these complex scripts. Although many of the typefaces were not commercially available outside of these large customer bases in the publishing world, they nevertheless have made their way into the marketplace in these regions.

For example, Linotype Bengali, which Fiona worked on with designer Tim Holloway, was a custom project for Anandabazar Patrika, an influential newspaper in Kolkata, India. While never available for

1
Fiona Ross at the University of Reading

2/3
Non-Latin scripts
From metal to digital type. Edited by Fiona Ross and Vaibhav Singh.

4
Fiona Ross and team at Linotype in the early '80s.

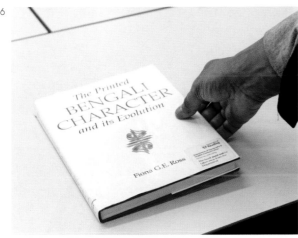

5
Ebela newspaper published by Ananda Bazar Patrika showing Sarkar Bold typeface designed by Tim Holloway, Neelakash Kshetrimayum and Fiona Ross.

6
The Printed Character and its Evolution by Fiona Ross. Published by RoutledgeCurzon.

7
Rubylith of ligature srii for production of digital photocomposition Linotype Bengali, ca. 1980

retail use, the fonts can be found used by Bengali speakers worldwide. That is the power of a design that strikes a chord with the audience that uses it. Originally, the design was criticized for being too traditional, looking too far back toward the manuscript tradition when people were accustomed to a version of the script that had been degraded by typesetting limitations. Today, decades of use has changed the view on this now-iconic design, and it is seen in many quarters as the defining representation of the Bengali script.

Fiona's working method—linguistic and historical research, challenging the perceived limitations of the medium, collaboration with talented designers and technologists—has raised the standard for the industry on the whole, thanks to projects clients such as Adobe, Apple, Monotype, Linotype, Bitstream, Dalton Maag, Vodaphone, Open University, and Quark. Much of Fiona's recent work has been in collaboration with Tiro Typeworks, working with John Hudson and a group of designers on a suite of typefaces for Harvard University's Murty Classical Library series, and new commissions from Anandabazar Patrika.

The other sphere of Fiona's substantial influence in our industry has been as an educator, working at the University of Reading in the UK since the late '90s. Fiona has taught a generation of type designers, guiding them not only about issues of design and linguistics, but also in research methodology. Her mentorship encourages them to draw on their own experience and perspective to help them make their own contributions with new typefaces for markets that are often so underserved by contemporary design. It is to Fiona's credit that so many of her students have gone on to well-placed positions working on typefaces for complex scripts, not simply replicating what she had to teach but having learned to take seriously the responsibility to support the world's languages. Rather than teaching style, Fiona teaches her students how to do the necessary work to treat these writing systems with respect while bringing new design sensibilities to them.

Fiona's keen eye, her teaching, her criticism, and her writing have made an incredible mark on many corners of the type industry, primarily for the benefit of the parts of the world that we in the West have not necessarily treated with parity. This has had an outsized impact on the regions that really benefit from the care she has practiced and championed during her long and influential career.

Dan Rhatigan

c — TwoBit A, Light by MuirMcNeil
d — Galapagos A, Regular by Felix Salut

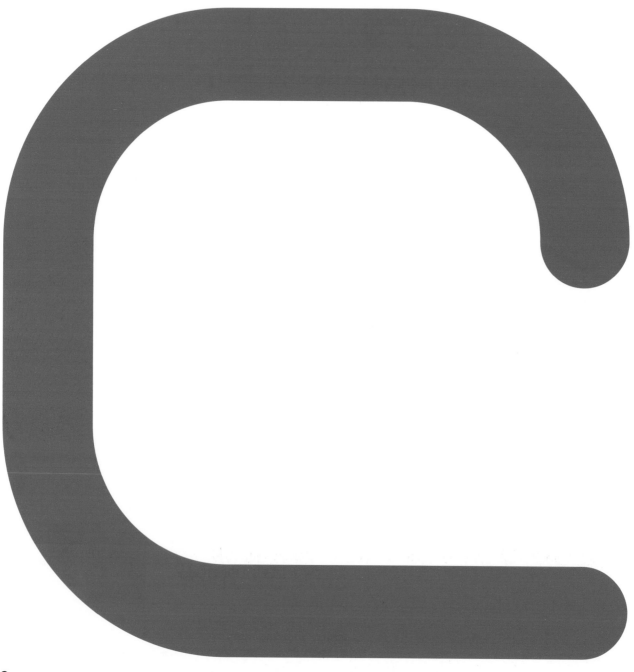

TDC65
Chair Statement

Meet the Judges

When TDC awards season is upon us, there's an excitement in the air. Carol Wahler, executive director of the Type Directors Club, initiates the methodical process that she has developed over her thirty-five years of running the competition.

A dedicated team of type lovers begins to gather, including Diego Vainesman, Matteo Bologna, Abby Goldstein, Deb Gonet, Gary Munch, Graham Clifford, Chris Andreola, and Allan and Adam Wahler. And an army of volunteers pitches in to collect and organize a dizzying number of posters, books, logos, and websites from all over the world.

It takes a village to pull off the preeminent competition showcasing The World's Best Typography.

I had only heard about this legendary process until it was my turn to get involved. It has been my honor to serve as chair of the Communication Design competition, in partnership with Nina Stössinger, chair of the Typeface Design competition. This year we celebrated the sixty-fifth annual Type Directors Club competition.

To develop the identity system, the campaign, and this annual, we reached out to international creative agency BOND, led by Hugh Miller and Ty Lou in their London office. They then reached out to Grilli Type and more than twenty other type designers from around the globe to deliver an appropriately representative visual system.

It was my responsibility to appoint a jury of the very best global thought leaders working in design today.

Karin Fong,
Leo Jung,
Eddie Opara,
Paulina Reyes,
Ian Spalter,
Annik Troxler and
Zipeng Zhu

agreed to give us their time and consideration. With this group of judges, the criteria we set for selection was simple: To be considered "The World's Best Typography," submissions had to feature type and typography in ways that raise the bar for those to come and push the industry forward.

Thousands of entries were narrowed to just 253 examples of typographic excellence. Wondering what that looks like? Catalina Kulczar documented the competition weekend for you.

It's incredible to me that for more than sixty-five years, so many have worked so tirelessly to pursue excellence in typography. The competition is not only incredibly important to sustaining the Type Directors Club, but it also is one of just a few unbroken records of our ever-changing industry. It is up to all of us to keep it going.

Bobby C. Martin Jr.
Chairman, TDC65
Communication Design

1
Grilli
Type

2

3

1. GT Walsheim by Grilli Type.

2. Ian, Leo and Zipeng - judging in progress.

3. Comunication Design social post by BOND.

4. Bobby C Martin Jr. and the Comunication Design Judges.

Karin Fong
Leo Jung
Eddie Opara
Paulina Reyes
Ian Spalter
Annik Troxler
Zipeng Zhu

Shot on location at Fordham University-Lincoln Center,
New York, by Catalina Kulczar

Karin Fong

Karin Fong is an Emmy Award winning director and designer working at the intersection of film, television, and graphic design. A founding member of Imaginary Forces, she is known for designing iconic title sequences. Her projects include the opening credits for the TV series Boardwalk Empire, South Park, and Black Sails, and most recently Lost In Space and Counterpart, as well as numerous feature films. She has helmed spots for major brands, including LEGO, Lexus, Target, Sony PlayStation, Toyota, and Herman Miller. From large scale video installations to video game trailers, Karin's diverse projects showcase her unique voice in visual storytelling.

Named by Fast Company as one of its 100 Most Creative People in Business and the recipient of the 2018 AIGA medal, she has won numerous awards in both advertising and entertainment. Her work has been featured at the Cooper-Hewitt National Design Museum, The Walker Art Center, The Wexner Center, SXSW, and in many publications about design and cinema.

imaginaryforces.com
@imaginary_forces_

1
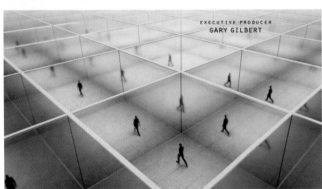

2

3

4

1/2
South Park
Main Title
Client: Comedy Central

3
Counterpart Main Title.
Client: STARZ

4
Rubicon Main Title
Client: AMC

Leo Jung

Leo Jung is Creative Director for the acclaimed live series Pop-Up Magazine and The California Sunday Magazine, which won the Society of Publication Design's award for Magazine of the Year in 2018. He is the former design director at Wired and deputy art director at The New York Times Magazine. His work has been recognized by the Art Directors Club, Type Directors Club, and the Society of Publication Designers.

leojung.com
californiasunday.com
popupmagazine.com

1

2

THE MAN

IN THE

3

DECK

BELOW

1,2,3.
Editorial spreads for
Califonia Sunday
Magazine.

Eddie Opara

Eddie Opara is a multi-faceted designer whose work encompasses strategy, design and technology. He is a partner in the New York office of Pentagram, where his projects have included the design of brand identity, publications, packaging, environments, exhibitions, interactive installations, websites, user interfaces and software, with many ranging across multiple media. His clients have included Samsung, Cooper Hewitt, Smithsonian National Design Museum, Nike, Quinnipiac University, Grace Farms, the Menil Foundation, The Baffler, Halstead, the Studio Museum in Harlem, Queens Museum, the Corcoran Group, New York University and Morgan Stanley.

Opara was born in Wandsworth, London, and studied graphic design at the London College of Printing and Yale University. He began his career as a designer at ATG, Imaginary Forces and 2×4, and ran his own studio, The Map Office, before joining Pentagram in 2010. He is a senior critic at the Yale University School of Art and a member of the Alliance Graphique Internationale. His work is represented in the permanent collection of the Museum of Modern Art. He is the author of Color Works (Rockport, 2014). He is the recipient of many awards and has been featured in Fast Company's 100 Most Creative People in Business, Ebony Magazine's Power 100 and Adweek's Creative 100.

pentagram.com

1
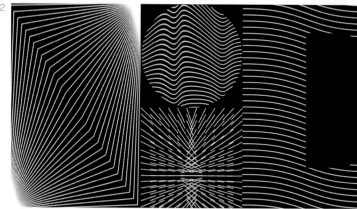

2
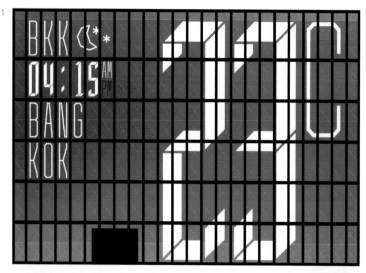

3

1
MahaNakhon
A dynamic seven-story digital installation at Bangkok's tallest tower activates its neighborhood and integrates the building into the surrounding cityscape.

2
FIT DTech Lab
Identity for the Fashion Institute of Technology

3
rə—inc
New lifestyle brand founded by members of the U.S. women's national soccer team.

Paulina Reyes

Paulina Reyes is the VP of Photo and Design at Refinery 29 in New York City. Over the last 20 years, Paulina has lent her creative expertise to prestigious companies, including: Plated, Mother New York, Collins, Kate Spade, Duffy Design, and Laurie DeMartino Design. In addition to her full-time work, Paulina has taught illustration at MCAD in Minneapolis and design at SVA in NYC.

Paulina's eclectic background has earned her recognitions from organizations such as ADC (Young Guns), Print Magazine (New Visual Artists), TDC, AIGA. Her work has been exhibited in national and international museums such as The Cooper Hewitt National Design Museum in New York City, The Field Museum of Natural History in Chicago and the Museo de Artes Populares in Mexico City where she's from.

paulinareyes.com

1

Jan 22 – Feb 1, 2015　　Park City, Utah

Sundance Film Festival

sundance.org/festival

2

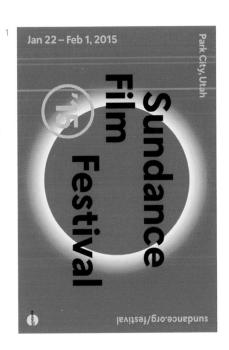

3

19/60　　　　Paulina

1
Sundance Film
Festival poster

2
Textile print for
WHIT spring

3
Snake Litho

Ian Spalter

Ian Spalter is Head of Design at Instagram, where he leads the team responsible for all things design ranging from cross-platform app experiences to brand & identity. Ian was previously a Sr. UX Manager at YouTube, and prior to that, Director of UX & Design at Foursquare.

Ian also spent four years at R/GA where he oversaw design development projects such as the Nike+ Fuelband and Nike Running, Basketball, and Training products. Ian was born and raised in New Rochelle, New York and graduated from Hampshire College.

instagram.com

1

2

1
Iconic Instagram
App Icon

2
Boomerang, Hyperlapse
& Layout icons

Annik Troxler

Annik Troxler is a Swiss graphic designer born 1979 in Willisau. She studied graphic design at the ECAL in Lausanne; now she works in the cultural field and teaches at the Basel School of Design. With a strong focus on content, narrative and visual quality, Annik Troxler creates posters and visual identities that use typography and images in unusual ways.

Her design methods combine a significant use of playful techniques and experimentation but a strong connection to the minimalistic functionalism is still apparent. Annik Troxler gives lectures and workshops in Europe and abroad and she has won several prizes such as in 2006 the Grand Prix of the International Poster Triennale of the Museum of Modern Art Toyama and the first prize at the International Poster Festival in Chaumont in 2007.

anniktroxler.ch

1

2

3

1—3
Expressive abstraction.
Jazz Festival Willisau
posters.

Zipeng Zhu

Zipeng Zhu is a Chinese-born designer, art director, illustrator and animator in New York City who wants to make everyday a razzle-dazzle musical. His clients include Coca-Cola, Microsoft, Netflix, Viacom, The New Yorker, Fox, CNN, Refinery29, Chobani, and Samsung. After he graduated from the School of Visual Arts in New York City, he has worked at Pentagram and Sagmeister & Walsh. He was one of the Art Directors Club Young Guns 13 winners and has been recognized as Print magazine's New Visual Artist and The One Show Young Ones. He has recently started his own creative studio Dazzle to make everything dazzling.

zz-is.it
@zzdesign

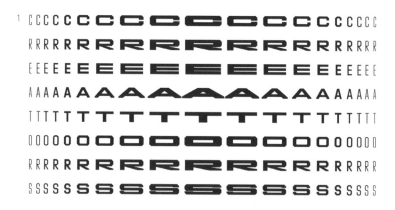

1
Creators
Design & Animation for Adidas commissioned by MCKL

2
New York
Graphic for Show Us Your Type

3
HongKong
Custom Lettering for Airbnb Magazine

Judging Cups
TDC Executive Director Carol Wahler introduced these charming and decorative cups in 1983 and has been using the same set of cups for the judging ever since. This is a continuation of the use of cups since the first judging in 1955.

e — TwoBit D Black. TwoBit A Extra Light by MuirMcNeil
f — Galapagos A, Regular by Felix Salut

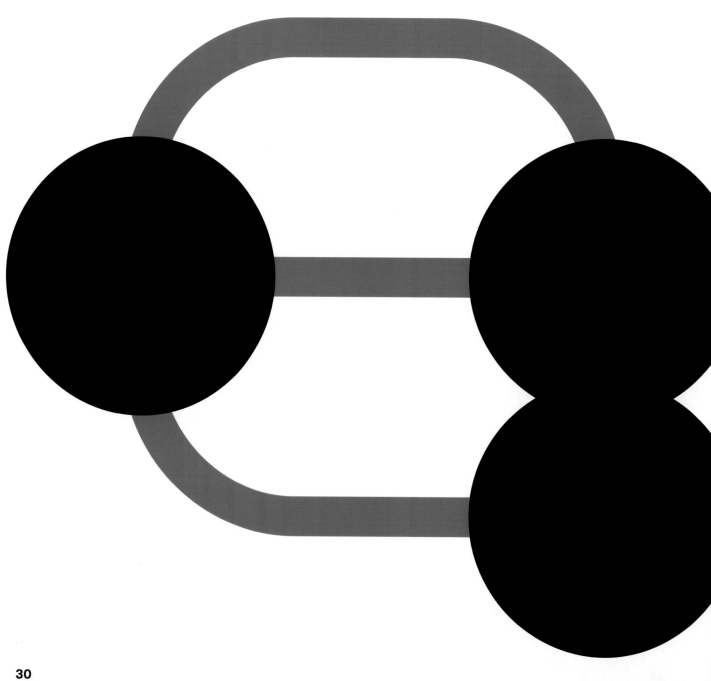

The World's Best Typography®   **The 40th Annual of the Type Directors Club**

e — TwoBit D Black. TwoBit A Extra Light by MuirMcNeil
f — Galapagos A, Regular by Felix Salut

Communication Design

Best in Show
Student Work
Judges' Choices

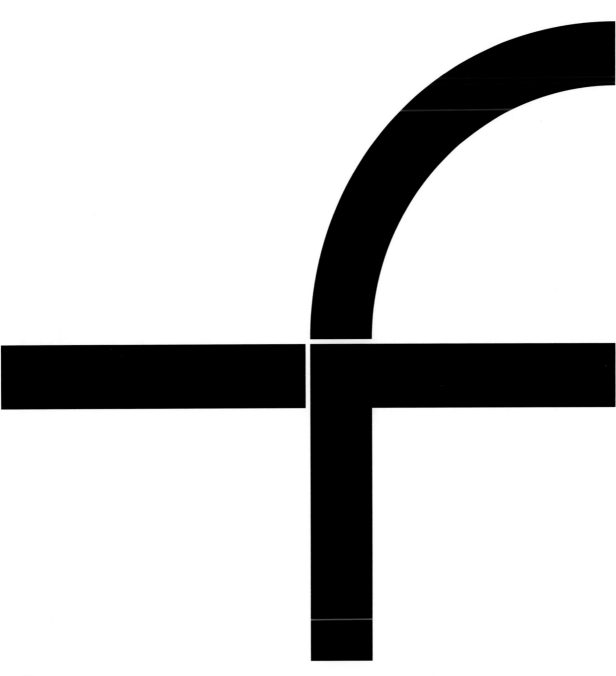

I knew this set of posters would be my Judge's Choice when I saw them across the room. Everything about them drew me in.
Paulina Reyes

I knew this set of posters would be my Judge's Choice when I saw them across the room. Everything about them drew me in. The bold compositions show an effortless play between type and illustration, executed in a wonderful color palette that recalls the fearless color sensibility of Latin America. The type is raw and graphic, its letterforms' varied widths interacting beautifully with the handcrafted nature of the illustration. The scale is impactful, and the projection of the series is at once playful and sophisticated.

The posters are not only exquisite in their execution, printed on really nice paper with inks that do the color palette justice, but they also do an excellent job of communicating the creative nature of the workshops they announce.

Paulina Reyes

This series of posters, with the theme of creativity, announces workshops taking place in Sesc Pompeia's "oficinas" (the iconic building designed by the Italian-Brazilian architect Lina Bo Bardi, in São Paulo).

Designed by Bloco Gráfico with illustrations by the artist Andrés Sandoval, the posters show hands interacting with the letters of the words that are the concept of the workshop of the month and, at the same time, express the main idea of the oficinas: manual work.

Gabriela Castro,
Paulo André Chagas,
and Gustavo Marchett

POSTERS

Oficinas de criatividade
Sesc Pompeia 2018

Design
**Gabriela Castro,
Paulo André Chagas,
and Gustavo Marchetti
São Paulo**

Illustration
Andrés Sandoval

URL
blocografico.com.br

Design Firm
Bloco Gráfico

Client
Sesc São Paulo

Dimensions
17 x 26 in. (44 x 66 cm)

Principal Type
Cindie Mono

Best in Show and Judge's Choice

Unrefined, barely legible, and, as TLC would say, damn unpretty, this piece seems to be the antithesis of beauty and craft in typography.

Leo Jung

With access to software that gives us the ability to manipulate form, perspective, and space like never before, the potential for pushing typography to new creative heights is inevitable. It's happening already. And I voted for many of them! At the same time, this capability can sometimes lead to an unplanned path toward sameness. It can also put emphasis on aesthetics and form over an underlying function. And with anything machine-made, its form can often feel cold and mechanical.

I found myself questioning why I liked certain pieces. And often those reasons felt hollow and superficial. Having said that, I'm always drawn to work that solves a problem in a way that feels different from all the rest— and, at the same time, challenges my own sense of biased visual preferences. After viewing thousands of entries, I realized why I kept coming back to this oddity. I was charmed by its simple, gestural, and lyrical form—in direct contrast to many of its technically complex counterparts. It's a reminder that no matter how far we develop our tools to create things that are beyond our imagination, a strong and simple idea is often what carries a piece beyond what form can do alone.

Unrefined, barely legible, and, as TLC would say, "damn unpretty," this piece seems to be the antithesis of beauty and craft in typography. But it's for all of these reasons that the solution works so effectively. Bacteria are unpretty. They're gross. And creepy. And yet—as the focus of a museum, bacteria look undeniably fun and intriguing. They're ugly in a beautiful way. The design ignores idealism and embraces imperfection. But more important, it feels human-made.

Leo Jung

This is a visual identity design for an imaginary Bacteria Museum. The use of playful colors conveys that bacteria are not necessarily all bad but that there are good bacteria as well. I wanted to make this museum children-friendly so that they could come explore and have fun at the same time.

The logo was created in an organic form with handwritten letters, relating to the ever-changing forms of bacteria. My inspiration came from the four most common bacteria in our living houses. The circular forms are meant to depict bacteria as seen through a magnifying glass. The use of neon colors and the organic feeling of the whole visual identity work well together to catch people's eyes.

Sunnie Lee

IDENTITY
Bacteria Museum

Design
Sunnie Lee
New York

Instructor
Natasha Jen°

School
School of Visual Arts,
New York°

Principal Type
Custom

UNNAMED FOLDER

Concept This calendar uses visual symbols and colors to communicate the meaning of the new year: unknown, uncertain, and various. We used Risograph printing and different post-printing methods to present the concept.

Design
**Chih-Wei Hsu,
Chen-Wei Lin, and
Xao-Wen Su
Taipei**

Professor
Sih-Wei Jheng

School
**National Taiwan
University of Science
and Technology**

Dimensions
10.2 x 6.7 in. (26 x 17 cm)

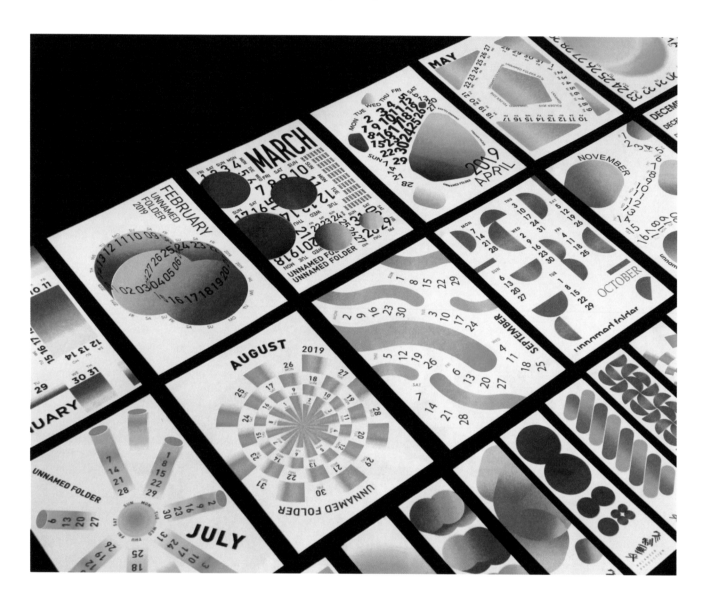

THE JUILLIARD SCHOOL

Concept   The Juilliard School's performative
logotype consists of modular dynamic forms that
can be applied as a flexible tool to communicate
information in a number of ways. The expansion
and retraction of graphic forms uses compositional
arrangements to emphasize spatial cognizance,
similar to musical scores and dance Labanotation.
The proposed identity delivers a visual performance
of forms and color for both the students and faculty
while providing a sense of clarity to the daily rigors
of school life.

Design
Karlo Fuertes Francisco°
Pasadena, California

URL
karlofrancis.co

Instructor
Brad Bartlett

School
**ArtCenter College
of Design**

Dimensions
Various

Principal Type
**Juilliard Display
and Univers**

I chose this project because it points to a way in which we can start thinking of type systems that relate to new technology.
Karin Fong

ZZ and I had to arm wrestle over who was going to write about this one! Smart and playful, this typographic system beautifully references the language of virtual reality.

I immediately connected with the way the type changed with motion. What impressed me was that it really conveys the ideas of depth and space elegantly, while providing lots of variation in both looks and usage. By making the extrusion and rotation reactive, the Gravient typefaces use z-space to make more "weights"—if you can call them that (part of my excitement is that perhaps ideas like this usher in even more choices in type systems). The interaction seems intuitive; type appears the way you move when you explore the space with your headset or device.

As someone who constantly uses typography in motion, I was struck by the idea of a typeface that changes with the user's—or the camera's—point of view. I enjoyed how dynamically the letterforms could animate, changing from something that could be very flat to sculptural over time. It's a simple idea that is successfully executed—while high concept, it avoids being cartoony or limited. There are moments when it seems classically modern; others seem almost calligraphic. In short, I could see using it.

I chose this project because it points to a way in which we can start thinking of type systems that relate to new technology. It's an exciting time to think about how letterforms will interact with new ways of seeing and creating content. As our lens on the world becomes more dimensional, so can typography. It's a reality I'm looking forward to!

Karin Fong

Gravient, a virtual and augmented reality company, asked us to develop their brand identity. Their main objective is the creative use of technology for commercial purposes. Building from a standard typeface, we developed a typographic behavior using interaction and three-dimensionality. Letters are set to change depending on the angle from which they're viewed—this way, the user's point of view becomes key in determining the shape of the typography.

David Galar Design and Pràctica

IDENTITY

Concept, Design, and
Art Direction
David Galar Design and
Pràctica
Barcelona

Code
Thomas Hoek

Typeface Development
Mikel Romero

Music
Reykjavik606

Photography
Kiwi Bravo

Voiceover
Ane Guerra

Video
Liten Studio

Cast
Mireia Farran

Design Firms
David Galar Design

URLs
davidgalar.com
practica.design

Instagram
@davidgalardesign
@practica.design

Client
Gravient

Principal Type
Gravient Diagonal,
Gravient Horizontal,
Gravient Vertical, and
interactive typography
and lettering

Behold the incredible surprises that greet you when you open the book.
Eddie Opara

At first glance, the cover is extremely unassuming. Upon closer examination, you see that its apparent pixelated title in all caps wears a distorted, woven-textured effect with its added hybrid brew of Anglo-German: "Pixel, Patch und Pattern." As your eyes peer down to the bottom of the cover, innocuously set in Futura, Typeknitting leaves you intrigued and you are overcome with curiosity.

Behold the incredible surprises that greet you when you open the book: You are taken into an alternative culture of typography that is knitted. The different stitching techniques are endless and transformative. The open, playful, thought-provoking, effortless, enterprising, and dynamic qualities are profound. You relish the fact that every design is made by hand, and the end results are awe-inspiring. It brings life to modularity and systems. After viewing this book, you have to ask yourself, "Why do I sit at my computer, hour after hour? Am I really making something that is tangible?"

Eddie Opara

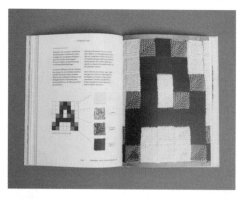

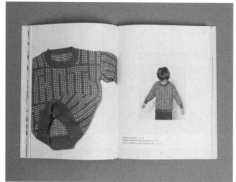

BOOKS

Pixel, Patch und
Pattern: Typeknitting

Design, Creative
Direction, and Author
Rüdiger Schlömer
Zürich

Photography
Linda Suter

Publisher
Bertram Schmidt-
Friderichs° and
Karin Schmidt-Friderichs

URL
rudigerschlomer.com

Client
Verlag Hermann Schmidt

Dimensions
6.7 x 9.1 in. (17 x 23 cm)

Principal Type
Futura LT and
Nexus Serif

While exploring different knitting techniques, I discovered many parallels to writing and typography: similar grid patterns that can be found in both areas, methods like patchwork knitting with many parallels to modular typography, and hand knitters who all have distinctive personal fingerprints.

I experienced knitting as a technical and logical practice, like analog programming. But looking only at the knitted artifacts, this is often rarely visible. I wanted to show this perspective to initiate a fresh, unbiased dialogue between knitting and typography. I chose to reduce the techniques to their structural basis using an instruction manual-inspired aesthetic. The two contrasting colors, blue and orange, distinguish between instructions and outcomes, between source code and artifact. In this way, the hope is that this book appeals to knitters and typographers equally.

Rüdiger Schlömer

Each layout has a kind of lyricism, using a spare and consistent set of elements that celebrates the magical beauty to be found in contrasts.

Ian Spalter

This second issue of Pan & The Dream is dedicated to the topic of beauty and is subtitled "La Belle et la Bête" or "The Beauty and the Beast"— a reference to Jean Cocteau's surrealist film. This surface-level dichotomy points to the worthy battleground that is the complicated topic of beauty.

There are, of course, many cliché examples of beauty in the world; however, there is also beauty to be found in the grotesque. It is about how something beautiful has been constructed or the context it is presented within. Often the most beautiful things stand out when we pay attention to details.

The imagery in this issue is meant to challenge what is beauty and where it can be found. You could imagine an alternative approach to the typographic decisions that stepped completely out of the way, becoming little more than a caption. Instead, the typography is both elegant and voluptuous. It works as a dignified narrator with a point of view, pushing the overall work away from a mere visual catalog or feed. A clear grid paired with SangBleu Empire creates a lovely system. Each layout has a kind of lyricism, using a spare and consistent set of elements that celebrates the magical beauty to be found in contrasts.

Ian Spalter

MAGAZINES

La Belle et la Bête

Design
Mike Abbink°
New York

Design Director
Jeanette Abbink°

Editor
Nathalie Agussol

URL
rationalbeauty.com

Twitter
@rationalbeauty

Design Firm
Rational Beauty

Dimensions
11 x 14.5 in. (28 x 37 cm)

Principal Type
SangBleu Empire and
SangBleu Republic

Client
Pan & The Dream

Jean Cocteau's surrealist 1946 film "La Belle et la Bête" was our muse for the beauty issue of Pan & The Dream. The design seeks to balance the emotional and the rational, and to help the reader navigate the often expressive content .

A simple grid structure and single font family create a consistent design, girded by Sang Bleu Empire and Republic. At once approachable and magical, the hybrid character of the letterforms are essential to the overall typography, particularly in the feature titles.

Oversized spreads are animated by changes in scale between headlines, pull quotes, and body copy, while minimal use of color allows the reader to focus. In keeping with the cinematic inspiration, there is an asymmetrical interplay between images and typography that amps up the spectator's experience.

Mike Abbink

PHOTOGRAPHY
Stephen Lewis

STYLIST
Sara Wacksman

pla sti que

Stephen Lewis
stephenlewisstudio.com
artandcommerce.com

Sara Wacksman
kingmanagementagency.com

BENOIT DELHOMME

LA BÊ TE

Portraits of Birds on old English
furniture and in old French interiors,
acrylic on vintage book pages.

87

This poster is a fresh, unique, and excellent example of innovative type design. In its simplicity, it is both bold and emblematic, clearly communicating the essence of its purpose is the magical beauty to be found in contrasts. Annik Troxler

The three beautifully designed letterforms are rounded and sensuously fluid, filling the entire poster's surface. It is not just the powerful presence of the image that attracts me, but also the elegance of the single blue color printed on white, with the black informational text acting as a counterpoint to the expressive shapes.

By combining the letters "bvh" in this way, the image references the studio's name with its flexibility, movement, and fluidity throughout innovative design processes, while keeping the connection between the group's individuals.

Annik Troxler

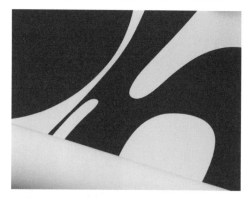

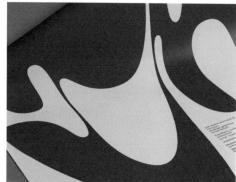

In 2018 we were invited by the contemporary art center Le Portique in Le Havre, France, to do a solo show of our work during the graphic design festival Une Saison Graphique. It was the tenth anniversary of the festival and also of our studio. That meant it was time to look back on our working manner and give it a visual form for the exhibition poster.

We invent flexible systems during our design process, moving between disciplines and navigating fluidly through different supports. Typography always plays a key element in our work. The design of the first three letters, "bvh," from our studio name, baldinger•vu-huu, reflects our flexibility, movement, and fluidity in the design process, while preserving the everlasting connection between us.

André Baldinger and Toan Vu-Huu

POSTERS

bvh

Design and Art Direction
André Baldinger and
Toan Vu-Huu
Paris

URL
baldingervuhuu.com

Studio
baldinger•vu-huu

Client
Le Portique

Dimensions
47.2 x 69.3 in.
(120 x 176 cm)

Principal Type
Handlettering

UNE SAISON GRAPHIQUE 18
Parcours
de design graphique
contemporain

Expositions, conférences,
événements
14 mai – 9 juin, 10e édition

unesaisongraphique.fr

BALDINGER • VU-HUU
Le Portique

ABM STUDIO
Bibliothèque universitaire

ABRACADABRA ÉSAD AMIENS
Le Tetris

MARION BATAILLE
Bibliothèques
O. Niemeyer & A. Salacrou

VALENTIN DANIEL
La Consigne

RAPHAËL GARNIER
ESADHaR
& Maison de l'Étudiant

MOREPUBLISHERS
Artothèque ESADHaR

Ra DESIGN
Carré du THV

UNE KERMESSE GRAPHIQUE
fort !

The reverse contrast in Anger especially stood out for me—its unusual proportions and inverted weight distribution caught my eye.

Zipeng Zhu

As a communication design judge, I look for one thing: Does the work communicate excellently through typography? My Judges' Choice not only met that standard, but it also completely exceeded my expectations in concept and execution.

As a variable typeface said to be inspired by human emotions, State not only has a thoughtful concept but has also been drawn exquisitely with beautiful experimental letterforms. The reverse contrast in Anger especially stood out for me—its unusual proportions and inverted weight distribution caught my eye. I can't get it out of my head.

I have such admiration and appreciation for the decision to pursue both innovation in technology and experimentation in typography. I wish there was another scale for excitement for what I'm feeling at the moment.

Zipeng Zhu

State is a variable typeface whose styles are inspired by human emotions. The typeface explores the new Variable Font format, an innovative technology that allows the user of a typeface to control the style of the font by adjusting a set of sliders.

The three axes of State are Greed, Pride, and Anger. Each axis consists of a pair of opposing emotions: desired and fulfilled for Greed, shy and confident for Pride, and calm and angry for Anger. A neutral type style—free of emotional expression—appears when all three axes are set in the middle. Variable typefaces are establishing a new relationship between type designers and graphic designers.

Potch Auacherdkul

TYPOGRAPHY

State

Design
Potch Auacherdkul°
Baltimore

URL
statesoftype.com

Instructors and Design
Direction
Jason Gottlieb, Ellen
Lupton, and Jennifer
Cole Phillips

School
Maryland Institute
College of Art

Principal Type
State

g — Galapagos A Light by Felix Salut
h — TwoBit D Bold. **TwoBit B Extra Light by MuirMcNeil**

g — Galapagos A Light by Felix Salut
h — TwoBit D Bold. **TwoBit B Extra Light by MuirMcNeil**

Communication Design Winners

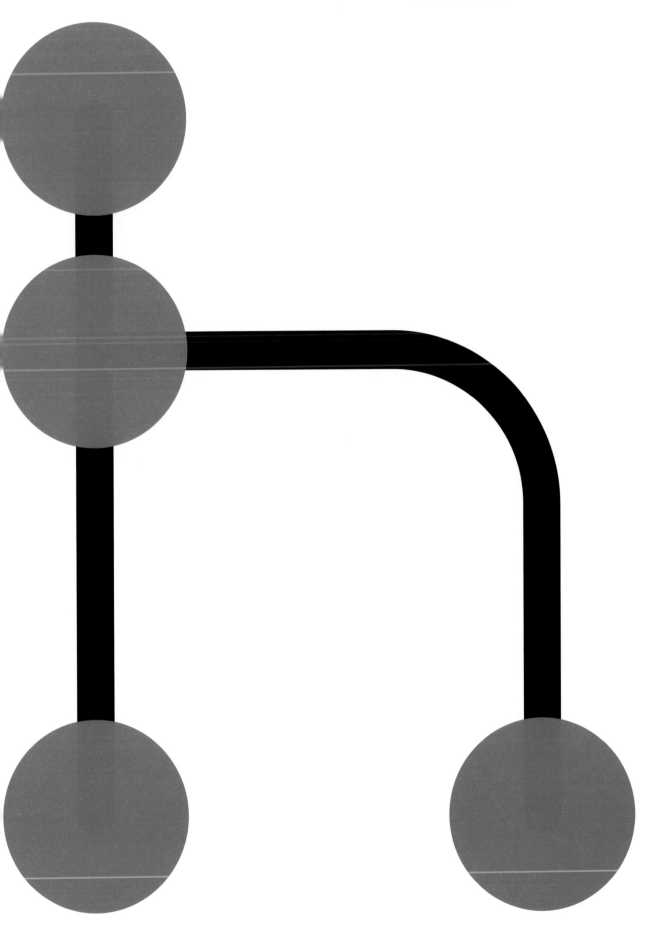

TV Makes Home Fun

Concept This is an advertisement for Japan's largest digital satellite broadcasting service provider. We used the main copy "TV makes home fun" in this ad that shows a snippet of a family enjoying TV. The typography, created by Yasaburo Kuwayama, is called Kodomo Shotai ("Children Font" in English). To try to express the fun the family is having while watching TV, we used a font inspired by kids that is both bold and playful.

Design
Keita Asaoka,
Sota Kitaura,
Toshichika Ono,
and Rina Sahoda
Tokyo

Creative Direction
Takuya Isojima

Art Direction
Taichi Tamaki

Copy Writer
Yukio Hashiguchi

URL
dentsu-crx.co.jp

Design Firm
Dentsu Inc., and
Dentsu Creative X Inc.

Client
SKY Perfect JSAT
Corporation

Dimensions
6.75 x 47.75 ft.
(2.1 x 14.6 m)

Principal Type
Kodomo Shotai

たまった録画を
消化する。
母のストレス
解消法。

母がなくした
リモコンを見つける。
父の特技です。

夫婦の空気が
微妙なとき、
娘はそっと
テレビをつける。

あなたのコピーが広告に。詳細は #スカパーコピー大賞

Zumtobel Annual Report 2017/18

Concept   Zumtobel is a lighting manufacturer based in Dornbirn, Austria. Inspired by light and shadow, we designed Zumtobel's 2017/18 annual report. We created a visual language synthesizing typographic play with gradients. Each chapter possesses unique covers of Zumtobel Group subsidiaries. Annual reports are further arrayed with twenty prints exhibiting typographic phrases. The report comes in the standard and limited editions—the standard has the report sandwiched between two cover boards, while the limited-edition versions are specially equipped in a box. Each edition is wrapped by bands that form the letter Z.

Creative Direction and Copywriting
Jessica Walsh
New York

Production
Erica Grubman and HeeJae Kim

Book Design
Shy Inbar
and HeeJae Kim

Print Design
Daniel Brokstad,
Juan Carlos,

Lina Forsgreen,
Fatih Hardal,
Stefan Hurlemann,
HeeJae Kim, Shy Inbar,
Cory Say, and
Anthony Velen

Animation
Anthony Velen
and Yaya Xu

URL
sagmeisterwalsh.com

Twitter
@sagmeisterwalsh

Studio
Sagmeister & Walsh

Client
Zumtobel

Dimensions
12 x 16.5 in.
(30.5 x 41.9 cm)

Principal Type
Minion Pro,
Untitled Sans,
and Untitled Serif

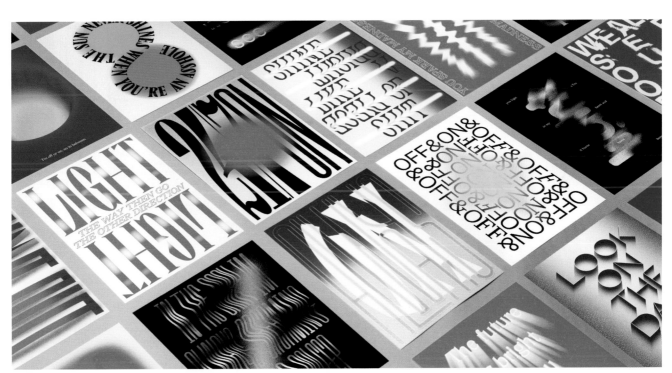

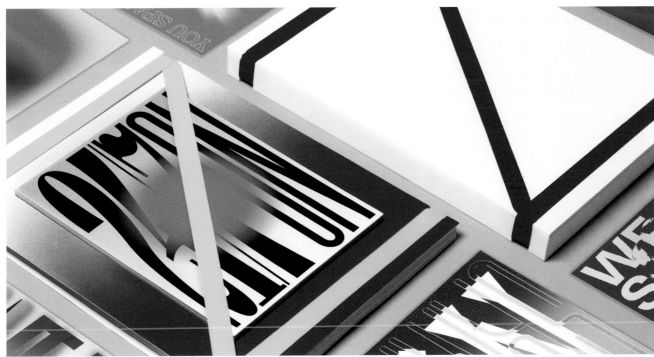

The Human Rights Campaign
Annual Report 2017

Concept The Human Rights Campaign is America's largest civil rights organization working to achieve equal rights for the lesbian, gay, bisexual, transgender, and queer community. Our objective was to create a visual language and message that would ignite participation. Through design and language, we looked to funnel fear and outrage into something meaningful. We designed a large-format magazine using only HRC's brand color with crisp black on newsprint. We made typography the primary vehicle to strengthen the central message of "unite, resist, and enlist." The piece is visually striking—but, more important, it energizes the reader to do something "more."

Design
Joe Letchford
Washington, D.C.

Art Direction
Sucha Becky

Chief Creative Officer
Pum Lefebure°

Account Director
Jake Lefebure

URL
designarmy.com

Instagram
@designarmy

Design Company
Design Army

Client
**Human Rights
Commission**

Dimensions
**12.5 x 22 in.
(31.8 x 55.9 cm)**

Principal Type
**Druk, Swiss BT,
and Swiss 721 BT**

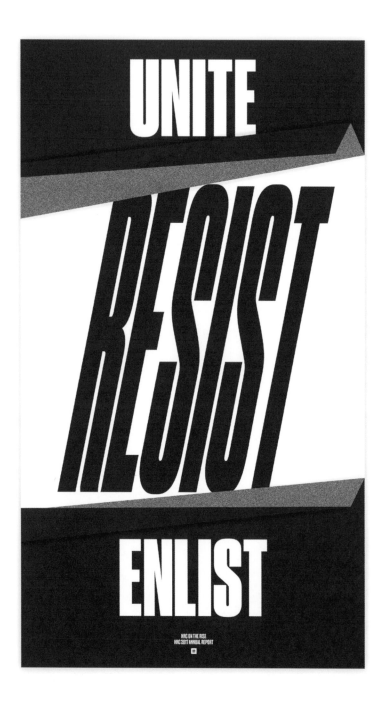

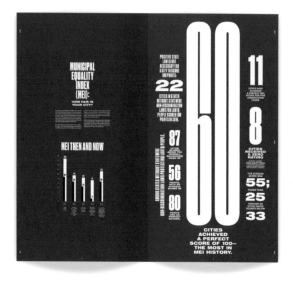

Deadly Ponies Silks

Concept Deadly Ponies is one of New Zealand's most iconic fashion labels. The brand is synonymous with subversiveness and fantastical adventures into other realms. "Gaga for Gala" and "Smokey and the Gambit" juxtapose spaghetti western themes with Salvador Dali's obsessive love for his tempestuous wife, Gala, as well as the wild adventures awaiting in their surreal dreams. "Obsessions and passions collide in the horizons, my sweet. In a world of surreal dreams is where we will live forever, my love." By embracing a frothy and luxurious sense of the absurd, these scarves indulge our surreal fantasies.

Creative Direction
Lloyd Osborne°
and Shabnam Shiwan
Auckland, New Zealand

Illustration
Lloyd Osborne
and Shabnam Shiwan

URL
osborneshiwan.com

Twitter
@OsborneShiwan

Agency
Osborne Shiwan

Client
Deadly Ponies

Dimensions
59.1 x 59.1 in.
(150 x 150 cm)

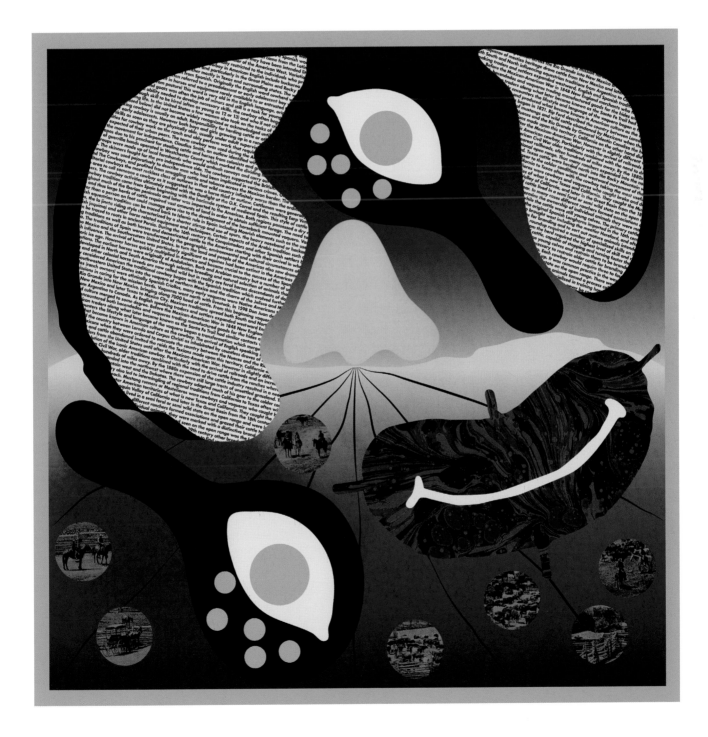

Beauty Book

Concept Stefan Sagmeister and Jessica Walsh set out on a mission: to find out what beauty is and the many ways it affects our lives. They turned to philosophy, history, and science to understand why we are drawn to beauty and how it influences the way we feel and behave. Determined to translate those findings into action, Sagmeister & Walsh shows us how beauty can improve the world.

Design
Kevin Brainard,
Cybele Grandjean,
and Tala Safié
New York

Art Direction
Kevin Brainard
and Cybele Grandjean

Creative Direction
Stefan Sagmeister
and Jessica Walsh

Editor
Sara Bader, Phaidon

Production Director
Elaine Ward, Phaidon

Production Artist
Joao Mota

Illustration
Daniel Brokstad,
Matteo Giuseppe Pani,
and Chen Yu

3D Artwork
David McLeod
and Fran Rossi

Production Coordinators
Erica Grubman,
Megan Oldfield,
and Gosbinda Vizarretea

URLs
sagmeisterwalsh.com
area-of-practice.com

Twitter
@sagmeisterwalsh
@areaofpractice

Studios
Sagmeister & Walsh
and Area of Practice

Clients
Sagmeister & Walsh
and Phaidon

Dimensions
7 x 9.5 in.
(17.8 x 24.1 cm)

Principal Type
Beauty, Gräebenbach,
Gräebenbach Mono,
Lyon and Lyon Display,
and Rando Display

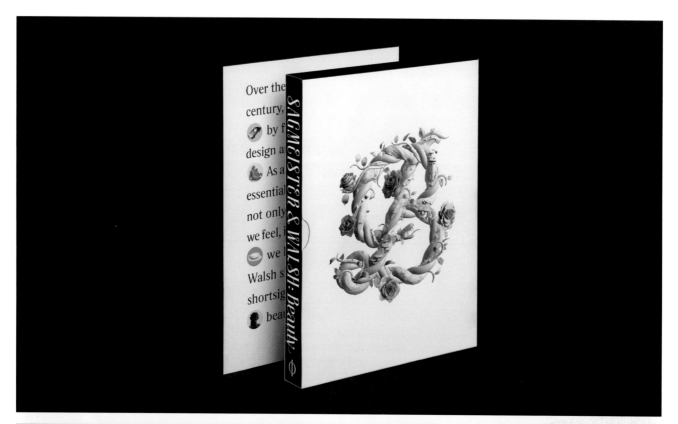

Mizdruck

Concept Unlike my fellow printers, I don't see any fault in the imperfect. On the contrary, differences and dissimilitudes fascinate me. They create a new dynamic on paper, a human touch to the formalities of the mechanical. In a world where industrial reproduction wants to smoothen anything and everything, I find comfort in the quirks of a (mis)print—and this isn't even my hobby. Idiosyncratically, I am neither artist nor craftsman. I experiment with the unknown, playing with tools from the past, teaching them new tricks. Old machines, new ink. Spontaneous, uncompromising, and maximalist. This is how I print.

Print and Design
**Jan-Willem van der Looij
Eindhoven,
The Netherlands**

Graphic Design (Text)
and Editor
Melani De Luca

Text and Translation
Megan Denius

URL
mizdruk.nl

Letterpress Design
Studio
Mizdruk Ink'orporated

Dimensions
**6.3 x 9.5 in.
(16.5 x 24 cm)**

Principal Type
**Ancient wood and metal
type, as well as new
"analogue pixels"**

Nocturne

Concept   Nocturne is a book painted full of black ink. Opening it is just the experience of walking into the dark night. The book is divided into four chapters, representing the four seasons: "Yuhua," "Water Forest," "Hill," and "Night Sky." There are thirteen pieces in each chapter, for a total of fifty-two, corresponding to the number of weeks in one year. Each poem is designed three ways: the first edition is easy to read; the second is very loose so as to recognize at night; and the third is abstract, using design language to express poetic meanings. All of the poems on the cover are printed with fluorescent ink.

Design
Zhao Qing
Nanjing, China

Design Firm
Nanjing Han Qing
Tang Design

Client
Zhejiang People's Fine
Arts Publishing House

Dimensions
5.1 x 9.1 in. (13 x 23 cm)

Principal Type
方正风雅宋

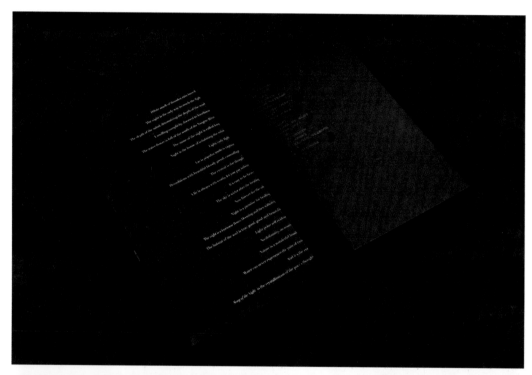

A is van Os

Concept Anyone who can read knows the twenty-six letters of the alphabet. But where do those letters come from? How long do they exist? Autobahn takes you back to the time of our distant ancestors, who made a drawing if they wanted to "write" something. Over time, their drawings evolved into the first letters. If you look closely, you'll recognize our current alphabet. And guess what? A is not for Apple at all, but for Ox! You will also understand why, whenever we send emoji to one another, we are actually doing the same thing our distant ancestors did over five thousand years ago.

Initiator and Design
Autobahn
Utrecht,
The Netherlands

URLs
autobahn.studio
autobahn.gallery

Studio
Autobahn

Dimensions
9.5 x 9.5 in. (24 x 24 cm)

Principal Type
Aperçu Medium,
Gotham Rounded
Medium, Autobahn
Greek Medium,
Autobahn Phoenician
Medium, and Autobahn
Proto-Sinaïtic Medium

Autobahn & Bette Westera

A is van Os

Waar komen onze letters vandaan?

GOTTMER

Brueterich Press-Lyrik Edition

Concept   Specializing in lyrical works, Brueterich Press wants to promote talented poets and offer them a controversial editing platform. Gold & Wirtschaftswunder was asked to translate this aspiration in the design. The result applies a graphic language of abstract forms and patterns that can be applied to various subjects while still offering enough freedom for the design of the individual covers. The content of the books is crafted in accordance with the rhythm and structure of the text. The focus lies on the possibilities of typography to create an emotional image rather than to display pure information.

Design
Flore de Crombrugghe,
Lena Haase,
Elena Mollenkopf,
and Maximilian Semmler
Stuttgart and Berlin

Creative Direction
Julia Kühne
and Christian M. Schiller

URL
gww-design.de

Agency
Gold & Wirtschaftswunder

Client
Brueterich Press

Dimensions
4.1 x 5.8 in.
(10.5 x 14.8 cm)

Principal Type
Contemporary Sans,
GT Eesti, Medusa,
Milieu Grotesque,
GT Sectra,
and GT Walsheim

The Door of Luban: Square, Circle, Line, Angle

Concept   My research into traditional Chinese architecture showed me that Chinese characters are essentially building blocks. So I imagined the logotype as the space of a building, dragging part of the characters and putting a "space" in the character for "DOOR" 門. The core of the magazine is "THE ART OF LIFE". The cover photographs are about daily stuff, with two photos combined as one story. I made use of more modern colors, and every volume has a color theme.

Design
Gu Hanyu
and Ren Huiya
Beijing

Art Direction
Gu Hanyu

Editors
Gu Hanyu,
Ren Huiya,
Editorial Board

Design Studio
T-Workshop

Clients
Beijing United
Publishing, Co., Ltd.
and Beijing Urban
Construction Design
& Development Group
Co., Ltd.

Dimensions
6.1 x 8.3 in.
(15.5 x 21 cm)

Principal Type
NotoSansHans, Palatino,
Source Han Serif, and
Times New Roman

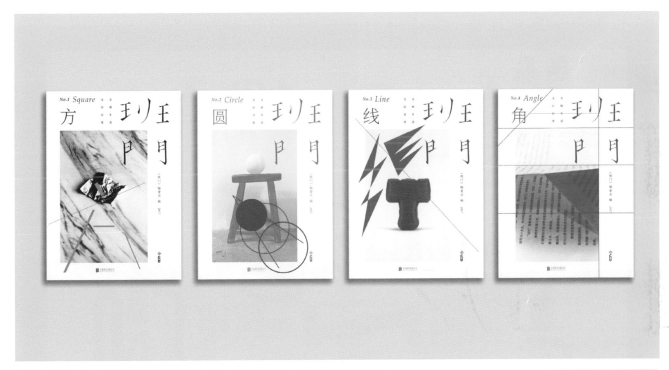

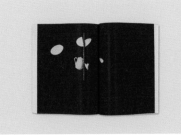

Wordplay / Gioco di parole / Wortspiele

Concept Wordplay / Gioco di parole / Wortspiele is a collaborative project undertaken by the participants of the 2017 "Legacy of Letters" letterpress workshop led by Erik Spiekermann and p98a at the Tipoteca in Cornuda, Italy. Each participant created a design that played verbally and/or visually with language.

URLs
paulshawletterdesign.com/category/tours-events/legacy-of-letters/
p98a.com

Design Firms
Legacy of Letters and p98a

Design
Tim Allen,
Raffaela Canu,
Elizabeth DeLuna°,
Susanna Dulkinys,
Maryam Hosseinnia,
Jeryl Jones,
Gloria Kondrup,
Linda Kwon,
Amy Chow Yuen Mei,
Lian Ng, Alta Price,

Sibylle Schneider,
Paul Shaw°,
Erik Spiekermann°,
Jessica Spring,
Ray Tomasso,
Ferdinand Ulrich, and
Marcela Paula Ávila
Vivero
Berlin; Como, Italy;
Englewood, Colorado;
Frankfurt; New York;
Long Island City,
New York;
Pasadena, California;
Safat, Kuwait;
San Francisco;
Santiago, Chile;
Scottsdale, Arizona;
Tacoma, Washington;
and Urbana, Illinois

Project Directors
Alta Price
and Paul Shaw

Art Direction
Susanna Dulkinys,
Erik Spiekermann,
and Ferdinand Ulrich

Client
Legacy of Letters

Dimensions
10 x 14 in.
(25.4 x 35.5 cm)

Principal Type
Wood and metal type from the Tipoteca collection

Die Wahre Geschichte

Concept   Die Wahre Geschichte ("The True Story") is an editorial piece on Klassik Radio, one of the most popular radio stations in Germany. It's a "nice-to-know" story that provides background into certain celebrities, major events in world history, or the meaning behind a phrase. The narrative always comes across in an amusing "Did you know?" tone of voice. The pun and wit of the short stories were enhanced by expressive typography and humorous illustrations. All illustrations are from three selected illustrators of the 100for10 art book series curated by Melville Brand Design.

Design
Florian Brugger,
Lars Harmsen,
and Yumi Kimoto
Munich

Creative Direction
Lars Harmsen

Art Direction
Florian Brugger
and Yumi Kimoto

Illustrators
Dario Forlin,
Thomas Hedger,
and Joni Majer

URL
melvilledesign.de

Behance and Vimeo
@melvilledesign

Facebook and Instagram
@melvillebranddesign

Agency
Melville Brand Design

Client Name
Klassik Radio

Dimensions
8.3 x 11 in.
(21.5 x 28.5 cm)

Principal Type
Akzidenz Grotesk
Medium Extended,
bb-book A-bold,
and bb-book A-regular

Xing Shu

Concept   In Mandarin, "Xing Shu" also means a style of traditional Chinese calligraphy. We believe design is one form of writing. When the main characters' characteristics are crafted, stories naturally flow. The cover was intended to deliver the message of this book: "what people said." It works in concert with the book. "Where there is a city, there are people and there are stories about those people."

Art Direction,
Executive Creative
Director, and Professor
Fa-Hsiang Hu
Taipei

Design Director
Alain Hu

Copy Director
Yun Liu

Typographers
**Alain Hu, Di Hu,
and Fei Hu**

Account Managers
**Natasha Liao
and Gayle Wang**

Cooperation School
CUTe, FJCU

Design Firm
hufax arts

Client
Ding Ding Co., Ltd.

Dimensions
5.1 x 7.5 in. (13 x 19 cm)

Principal Type
Custom

The 9th National Book Design Art Exhibition Excellent Works Collection

Concept   This book records the outstanding award-winning works of the 9th National Book Design Art Exhibition. The segregated dimensions are engraved on the cover with nine exhibition logos, forming an abstract Arabic numeral 9, symbolizing these nine exhibitions. The split graphics combine the letters B and D, which represent Book and Design, respectively. This book first tried a chronological style of presentation—collecting information on previous exhibitions, making a "memoir" in the timeline, telling the history of the previous eight exhibitions—and the guide bar is specially set on the outside of the book cover for easy access.vem spimum.

Design
Zhao Qing and Zhu Tao
Nanjing, China

Design Firm
Nanjing Han Qing Tang Design

Client
Nanjing Press

Dimensions
7.5 x 10.2 in. (19 x 26 cm)

Principal Type
DIN, 汉仪瑞意宋, and 方正纤雅宋

Une Historie de l'Orthopédie

Concept   Based on the history of the Orthopedic Hospital of western Switzerland, founded in Lausanne in 1876, this book illustrates the advances of orthopedics as a discipline and technique from the mid-eighteenth century to the present day. We wanted a book so sleek and smart in itself that it could almost be mistaken for a slipcase. The main content throughout the edition is rhythmed by a generous amount of quotations that flow out independently from the text. A small yet key element are the footnotes, which stand out vertically in the center of the pages supporting all the content, just like a spine.

Design and Art Direction
Aris Zenone
Lausanne, Switzerland

Author
Mariama Kaba

Editor
Éditions BHMS

URLs
ariszenone.ch
sam-chuv.ch

Twitter
@ariszenone

Studio
SAM-CHUV

Client
Centre hospitalier
universitaire vaudois

Dimensions
8.5 x 12.5 in.
(21.6 x 32 cm)

Principal Type
Ivar and NEXT

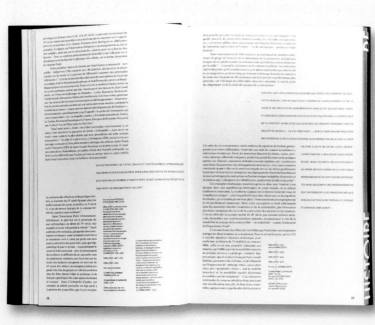

Watching Paint Dry

Concept The book combines, as an exhibition catalog, the contemporary works of the artist Arvid Boecker. The catalog is printed on two types of paper: The forty-seven works are printed on coated paper, while the introduction and appendix are printed on uncoated natural paper. We have chosen Apocalypse and Favorit, respectively—and just like the paint on the pictures, so these two typefaces confront each other, producing a tension full of contrasts. The pictures are numbered, and the numbers can be found opposite the pictures. The colors black, white, and gray have deliberately been chosen to give the pictures room to unfold.

Creative Direction
**Markus Artur Fuchs
and Patrick Hubbuch
Berlin and Heidelberg**

Art Direction
Francesco Futterer

Photography
Sabine Arndt

Editor
**Verein für aktuelle Kunst
Ruhrgebiet e.V.**

URLs
**kontext-kom.de
vfakr.de
wunderhorn.de**

Instagram
@kontextkommunikation

Design Firm
**KontextKommunikation
GmbH**

Publisher
Wunderhorn

Client
Arvid Boecker

Dimensions
**9.7 in x 11.6 in.
(24.5 x 29.5 cm)**

Principal Type
Apocalypse and Favorit

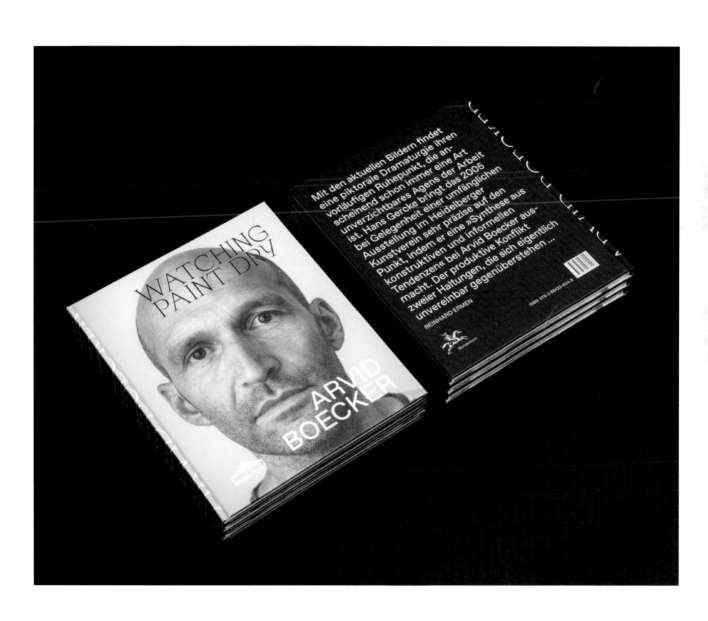

Memórias Póstumas de Brás Cubas

Concept   Memórias Póstumas de Brás Cubas, by the Brazilian writer Machado de Assis, was originally published in 1881. The novel is narrated by the dead protagonist Brás Cubas, who tells his own life story from beyond the grave, noting his mistakes and failed romances. The project took inspiration from the typography and ornaments encountered in gravestones. The illustrations were made by combining a small collection of type ornaments with woodcuts.

Design
Tereza Bettinardi
São Paulo

Illustration
Heloisa Etelvina

Print Production
Lilia Goes

URL
terezabettinardi.com

Twitter
@tbettinardi

Client
Carambaia

Dimensions
4.7 x 7.2 in.
(12 x 18.5 cm)

Principal Type
Chiswick Text and
the Pyte Foundry fonts

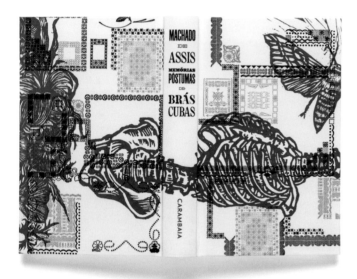

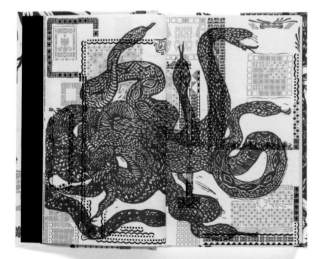

Typography Basic

Concept   This book aims to be a textbook for typography for both young designers as well as students and business people. I introduced a grid system that is central to the teaching of Swiss typography master Josef Müller-Brockmann, who was a visiting professor when I attended Osaka University of Arts.

Design and Art Direction
Yukichi Takada°
Osaka, Japan

Client
Osaka University of Arts,
and PIE International

Dimensions
8.3 x 11.7 in.
(21 x 29.7 cm)

Principal Type
GothicMB101
and Helvetica

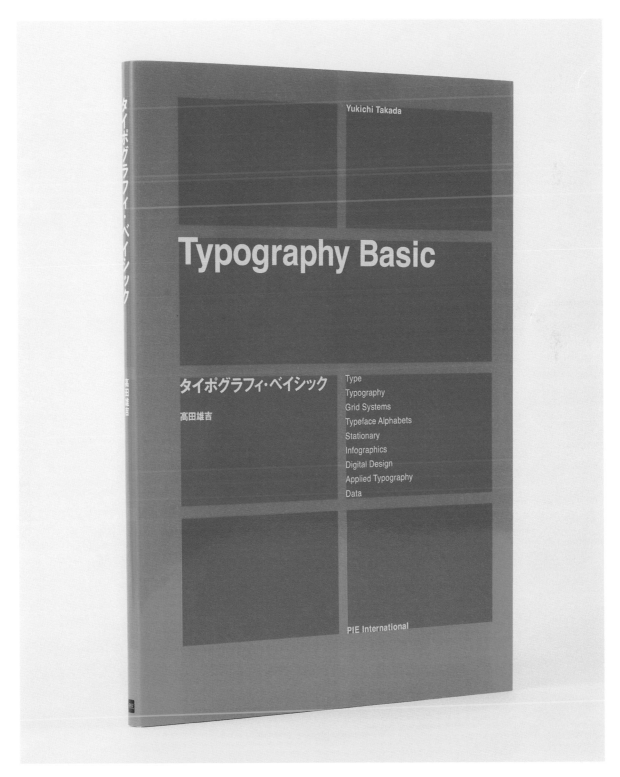

A Fantástica Tipografia do Companheiro Matias

Concept A Fantástica Tipografia do Companheiro Matias ("The Fantastic Letterpress Shop of Our Fellow Matias") is a book about the letterpress printer Ademir Matias. Working since 1955 at the same place, Matias is one of the last traditional printers in Brazil who still works only with letterpress. To honor his legacy, designers Olavo D'Aguiar and Gabriel Nascimento decided to make an experimental project using Matias' quotes. "Anything with the height of a movable type can be printed," he says. Stamps, vinyl discs, coffee mugs, hands, ink rollers, bubbles, tires, smoke, wood and metal types, and other materials were printed. Each book is unique, like every moment with Matias.

Editor, Producer, Art Director, Artist, and Printer
Olavo D'Aguiar and Gabriel Nascimento
Belo Horizonte, Minas Gerais, Brazil

Editor and Printer
Ademir Matias

Invited Artists
Ágatha Araújo Andrade, Débora Colares, Pedro Leitin, Luis Matuto, Maria T. Morais, Vitor Paiva, Thales Ramonielli, Ana Letícia Rodrigues, and Flávio Vignoli

URL
62pontos.com

Studio
62 Pontos

Client
Tipografia Matias

Dimensions
7.2 x 8.9 in.
(18.5 x 22.5 cm)

Principal Type
Lead and wood types including Antiga Oficial, Bodoni Preta, Grotesca Reforma Preta Estreita, Kabel, Grotesca Reforma Gorda Apertada, Orplid, and Manuscrita

I Believe I Can Fly

Concept Inspired by work from the artist, we placed text in various geometric shapes throughout Nina Rike Springer's book.

Design
Sebastian Fischer and Philipp Hubert
New York and Berlin

URL
hubertfischer.com

Twitter
@HubertFischerNY

Design Firm
Hubert & Fischer

Client
ZF Art Foundation

Dimensions
9 x 11 in. (23 x 28 cm)

Principal Type
Basis Grotesque

The films last no longer than it takes to perform a joke, but in both cases the punchline is felt long afterwards. This is because the humour in Nina Rike Springer's work is always so profound and thought-provoking. We are reminded of the cow that is literally fed up with the constant grazing and ruminating. And we observe the animated grass in Nina Rike Springer's stop-motion film that takes its thrown-into-the-world existence in its own hands and searches for a new purpose: the grass is not just grass, but does something – it grazes! This makes a big difference if one believes Martin Heidegger, that other great existential philosopher: "Being always sees itself from its existence, the possibility of the self to be or not to be itself." [3] Measured by the seriousness of the situation one must also consider that even grass could be capable of deciding to be or not to be itself. —— Through alienation and defamiliarization Nina Rike Springer throws things into a mighty jumble. But what is alien about making a couch dance together with its cushions (*Couch Polka*, 2006) or having some petits fours magically perform a *Mehlspeis Tango (Pastry Tango)* (2011) in formation on the dance floor? It is a question of imagination and intuition, how much freedom one allows things, and above all the mental picture that we have of them. —— At the same time Nina Rike Springer in her animations and tableaux has departed more and more from things in order to devote herself to the possibilities and the purpose of her person as a human being and artist. In 2014 she staged herself in the photo series *Schöne neue Welt (Beautiful New World)* as *Triad*, as *Müde Heldin (Tired Heroin)*, as *Salonfähige Einheit (Socially Acceptable Entity)* or in *Blindflug (Blind Flying)*. For this she created virtual stage spaces that were formed and deformed by geometrical surfaces. Completely in white with a strange bathing cap on her head, the artist plays all the roles herself. The figures remain as enigmatic as the narration, which – particularly in the triptychs – takes place at different locations: absurd, fantastic, surreal, unreal, but quite possible. —— Exactly this is taken up by the three most recent animations and a photographic series, all of which emerged in 2018. In the short film *Skills* she reappears, the artist, this time in a yellow bathing cap, in mint green sweatshirt and blue jogging pants – color-matched to the reduced arrangement of the scenery and props. Whereas the vocational world demands from its qualified specialists every sort of possible skill, and even the youth has incorporated the 'skiller' admiringly into its vocabulary, Nina Rike Springer's film totally does without spectacular gestures or skills. Standing, she slides from the left into the picture, squats, stretches the arms out to the ringing of bells, and disappears again. She pushes a yellow cuboid into the room, slides from left to right while squatting on it, takes the cuboid with her and disappears. A short moment later she runs back through the picture. While the picture fades, we hear a thunder storm from afar.

16

3 Martin Heidegger: *Sein und Zeit (Being and Time)*, 17th German Ed., Max Niemeyer Verlag, Tübingen 1993, §4, p.12.

In *Artificial* the artist swallows a blue pompom, that grows several fold out of her head a moment later. The pompoms take on a life of their own, and like an industrious armada carry off the components of a geometric composition – until only a white area remains. It is to some extent the reversal of an artistic process that does not begin with an empty sheet, but ends with it. There is also nothing really spectacular in that – except the recording of that famous sentence sent to the Earth by Neil Armstrong on landing on the surface of the moon on July 21, 1969: "That's one small step for man, one giant leap for mankind." —— So high up is not what Nina Rike Springer has in mind, certainly not in the heroic and earth shaking dimensions of space travel. If weightlessness appears unattainable in the eyes of the artist, the dream of flying at least lies in the realm of the possible. Its pre-stage is found in the large format digital photographic work *Schwebeperformance (Hovering Performance)*. As in the photo series *Beautiful New World* – the setting is formed more by a virtual stage space in which coloured geometric forms function as backdrops. Small circular areas serve as props for the figures. Behind a neon pink rectangle the distinctive bathing cap of the artist peeps out, behind a further rectangle her stooped back, and above on the left backdrop the bodies of the artist lie on top of each other like laundry bags. Two figures appear to hold a kind of balance beam on which however no one is balancing. In the middle of the picture the artist hangs horizontally like a weather flag on a pole. —— If one wants, this *Hovering Performance* can be read as a multiple self portrait that keeps the being of the acting figure in a hover and instead distributes its purpose over several states: struggling and bracing, trying and failing, not necessarily leading to success. As an aid, in the series *Flugkörper (Flying Bodies)* Nina Rike Springer designs fantastic flying suits that in their expansive forms and bold colors inevitably bring to mind Oskar Schlemmer's *Triadic Ballet* of 1922. The round tableaux form the frame, a rectangular area of color the background, in front of which the artist poses with the various flying suits that she has digitally tailored. —— But is that sufficient for flying? In the stop-motion animation *I Believe I Can Fly* Nina Rike Springer firmly believes that it is. But flying we guess is far more arduous than hovering. The flight preparation is everything. The artist prepares for take-off, the hands simulating the alignment of the take-off and landing flaps, she checks once more the function of the landing gear ... and ... Cut! In the next shot the artist lies horizontally on an almost invisible pedestal with outstretched arms. She is flying! To the airy strains of the *Blue Danube Waltz* by Johann Strauss. "Super!" is how the artist finds it at the end of the film and, winking, flexes her non-existent muscles.

17

IMPRESSUM EDITION NOTICE Dieser Katalog erscheint anlässlich der Ausstellung *Nina Rike Springer. I believe I can fly* der ZF Kunststiftung im Zeppelin Museum Friedrichshafen vom 19. Oktober bis 2. Dezember 2018. This catalogue is published on the occasion of the exhibition *Nina Rike Springer. I believe I can fly* held by the ZF Art Foundation at Zeppelin Museum Friedrichshafen, October 19 until December 2, 2018.

Herausgeber Editors Matthias Lenz, Regina Michel, ZF Kunststiftung, 88038 Friedrichshafen, www.zf.com/kunststiftung — Redaktion Editing Regina Michel — Text Text Dr. Ralf Christofori — Übersetzung Translation Peter Lilley — Lektorat Copy Editing Maria Dressler — Gestaltung Design Hubert&Fischer, www.hubertfischer.com — Fotonachweis Photo Credits Rafael Krötz, www.rafaelkroetz.de — Gesamtherstellung Printed by DZA Druckerei zu Altenburg GmbH — Erschienen bei Published by modo Verlag GmbH, Freiburg i. Br.

Die Deutsche Nationalbibliothek verzeichnet diese Publikation in der Deutschen Nationalbibliografie; detaillierte bibliografische Daten sind im Internet über http://dnb.dnb.de abrufbar. The Deutsche Nationalbibliothek lists this publication in the Deutsche Nationalbibliografie; detailed bibliographic data are available online at http://dnb.dnb.de. — Copyright © 2018, für diese Ausgabe for this edition Kunststiftung der ZF Friedrichshafen AG und and modo Verlag GmbH, Freiburg i. Br. — für die Texte bei den Autoren for the texts belongs to the authors — für die abgebildeten Werke beim Künstler for the selected works rests with the artist © Nina Rike Springer / Bildrecht, Wien 2018 / VG Bild-Kunst, Bonn 2018 — modo Verlag GmbH, Freiburg i. Br., www.modoverlag.de

Printed in Germany
Auflage Number of copies 1.000
ISBN 978-3-86833-256-8

Nina Rike Springer
www.ninaspringer.com

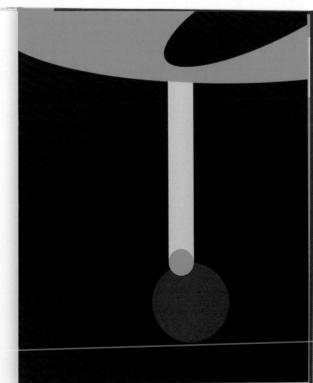

Graphik Booklet

Concept Graphik Latin, designed by Christian
Schwartz, has been expanded to support Arabic,
Persian, and Urdu. The booklet specimen was
designed to showcase the typeface in use.

Design
**Khajag Apelian
and Wael Morcos°
Beirut and New York**

URLs
**morcoskey.com
debakir.com
commercialtype.com**

Twitter
**@morcoskey
@waelmorcos
@debakir
@commercialtype**

Design Firm
**Morcos Key
and Khajag Apelian**

Client
Commercial Type

Dimensions
6 x 9 in. (15.2 x 22.9 cm)

Principal Type
**Graphik
and Graphik Arabic**

Lucas Albrecht Private Practice

Concept   "Back when Paul Rand wrote, 'There is no such thing as bad content, only bad form,' I remember being intensely annoyed. I took it as an abdication of a designer's responsibility to meaning. Over time, I have come to read it differently: He was not defending hate speech or schlock or banality; he meant that the designer's purview is to shape, not to write. But that shaping itself is a profoundly affecting form. (Perhaps this is the reason that modern designers—Rand, Munari, Leoni—always seem to end their careers designing children's books. The children's book is the purest venue of the designer/author because the content is negligible and the evocative potential of the form unlimited.)" —from "Fuck Content" by Michael Rock This project was done as a meditation on adulthood, debt, and learned responsibility.

Design
Lucas Albrecht
Brooklyn, New York

URL
lralbrecht.com

Dimensions
24 x 36 in. (61 x 91 cm)

Principal Type
Chartpak Vinyl Helvetica

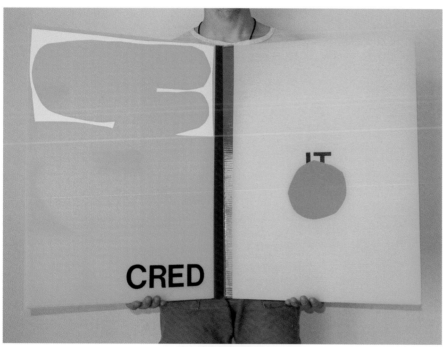

1984

Concept The book intends to embody the image of a totalitarian regime and the darkness of the dystopia in its overall form. For this purpose, the title was fitted in the iconic V letter, embedded into a metal plate, and placed on a black cloth cover. Taking the book out of its box, the reader immediately discovers the "Big Brother is Watching You" caption. Inside the book, discourses and slogans of the regime have been designed as typographic propaganda posters. Words in Newspeak, a language created to limit the freedom of thought, are highlighted with black foiling in the body text to denote censorship.

Design
Utku Lomlu°
Istanbul

URL
utkulomlu.com

Twitter
@utkulomlu

Design Studio
Lom Creative

Client
Can Publishing

Dimensions
6.3 x 8.9 in.
(16 x 22.5 cm)

Principal Type
Fedra Serif and custom

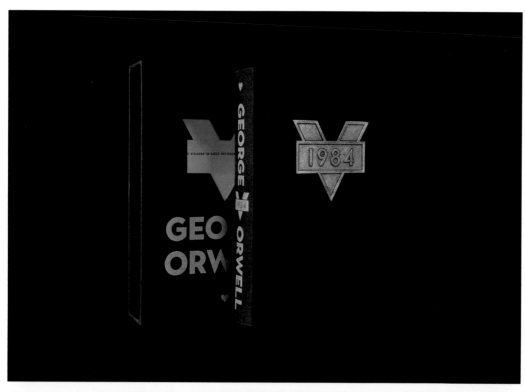

Imaginary Concerts

Concept Imaginary Concerts consists of two publications featuring the contributions of more than 160 artists, curators, and musicians. Each contributor submitted a fictitious concert lineup they'd like to one day see take place, regardless of how unrealistic or unrealizable. Each poster was designed in the style of the Colby Poster Printing Co., the LA-based print shop that famously churned out iconic "show print" posters for nearly sixty-five years before closing in 2012. Adam Turnbull carefully studied the layout process of the press and created a style of laying this out in InDesign, carefully tracking and kerning every letter to re-create the natural order of the original press.

Design and
Creative Direction
Adam Turnbull
New York

URL
pacificpacific.pub

Design Firm
Pacific

Client
Printed Matter,
Anthology Editions &
Peter Coffin

Dimensions
9 x 12 in.
(22.9 x 30.5 cm)

Principal Type
Various

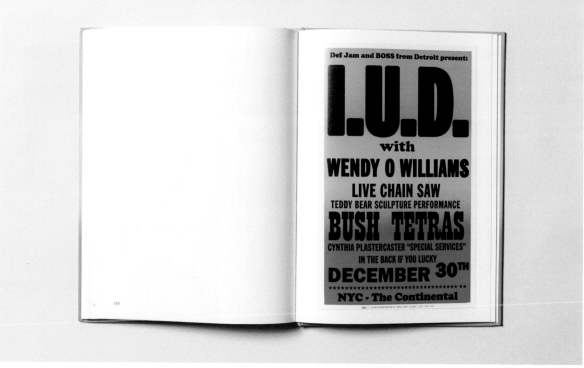

Force

Concept   The task was to present the work of Christian Falsnaes in a book. The Danish performance artist is known for strongly confronting his audience during his performances centered around power, authority, energy, and violence.
To reflect these themes through design, the layout was mirrored, but content was inconsistently reflected in a challenging manner. The cover for Force is split into red and black—both strong, aggressive hues—to differentiate German from English. The reader begins from either side and progresses toward the middle, where images are showcased. This representation allows both languages to be perceived as primary while creating contrast.

Design
Rubina Schafer
Berlin

Art Direction
Jessica David

Creative Direction
Sven Hausherr
and Nina Trippel

URLs
ceeceecreative.com
kunstmuseenkrefeld.
de/de

Agency
Cee Cee Creative

Client
Sylvia Martin,
associate director/
curator of Kunstmuseen
Krefeld, Germany

Dimensions
7.9 x 10.6 in.
(20 x 27 cm)

Principal Type
Favorit and Space Mono

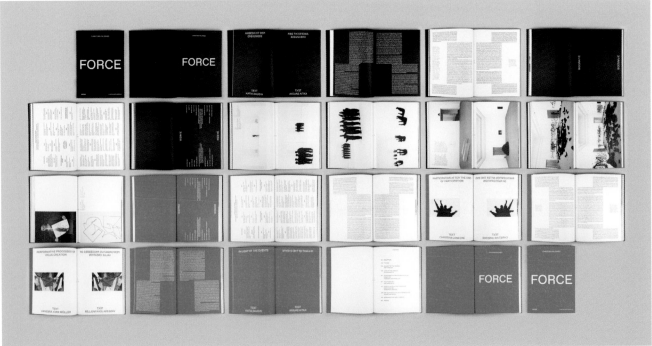

Acervo Carambaia

Concept   Unlike the conventional editions made by this book publisher, in which a different graphic design project is created for each book in a limited edition, the Carambaia Collection seeks to be a kind of "catalog" capable of uniting all the publisher's titles under a single graphic project. The goal is to reach a wider readership at an affordable price. The starting points for the project were neutrality and economy. The Untitled font was chosen for having in its family both a serif and sans serif version. The catalographic card on the cover reinforces the catalog feature of the collection.

Design
**Gabriela Castro,
Paulo André Chagas,
and Gustavo Marchetti
São Paulo**

URL
blocografico.com.br

Design Firm
Bloco Gráfico

Client
Carambaia

Dimensions
5 x 8 in. (13 x 20 cm)

Principal Type
**Untitled Sans
and Untitled Serif**

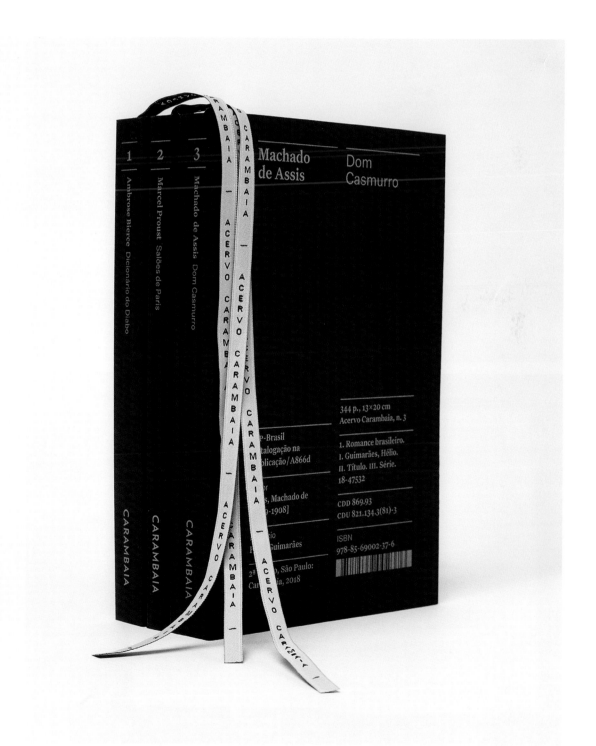

Siah Armajani: Follow This Line

Concept The design of the book was inspired by lexicography, a practice that has reappeared over the course of Siah Armajani's oeuvre, as well as ideas of tracing, layering, and obscuring, also common techniques used by the artist throughout his career. Emulating the mylar paper that Armajani uses in many of his works as well as bible paper used in dictionaries, I selected a very thin paper, utilizing the show-through as a design element that would formally tie the book together. The translucent paper obscures the text and imagery ever so slightly while also illustrating, several layers (or pages) deep, more than sixty years of Armajani's diverse career.

Designer
Aryn Beitz
Brooklyn, New York

Studio
Walker Art Center

Client
Walker Art Center

Principal Type
Janson Max Neue
Century Schoolbook
Swiss 721

Dimensions
7.5 x 10.5 in.
(19.1 x 26.7 cm)

Frankenstein in Baghdad

Concept   I really wanted to fuse (or, in this case, stitch and staple) together the two main elements of the book, hinting at both the monster created and the "wartorn" aspect of the novel. My hope was to capture the white-knuckle horror and black humor, which is the surreal reality of a city at war, by using staples to piece the title together. The final cover features embossing on the staples to create a tactile feel.

Design and Art Direction
**James Paul Jones
Buckinghamshire,
England**
URL
**jamespauljones.
tumblr.com**
Twitter
@JamesPaulJones
Instagram
@jamespauljones

Client
Oneworld Publications

Dimensions
**5.3 x 8.5 in.
(13.5 x 21.6 cm)**

Principal Type
**D-Day Stencil and
Typographer Textur Bold**

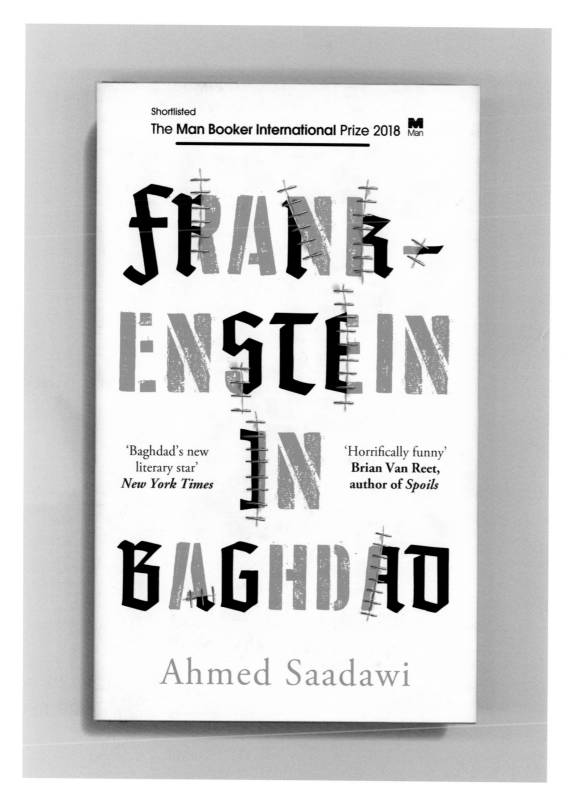

Literacy Classics

Concept   Illustrations are distinctively used to create a wide space for the reader's imagination as well as to make classics more appealing to younger readers through a contemporary graphic style.

Design
Geray Gencer, Istanbul

URL
geraygencer.com

Studio
Studio Geray Gencer

Client
Dogan Egmont Publishing

Dimensions
5.3 x 7.7 in.
(13.5 x 19.5 cm)

Principal Type
Futura PT

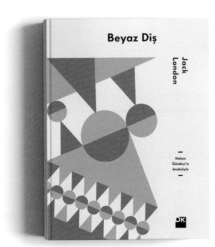

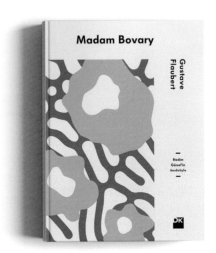

Fukt Magazine #17:
The Words Issue—Written Drawings

Concept The seventeenth issue is a celebration of words and their presence in the medium of drawing. The cover design expresses the theme and title of the magazine, "Written Drawings," as purely as possible—the letters F, U, K, and T are shaped by letters reading the line directions. Compass directions are noted, as are various formatting and cover treatment details ("TOP RIGHT ROUNDED CORNER," etc.). And here or there you'll find a little word of dust or dirty fingerprint spelled out.

Design
and Creative Direction
Ariane Spanier
Berlin

URL
arianespanier.com

Studio
Studio Ariane Spanier
Design

Client
Fukt Magazine

Dimensions
6.5 x 9 in. (16.5 x 23 cm)

Principal Type
Acumin

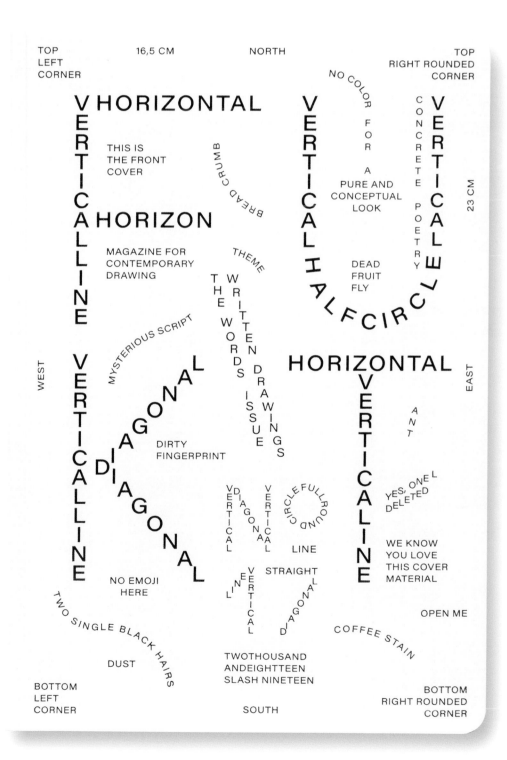

100 Years of Bauhaus

Concept   The cover displays a mere forty-two of the nearly six hundred glyphs that Sascha Lobe and his team have created so far while designing the identity for the Bauhaus Archive. It is available in three colors and, as a little bonus, the cover artwork comes to life in augmented reality when viewed using the Artivive app.

Partner
and Creative Direction
Sascha Lobe°
London

URL
pentagram.com

Twitter
@pentagram

Design Firm
Pentagram

Client
It's Nice That
Printed Pages

Dimensions
7.9 x 10.8 in.
(20 x 27.5 cm)

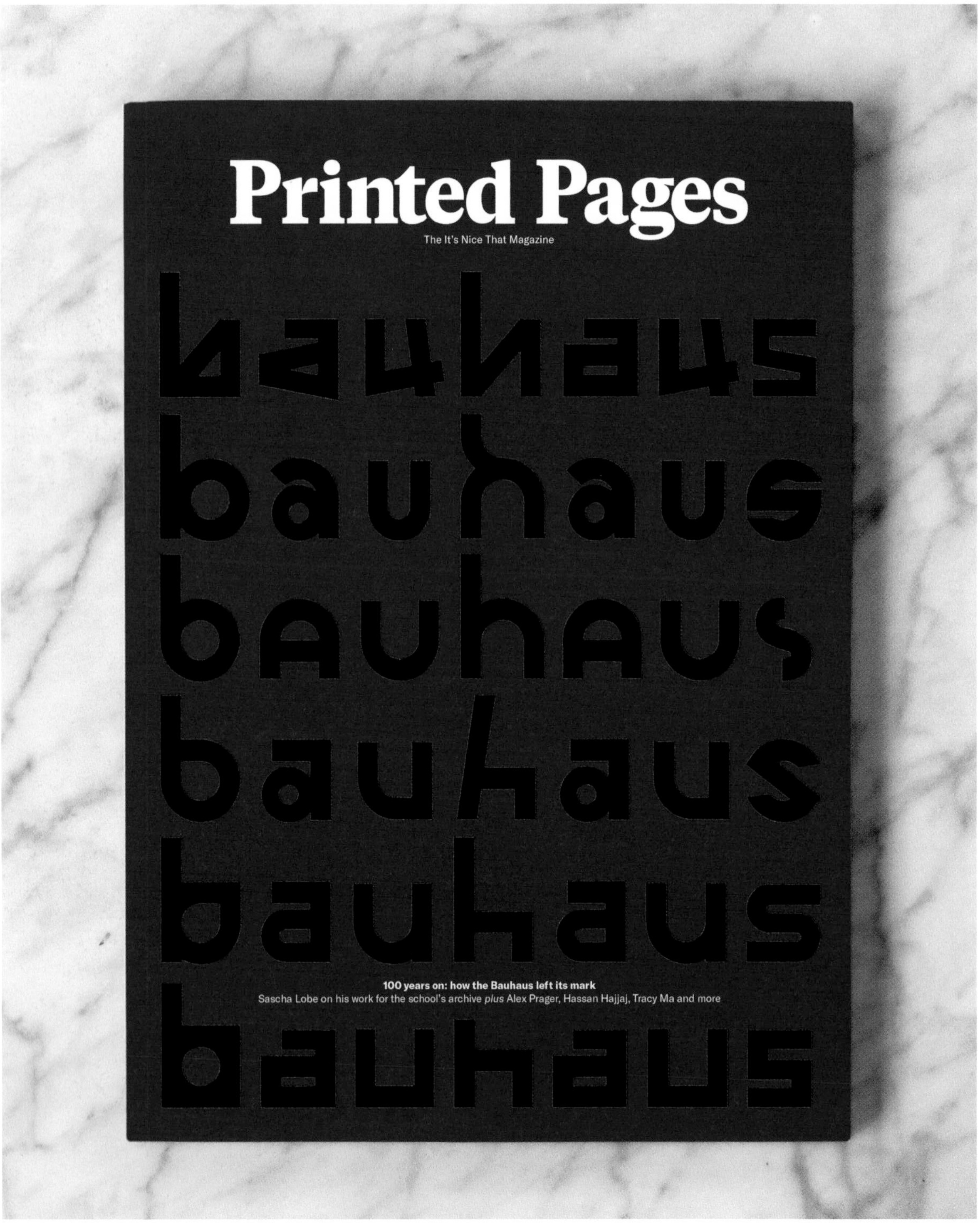

Roald Dahl Series

Concept Roald Dahl was known for his rule-flouting, witty children's books and fantastic stories for adults. On the covers of this series, his name is used as a key element that connects all books, and the content is placed in this binding structure. Typography is spread in masses at different angles to give a sense of animation. For each cover, characters and supporting details from the books are selected and used on this structure, which itself is also shaped and colored according to the story. The goal is a serial formulation that pays proper tribute to the colorful and fantastic imaginary world of Dahl's literature.

Design
Utku Lomlu°
Istanbul

URL
utkulomlu.com

Twitter
@utkulomlu

Design Studio
Lom Creative

Client
Can Publishing

Dimensions
4.9 x 7.7 in.
(12.5 x 19.5 cm)

Principal Type
Custom

The Lost Chapters

Concept   This memoir is an account of recovery
following a 414-day relapse into alcohol and drug
addiction after more than a decade of being clean
and sober. The type appears to be printed on one of
the last remaining pages in a book torn apart.

Design
Ben Denzer
New York

Art Direction
Jason Booher

Publisher
Penguin Random House

Client
Blue Rider Press

Dimensions
6 x 9 in. (15.2 x 22.9 cm)

Principal Type
Bodoni Classic

The Vanishing Frame:
Latin American Culture and Theory
in the Postdictatorial Era

Concept   This is the cover for a Latin American
Studies book that examines several prominent
writers and artists whose work is a critique of
economic inequality. The texture of ink on paper
points to a conceptual gray area—an indeterminate
conceptual frame where things are not always
black and white or easy to categorize.

Design
**Mitch Goldstein
and Anne Jordan
Rochester, New York**

Art Direction
Dustin Kilgore

URLs
**annatype.com
mitchgoldstein.com**

Twitter
**@annatype
@mgoldst**

Studio
**Studio of Anne Jordan
and Mitch Goldstein**

Client
**The University of
Texas Press**

Dimensions
**6 x 9 in.
(15.24 x 22.86 cm)**

Principal Type
DIN Medium

EUGENIO CLAUDIO DI STEFANO

THE VANISHING FRAME

LATIN AMERICAN CULTURE
AND THEORY IN THE
POSTDICTATORIAL ERA

Astral Weeks

Concept   The handlettering was inspired by The
Avatar, a biweekly publication published in Boston
from June 1967 to April 1968. The design calls to
mind a specific time and place (Boston, 1968).

Design
Ben Denzer
New York

Art Direction
Darren Haggar

URL
bendenzer.com

Studio
Penguin Art Group

Client
Penguin Press

Dimensions
6.25 x 9.5 in.
(15.9 x 24.1 cm)

Principal Type
Handlettering

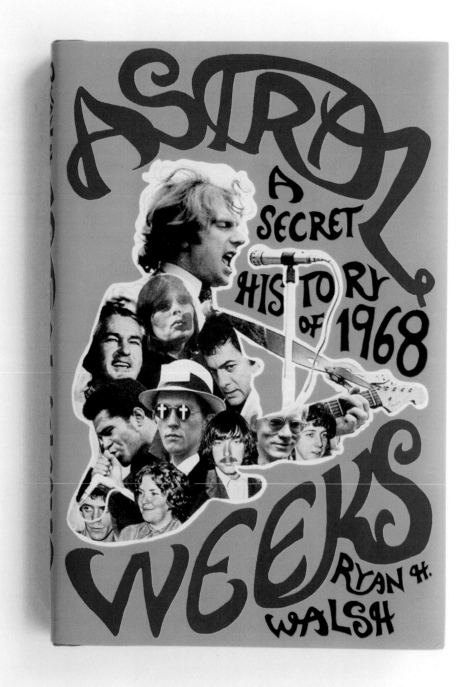

Franny en Zooey

Concept   J.D. Salinger covers require that no photos or illustrations be used. In addition, the title should always be above the name of the author and set in bigger type. To break the rigidity of these rules and bring expressiveness to the design, we decided to handletter the title instead of using a font. As an opposite, we set the author's name as serious as possible in stately Roman capitals.

Design and Calligraphy
**Henk van het Nederend
Amsterdam**

URL
mokerontwerp.nl

Twitter
@MokerOntwerp

Design Firm
Moker Ontwerp

Client
De Bezige Bij

Dimensions
**4.92 x 7.9 in.
(12.5 x 20 cm)**

Principal Type
**Canto Roman
and handlettering**

Virtude Cênica

Concept   Virtude Cênica ("Scenic Virtue") contains the work of street photographer Ricardo Perini. His work navigates among the strokes of light in the shadows of daily life—hence the use of black, white, and gold on the book cover. The strong presence of urban architecture in Perini's photos inspired this geometric/volumetric lettering that can be read in two directions.

Art Direction
Cyla Costa°
Curitiba and São Paulo,
Brazil

URL
cylacosta.com

Twitter
@cylacosta

Design Firm
Cyla Costa Studio

Client
Ricardo Perini
and Fotô Editorial

Dimensions
8 x 10.5 in. (20 x 26 cm)

Principal Type
Handlettering

Field Museum

Concept   The newly unveiled logo and brand system for The Field Museum is intentionally bold, modern, and forward looking. Mummies, an exhibit that showcased recently unearthed research into the ancient practice of mummification, set the tone for the brand. Our goal was to reset the visitor's perception of mummies from mysterious, dusty, and passive to engaging and awe inspiring.

Design
**Scott Cress
and Rob Schellenberg
Chicago**

Head of Design
Alisa Wolfson

Agency
**Leo Burnett Chicago
Department of Design**

Client
The Field Museum

Dimensions
Various

Principal Type
Druk and Graphik

CareerTrackers Advantage Report

Concept   CareerTrackers is an Australian nonprofit that addresses indigenous disadvantage by developing professional career pathways, internship programs, and links with private sector employers. We were briefed to create a "report" that shared data on some of the extraordinary outcomes that CareerTrackers is achieving in Australia. We proposed the idea of a set of cards in an interactive format that could be used as an orientation activity. The cards also added a tangibility to the data, which we felt would appeal to students, who might not get that engaged by something like a PDF or slide deck. The cards use bold graphic forms, unified by a simple color palette inspired by the Aboriginal and Torres Strait Islander flags.

Design
**Paul Garbett
Sydney**

Art Direction
Danielle de Andrade

URL
garbett.com.au

Instagram
@garbettdesign

Design Firm
Garbett

Client
CareerTrackers

Dimensions
5.9 x 4.3 in. (15 x 11 cm)

Principal Type
Future Mono

Fall Season 18

Concept This is a fall season brochure to highlight upcoming shows. The show-specific pages include indexical images to reference the plays. The general content pages include a variety of lively Public Theater performers.

Senior Graphic Designer
Tammy Shell
New York

Creative Direction
Paula Scher°
(Pentagram)

URL
publictheater.org

Twitter
@publictheaterny

Studio
The Public Theater

Client
The Public Theater

Dimensions
Folded 6 x 9 in. (15.2 x 22.9 cm); Flat 18 x 24 in. (45.7 x 61 cm)

Principal Type
Knockout

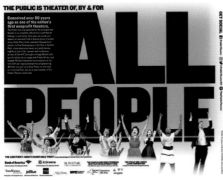

ZHU Carbon Toasted Tea

Concept   We were invited to help express the essence of the ZHU brand through a conceptual book. By intermixing fragmented pictures and text throughout, we broke up the timeline and the construction of space. In addition, we used a non-liner and loose-sheet construction. Finally, laser engraving technology gave us a great "toasting" effect on one side. Each book is presented as a different possibility.

Design
Zhang Jingrui
Beijing

Art Direction
Gu Hanyu

Editor
LEO

Design Studio
T-workshop

Client
ZHU Studio

Dimensions
6.3 x 8.7 in. (16 x 22 cm)

Principal Type
Avenir Next, Noto Sans S Chinese, and custom

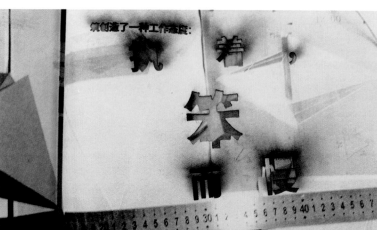

Circular Calendar

Concept   This circular calendar is a typographic exercise that looks at the 365 days of the year of 2018 from a different point of view. Each concentric circle brings the days of the months. They line up by the outer circle, which indicates the days of the week.

Design
Ralph Mayer
São Paulo

URL
estudiograde.com.br

Instagram
@estudiograde

Studio
Estúdio Grade

Dimensions
16.5 x 23.4 in.
(42 x 59.4 cm)

Principal Type
Simplon Mono

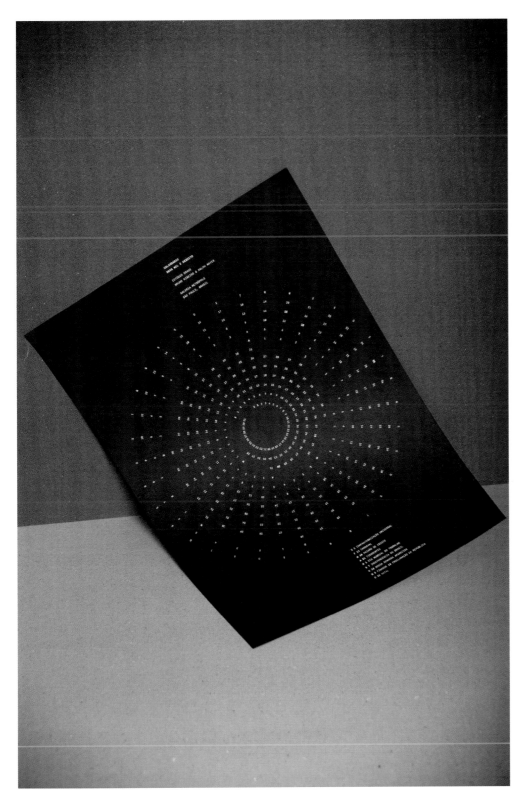

With Out Water

Concept The premise was to create a brochure that reflected the beauty of the photography and the botanical forms of flowers—a piece of work that elevated the creativity of the exhibition and spoke to those who might want to see it.

Design,
Creative Direction,
and Typographer
Derek Samuel
Melbourne, Australia

URL
dereksamuel.com

Design Firm
Derek Samuel Design

Client
Isamu Sawa
Photography

Dimensions
11.6 x 16.5 in.
(29.4 x 42 cm)

Principal Type
Din Round
and Port Vintage

Odd Apples Photobook

Concept Through photographs of rare and curious apples, this large-format photobook expands our perception of apples, what they look like, and what they taste like. Odd Apples was a limited, hand-numbered edition of two hundred.

Design and Lettering
**Andrea A.
Trabucco-Campos°
Brooklyn, New York**

Photography
William Mullan

Printer
PureprintGroup

URL
trabuc.co

Twitter
@trabuccocampos

Dimensions
**12 x 16 in.
(30.5 x 15.2 cm)**

Principal Type
**Traulha Regulara
and custom**

100 Years of Bauhaus

Concept   The animation displays the manifoldness of the Bayer Next glyphs. The concept was developed in collaboration with It's Nice That.

Design
Connor Campbell (It's Nice That) and Jonas Zieher London

Partner and Creative Direction
Sascha Lobe°

URL
pentagram.com

Twitter
@pentagram

Design Firm
Pentagram

Client
It's Nice That Printed Pages

Is Google Too Powerful?

Concept For Charles Duhigg's article on Google and antitrust lawsuits, an outsize logo rolls onto the cover, conveying the size and power of the tech behemoth as it displaces the cover language and even our own logo.

Design and
Design Direction
Gail Bichler°
New York

Art Direction
Matt Willey

Deputy Art Director
Ben Grandgenett

URL
**https://nytimes.
com/2018/02/20/mag-
azine/the-case-against-
google.html**

Publication
**The New York Times
Magazine**

Dimensions
**8.9 x 10.9 in.
(22.5 x 27.6 cm)**

Principal Type
NYT Mag Sans

No Man's Land

Concept   Pentagram has created a brand identity and editorial design for The Wing's first biannual magazine, No Man's Land, bringing The Wing's smart, edgy sensibility and emphasis on diverse voices to a broader audience. Stemming from the branding for The Wing, Pentagram's design for the magazine reflects its ethos with a multifaceted, punchy approach that is witty and self-referential. No Man's Land stylistically represents an unexpected, feminist-centric twist on standard magazine tropes, without veering into parody. The Pentagram team helped develop the publication's structure and flow, rendering each of its sections visually distinct and deeply considered.

Design
**Elizabeth Goodspeed,
Christina Hogan,
and Joey Petrillo
New York**

Partner
Emily Oberman°

Project Manager
Anna Meixler

Executive Editor
Deidre Dyer

Deputy Editor
Laia Garcia

Director of Photography
Emily Keegin

Photo Editor
Alis Atwell

URL
pentagram.com

Twitter
@pentagram

Design Firm
Pentagram°

Client
The Wing

Dimensions
**8 x 10.5 in.
(20.3 x 26.7 cm)**

Principal Type
**Agipo Condensed,
Berlingske Slab,
Clifton Italic, Knif Mono,
Maison Neue,
and Titania**

The Education Issue,
September 9, 2018

Concept   Teachers today are facing pressure
from all angles, whether it is standardized test
scores, chronic underfunding, or having to deal
with the horrors of school shootings. The cover of
our education issue takes visual inspiration from
old protest posters and very directly addresses just
how hard a task teaching has become.

Design
Claudia Rubín
New York

Design Direction
Gail Bichler°

Art Direction
Matt Willey

Deputy Art Director
Ben Grandgenett

URL
https://nytimes.com/
interactive/2018/09/05/
magazine/arizona-
teachers-facebook-
group-doug-ducey.html

Publication
The New York Times
Magazine

Dimensions
8.9 x 10.9 in.
(22.5 x 27.6 cm)

Principal Type
Franklin Gothic Std
Condensed,
Franklin Gothic Std
Extra Condensed,
Franklin Gothic Std
No. 2 Roman,
Onehunga,
and Univers Std 93 Extra
Black Extended

September 9, 2018

The New York Times Magazine

TEACHERS JUST WANT TO TEACH BUT THE CLASSROOM HAS BECOME A BATTLEGROUND

University of Toronto Magazine

Art Direction
Nicola Hamilton
Toronto

Creative Direction
Vanessa Wyse

URL
studiowyse.com

Design Studio
Studio Wyse

Client
University of Toronto
Magazine

Principal Type
Beaufort Condensed,
Beaufort Extended, and
Beaufort Pro

Dimensions
7.75 x 10.5 in.
(19.7 x 26.7 cm)

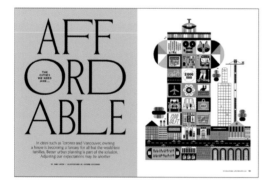

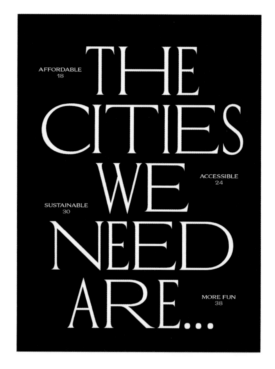

Food & Wine: The Photography Issue

Concept   The cover of Food & Wine's March 2018 Photography Issue features a gorgeous flan, shot by Gourmet's former in-house photographer Romulo Yanes. The flan is shot close up and evocatively cut into, bringing the tender, custardy dessert onto the viewer's plate. The arresting photo signals the "Cooks & Shooters" feature package within—forty pages celebrating the intersection of cooking and photography. Creative Director Winslow Taft extended the pools of caramel to integrate the logo, creating a single, cohesive image. Decadent yet playful, it steps outside the comfort zone of the traditional F&W cover while continuing our legacy of beautiful food.

Design and
Creative Direction
Winslow Taft
Birmingham, Alabama

Photography
Romulo Yanes

URL
foodandwine.com

Publication
Food & Wine

Dimensions
8 x 10.5 in.
(20.2 x 26.7 cm)

Principal Type
Benton Sans

Burnt Caramel
Flan (p. 89)

MARCH 2018

Oil of LA

Concept Los Angeles Magazine approached me to illustrate the headline for an article about oil in Los Angeles. The challenge was to create lettering that looked like oil, while being legible and visually interesting. I took inspiration from the density and dynamic behavior of oil itself and built the letters as if they were splashes in order to add movement and richness to the title.

Art Direction
**Jordan Williams,
Los Angeles**

Lettering
Ana Gómez Bernaus°

URL
anenocena.com

Studio
Anenocena

Client
Los Angeles Magazine

Dimensions
**8 x 10.5 in.
(20.3 x 26.7 cm)**

Principal Type
Custom

D1GIT

Concept   3D printers, microalgae, spores, parametrically programmed ultra-resistant materials, and dynamic volumes will change the way we design. Or will we continue to build houses in the form of ... houses? This issue of 120g Magazine explores the intersection between the digital world of new technologies and the oldest building materials, elevating traditional techniques to new horizons. D1GIT's imagery boldly transmutes raw matter into digital textures, while typography brightly organizes content and imagery into six articles about the future of building and living.

Design and Art Direction
Fabio Santaniello Bruun
Milan

URL
fsb.design

Twitter
@fabiosbruun

Design Firm
FSB Design

Client
120g Magazine

Dimensions
9.5 x 13.4 in.
(24 x 34 cm)

Principal Type
Liber Grotesque
and IBM Plex Mono

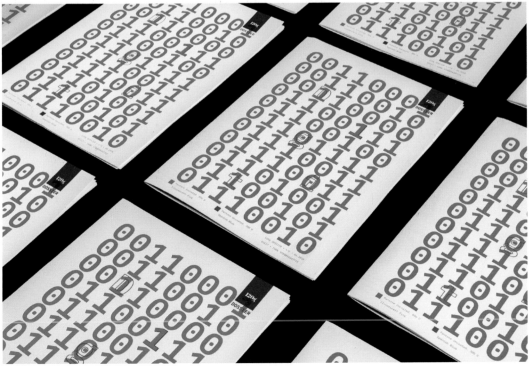

Emil Ruder's Typography in Chinese

Concept   Issue 13 of circle is a tribute to Emil Ruder and his masterpiece Typography, and an experimental project of Swiss typography manifested in Chinese/kanji. To fully bridge the two different writing systems and explore the possibilities of Chinese type design, the oblique and extended fonts—which don't yet exist in Chinese typography—were customized for the project. As a result, quoting from and derived from part of the nine chapters of Ruder's original book, the Chinese interpretation proves to be a reflection of his typographic principles combined with a completely different language, culture, time, and technology.

Design
Bei-En Wang
Taipei

Creative Direction
Jessie Chiuhui Chen

URLs
way2creative.com
circlezine.com

Design Firm
way2creative inc.

Client
circle zine

Dimensions
8.5 x 10.8 in.
(21.5 x 27.5 cm)

Principal Type
UD Shin Go

Golden Age

Concept   We created this type-led cover for the magazine's issue dedicated to free speech—more specifically, to illustrate how free speech has degraded in the digital age, with new kinds of censorship. The idea was to combine something pure with something eroded, through textures and color contrasts: a smooth base, destroyed by rust. We mixed a CG matrix with photographic textures from heavily oxidized metal sheets, as well as all the old peeling paints and scraps we could find. All of this was shot in macro, then applied piece by piece to our digital canvas to create a rich and tactile treatment.

Design and Photography
Sean Freeman
London

Art Direction
Frank Augugliaro

Creative Production
Eve Steben

Creative Direction
David Moretti

URL
thereis.co.uk

Design Firm
THERE IS

Client
Wired U.S.

Dimensions
8.1 x 10.9 in.
(20.6 x 27.6 cm)

Principal Type
Wired Pointy

FEATURING:
ZEYNEP TUFEKCI
ALICE GREGORY
VIRGINIA HEFFERNAN
STEVEN JOHNSON
DOUG BOCK CLARK

SPECIAL ISSUE:
TECH, TURMOIL,
AND THE
NEW CENSORSHIP
P.50

THE GOLDEN AGE OF FREE SPEECH

FEBRUARY 2018 | CAN WE TALK?

WIRED-26.02

CREATE. CONNECT. CONDÉ NAST

103

Back to Life

Concept This typography was for an article about deceased celebrities being reincarnated as holograms.

Design and Typography
**Rob Gonzalez
and Jonathan Quainton
London**

URL
madebysawdust.co.uk

Twitter
@SawdustStudio

Design Firm
Sawdust

Client
Wired UK

Dimensions
**16 x 10.9 in.
(40.6 x 27.6 cm)**

Principal Type
Bespoke

Mohawk Maker Quarterly 15: Materials

Concept   Materials are an emotional filter, informing how we should feel about what we touch and see. The fifteenth issue of Mohawk Maker Quarterly focuses on the object qualities that materials make possible. Each article is realized as its own object—made of material(s) and form that help communicate its point of view. Collectively, the issue speaks to the importance of object quality in our work, and the responsibility to use these qualities not as bells and whistles, but as design elements.

Design
**Sarah Jean Recht,
Carl-Hampus Vallin,
and David Weber**
San Francisco

Design and Illustration
Olivia Ward

Creative Direction
Caleb Kozlowski
Executive Creative

Director
Dora Drimalas

URL
hybrid-design.com

Studio
Hybrid Design

Client
Mohawk

Dimensions
9 x 12 in.
(22.9 x 30.5 cm)

Principal Type
Chalet and Sentinel

Dazzle

Design
Domenic Lippa°
London

Project Team
David Bhalla

Design Firm
Pentagram

Client
London Design Festival

Principal Type
Custom (based on Naval Pennant Numbers and Berthold Akzidenz Grotesk Light)

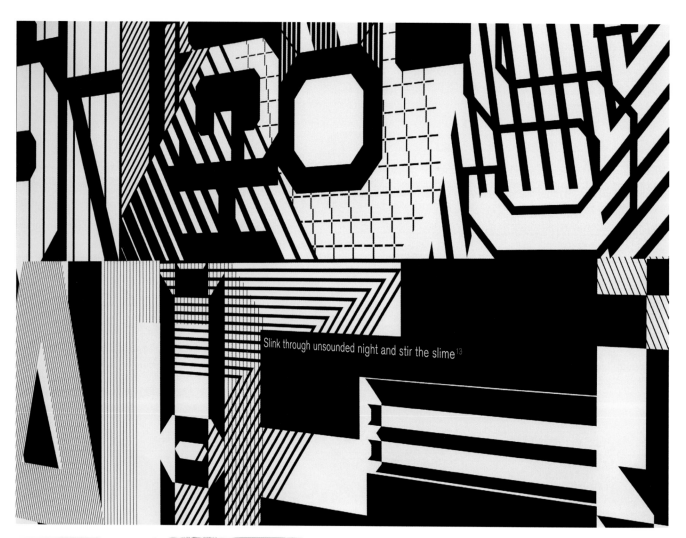

Slink through unsounded night and stir the slime [13]

Signage CO 4.0

Concept   Colombia 4.0 is the country's largest digital culture and technology event. For its 2018 version, we were commissioned to create the visual identity of the event, including interventions in space. We created a visual system full of powerful typographic compositions complemented by color and geometry, signifying the different representations of human thought on digital screens. This powerful system made it possible to generate impact and identity in such a large space as the Bogotá fair and helped the 45,000-plus visitors find the different contents.

Creative Direction
**Julian Jaramillo
and Oliver Siegenthaler
Bogotá**

Art Direction
**Silvia Camargo
and Nicolas Galeano**

Executive Director
Paula Martinez

URL
siegenco.com

Instagram
@siegenco

Design Firm
S&Co

Client
**Ministerio de
Tecnologías de la
Información y las
Comunicaciones
de Colombia**

Principal Type
GT America Expanded

Dimensions
Various

Avant Aprés

Concept Conceived from Porto, and focusing exclusively on the city of Le Havre, the installation is inspired by images, documents, books, architecture, music, films, stories, building materials, and momentary experiences of the city. It is a work that reflects the present by exploring the void between the two words "before" (avant) and "after" (après). It's an empty space that is construed through the links between the past and future, and it's open to multiple interpretations and perspectives.

Design and Art Direction
Lizá Défossez Ramalho and Artur Rebelo
Porto, Portugal

URL
r2design.pt

Studio
R2

Client
Ville du Havre, Le Havre, France and Une Saison Graphique 18

Dimensions
Letters 39.7 x 39.7 x 39.7 in. (100 x 100 x 100 cm); Total length 259.8 in. (660 cm)

Principal Type
Bespoke

Rent-Event-Tec

Concept   The urban planning authority wanted this façade to be decorated in its entirety. We persuaded them to let us do the honors by promising that it would feature their logo. The planners were not happy, though: According to their regulations, only ten percent of the façade can be used for advertising purposes. Our solution was to take the company logo and break it up into its component parts, which we then arranged loosely and indecipherably enough for the planners to approve—yet closely enough that it's just about legible. Now the client is happy. For everyone else, it's a giant graphic puzzle.

Art Direction
**Carolin Himmel
and Andreas Uebele°
Mannheim, Germany**

Project Manager
Christian Lindermann

URL
uebele.com

Design Firm
**büro uebele visuelle
kommunikation**

Client
City of Mannheim

Dimensions
**32.2 x 39.4 ft.
(98 x 120 m)**

Principal Type
Glaser Stencil

There Is No Such Thing as a New Zealand Typeface

Concept   National 2, a typeface by Klim Type Foundry, is at the heart of this exhibition that questions the way identities are formed through symbols, imagery, beliefs, and language. The exhibition interrogates the relationship between type and place, text and landscape, and ultimately identity. Across the exhibition title—a super graphic across the gallery walls—sixteen large-scale atmospheric photos with shared horizons trace a visual journey from the Valley of Darkness up Mount Inaccessible. Through vernacular road signs, National 2 is cast in a territory where design is intertwined with landscape.

Design
**Tim Gomez
Auckland**

Design Director
Janson Chau

Creative Directors
**Dean Poole, Alt Group;
and Kris Sowersby°
Klim Type Foundry**

Writer
Mike Barrett

Photography
Alistair Guthrie

Design Studio
Alt Group

Client
Klim Type Foundry

Principal Type
National 2

The Book of Genesis

Concept Over and over in the book of Genesis, God asks his people to follow him through difficult trials and unpredictable circumstances. Abraham, Isaac, Jacob, Noah, and Joseph each obey God solely in faith that God fulfills his promises. This Genesis piece is a metaphor for that faith: following the path of God even when the future is hidden from sight.

Design
Katie Tynes
Atlanta

Advisor
Hank Richardson

School
Miami Ad School
@ Portfolio Center

Dimensions
48 x 30 in. (122 x 76 cm)

Principal Type
Berthold Bodoni
Old Face

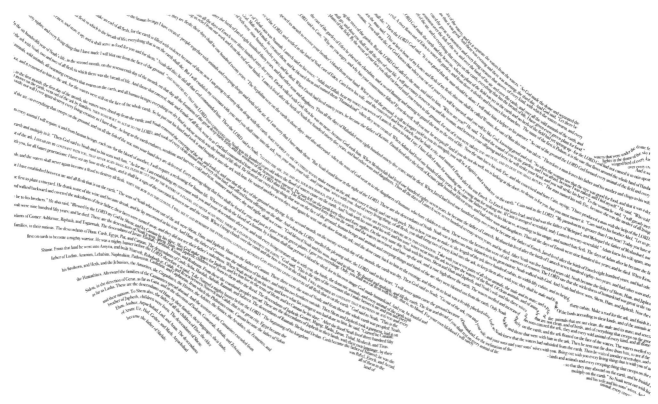

36 Days of Type

Concept   The 36 Days of Type series is an exploration of the boundaries between my expressive handwriting and legibility restrictions. I challenged myself to use as few lines and components as possible, based on quick sketches of simple ideas.

Design
Zuzanna Rogatty°
Warsaw

URL
rogatty.com

Instagram
**www.instagram.com/
zrogatty**

Dimensions
24 x 36 in. (61 x 91 cm)

Principal Type
Custom Lettering

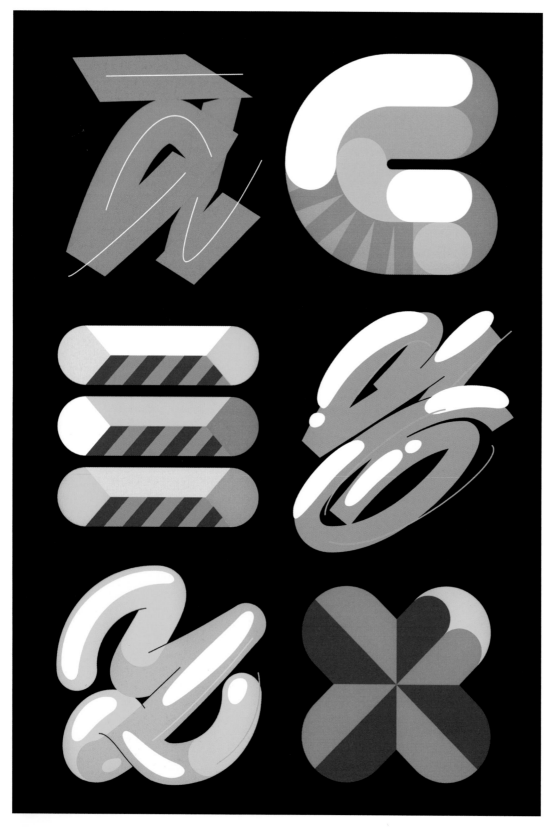

Planet Caravan

Concept **Planet Caravan is a noncommercial experimental typeface with an enormously high contrast and nontraditional strokes. It features a random sequence of horizontal and vertical line widths and jumping stroke heights for visual perception compensation.**

Design and Art Direction
Kirill Ratman
Ekaterinburg, Russia

URL
@kiratman

Principal Type
Planet Caravan

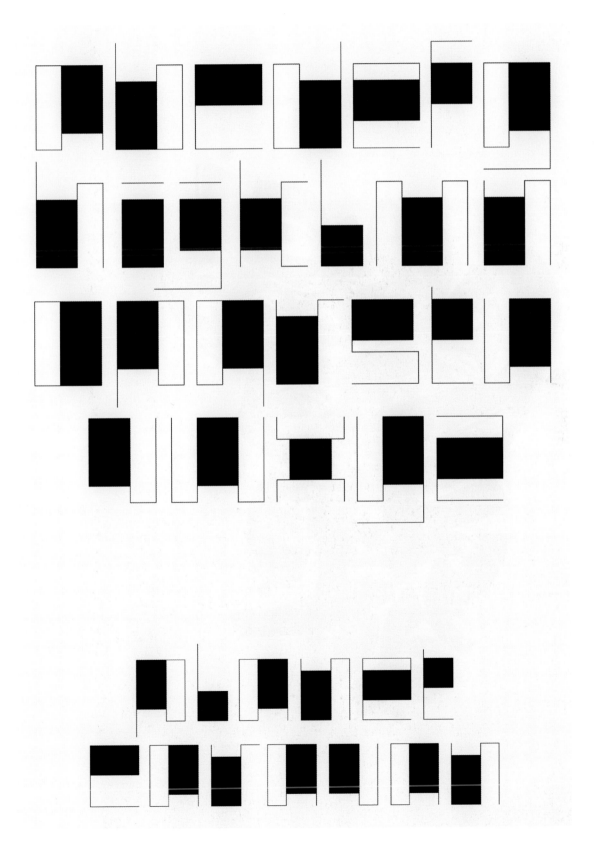

Ancestors

Concept   Juliette Abdallah Moshe. First name:
Juliette. Father's name: Abdallah. Grandfather's
name: Moshe. This is how my grandmother was
listed on her immigration papers to Israel, when she
arrived from Iraq in 1951. As was customary then,
her name was shortened to Juliette Dvora.
The moving discovery of her full name made me
wonder about the absence of my ancestors from
my name, and about my place in my family's
journey. The two works, Shany Abdallah Najiand
Shany Miriam Yocheved, were written in Hebrew
letters, based on calligraphy from manuscripts
written five-hundred years ago in Iraq, Yemen,
and Morocco.

Design and Lettering
Shany Dvora
Tel Aviv

Photography
Raz Silberman

URL
shanydvora.com

Dimensions
18 x 35.8 in.
(91 x 45.5 cm)

Principal Type
Handlettering

Posters of 365 Days
Font Design Exhibition

Concept In the past 365 days, I did have done one typographic design for each day. These words may be the festival of the day, solar terms, news, travelling anecdotes, or emotional feelings and inspirations of the moment. My daily attempts explored the immense possibilities of Chinese characters, which also led to a greater appreciation and understanding of the characters themselves.

Design
Lu Xiao Kun
Guangzhou, China

URL
waygen-design.com

Design Firm
Waygen Design

Dimensions
20.5 x 29.5 in.
(52 x 75 cm)

Principal Type
Custom

Ki-Lim Kim "Sea and Beauty" Concrete Poetry Book

Concept This book embodies the idea of falling into a deep, dark abyss. To express the effect of being drowned in the rough sea, it has a square-shaped vacant space and concrete poetry arranged at both ends. This concrete poetry uses thinner fonts as it ventures farther from the front part of the book, to emphasize the growing deepness of the abyss.

Design
Kunha Lee
Seoul

URL
graphicha.kr

Studio
Graphicha Studio

Client
Hongik University

Dimensions
8.3 x 11 x 7.5 in.
(21.5 x 28 x 19 cm)

Principal Type
Sandoll Gothic Neo1

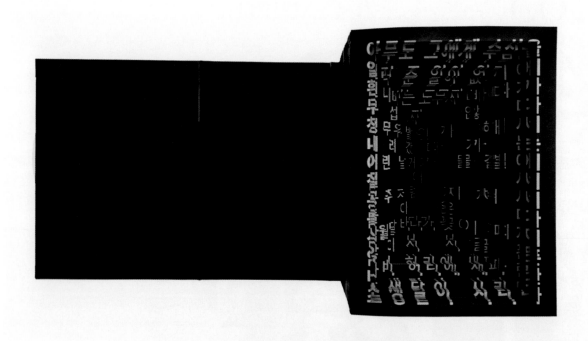

Ki-Lim Kim "Sea and Beauty" Concrete Poetry Book

Concept This book embodies the idea of falling into a deep, dark abyss. To express the effect of being drowned in the rough sea, it has a square-shaped vacant space and concrete poetry arranged at both ends. This concrete poetry uses thinner fonts as it ventures farther from the front part of the book, to emphasize the growing deepness of the abyss.

Design
Kunha Lee
Seoul

URL
graphicha.kr

Studio
Graphicha Studio

Client
Hongik University

Inna Art Space 10:
The First Decade

Concept
This is the visual design for the tenth-anniversary invitational exhibition The First Decade of Inna Art Space. Taking the ten-year exhibition timeline as a clue, it presents various aspects of the Inna Art Space over the past decade.

Design
**Cong Chen,
Xiaomei Liu, Fan Yang,
and Qiongjie Yu
Hangzhou, China**

Art Direction
Qiongjie Yu

URL
transwhite.cn

Design Studio
Transwhite Studio

Client
Inna Art Space

Dimensions
Various

Principal Type
Brutal

2018 International Garden Festival

Concept   Each year, the International Garden Festival invites artists to create contemporary garden projects. For this edition, the festival chose to reinstate the previous year's theme of playful landscapes, titling it "Playscapes 2." To communicate the event, we developed a system of shapes, colors, and typography—a concept that allowed us to address the playful aspect in an abstract fashion, all while hinting at various regional landscapes.

Design
**Marie-France Gaudet
Montréal**

Creative Direction
Patrick Pellerin

Art Direction
**Marie-France Gaudet
and Bryan K. Lamonde**

URL
principal.studio

Design Studio
Principal

Client
Jardins de Métis

Dimensions
36 x 24 in. (91.4 x 61 cm)

Principal Type
LL Circular

Hong Shi Ban Farmer's Market

Concept   The design was inspired by the original visual relationship and usage traces of the Hong Shi Ban Farmer's Market. Based on the arrangement of Chinese characters and Western words, the text sequence is disrupted to form a new flat language system and an interesting visual experience.

Design
Meng Ge, Ren Qianqian, Mei Shuzhi, Wu Xiaoyan, and Wu Yanying
Hangzhou City, China

Art Direction
Mei Shuzhi

Design Firm
702design

Client
H-Change Group

Dimensions
Various

Principal Type
Calibre,
Founder Lanting Black,
and Hiragino Sans

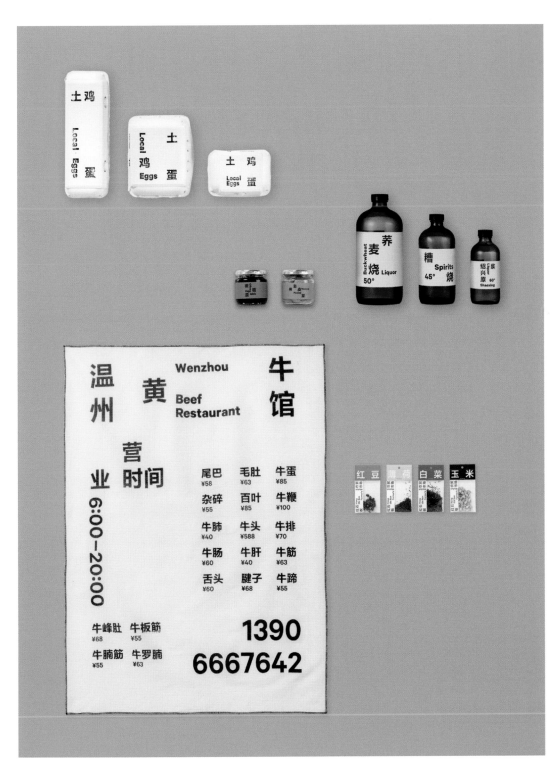

Origami X Material

Concept The key visual uses the technique of folding to change the characteristics of materials, allowing a two-dimensional material to acquire three-dimensional attributes. The letter O in the design exists between two-dimensional and three-dimensional space. The audience can also learn different origami folding techniques by interacting with the folding leaflet.

Design
Shui-Lun Fan
Hong Kong

URL
nottoolate.hk

Design Firm
NOT TOO LATE

Client
The Hong Kong
Polytechnic University
Material Resource
Centre

Dimensions
Various

Principal Type
MONT Bold,
SemiBold, and Regular;
and Xin Gothic, W8,
W6, and W4

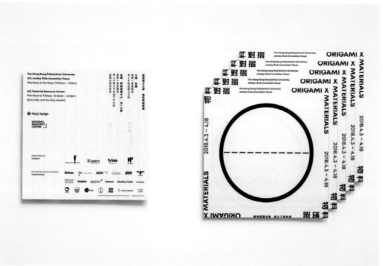

Montres KF

Concept   Montres KF is the new brand of the well-known watchmaker Karsten Fräßdorf, who specializes in the design of sophisticated tourbillon movements and handcrafted individual pieces or limited editions. The logo consists of Fräßdorf's initials in conjunction with minute and hour hands. The simplicity of idea and realization reflects the philosophy of his watchmaking—purism, craftsmanship, and respect for the historical roots of horology. This stance is underpinned by the use of letterpress printing and high-quality uncoated paper.

Design
Christopher Wiehl°
Düsseldorf

URL
wiehl-co.com

Design Firm
wiehl, Co.

Client
Montres KF

Dimensions
Various

Principal Type
Futura T and Sabon LT

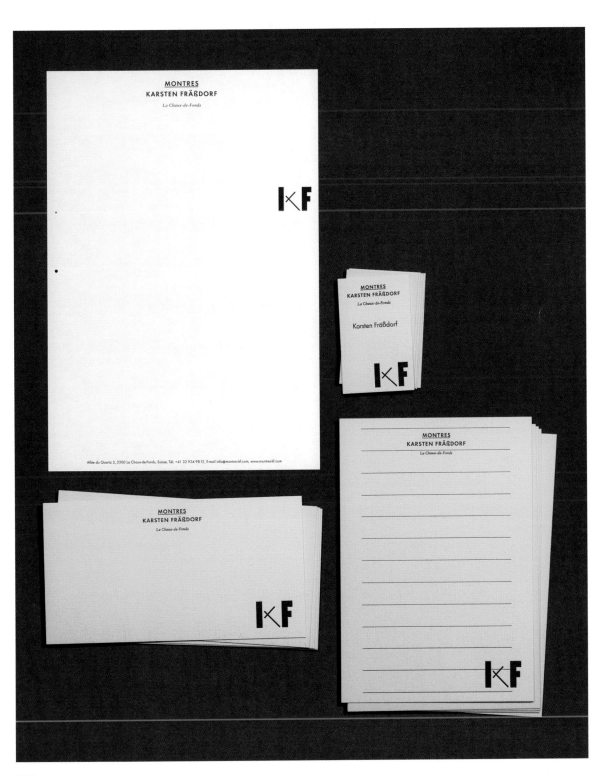

i dots

Concept **Die-cut dots floating free from their respective dotless i's visually reinforce the client's independent brand name.**

Design
Graham Clifford°
New York

Creative
and Art Direction
Colin Corcoran
Minneapolis

Typographer
Graham Clifford

Writer
Colin Corcoran

Printer
Angel Bomb Design +
Letterpress

Producer
Todd Thyberg

URLs
grahamclifforddesign.
com
independentcopywriter.
com
angelbomb.com
a2-type.co.uk

Client
Colin Corcoran
Independent Copywriter

Design Studio
Graham Clifford Design

Dimensions
3.5 x 2 in. (8.9 x 5.1 cm)

Principal Type
A2 Typewriter

Lugano Region Territorial Branding

Concept This is the territorial branding for the Swiss city of Lugano and its region. Lugano represents an atypical destination within Switzerland where Mediterranean weather and cuisine can be found in a safe, quiet, and efficient Swiss environment. The brand essence that emerged from this context is "differently Swiss," which has been translated visually in an alteration of the Swiss flag to form the letter L of Lugano. A graphic system that aims to display the variety of the region's offerings has been conceived by designing for each category a specific font in order to give each time a different connotation of the letter L of Lugano.

Creative Direction
Fabio Caselli
Mendrisio, Switzerland

Photography
Joseph Fortebraccio

Strategic Planner
Francesca Casati

Project Manager
Lilian Widdershoven

URL
caselli.ch

Design Firm
Caselli Strategic Design

Client
Ente Turistico del Luganese

Dimensions
Various

Principal Type
Garamond, Proxima Nova, and custom

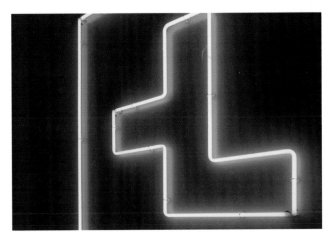

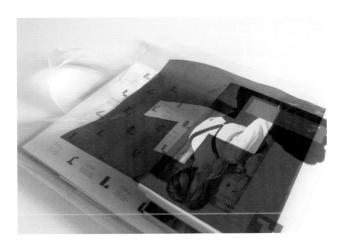

Future Exhibition

Concept Future Exhibition is a salon and exhibition led by new designers and artists that aims to explore the connection of art and explain the confusion toward future art. We set up a seemingly clear visual network for the exhibition and mixed it with the image of Chinese characteristics "未来". All areas are connected by lines but are also confused because of the texture of "未来"—creating an ordered yet disordered visual system.

Art Direction
Yinan Lyu
Beijing

Design Firm
Calx Station

URL
calxstation.com

Client
Future Exhibition

Dimensions
Various

Principal Type
Source Han Sans

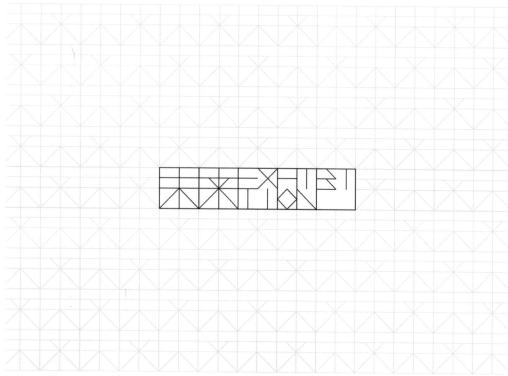

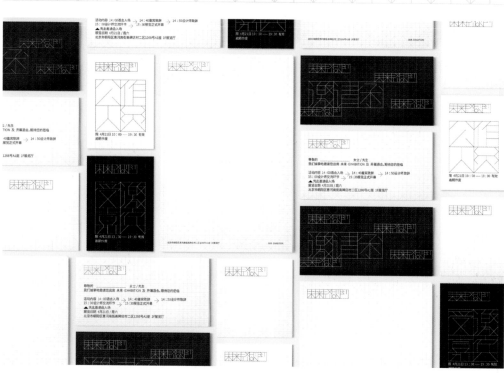

150 Media Stream

Concept 150 Media Stream is a sculptural video installation consisting of ninety-two LED screens that stream artwork created by internationally renowned artists. Our goal was to design an identity to attract artistic talent and connoisseurs of the arts, and to establish this installation as a Chicago cultural landmark. The Narrative developed an adaptable identity full of visual energy and movement to function alongside the ever-changing artistic styles of the curated video content. The identity was inspired by the space between the blades of the installation—the tension between separation and unity.

Design Directors and Partners
**Sofya Karash and Daniel McManus
Chicago**

150 Media Stream Director and Curator
Yuge Zhou

URL
thenarrative.design

Twitter
@thenarrativedes

Design Studio
The Narrative

Client
Riverside Investment & Development

Dimensions
Various

Principal Type
Neutraface

IDENTITY

Sydney Saké Society

Concept Sydney Saké Society aims to bridge the gap between the niche saké culture and Sydney's vibrant food and entertainment scene. The logo mark is a seal stamp (commonly seen on saké bottle labels) comprising three S's. A display typeface has been designed based on the letter S, mimicking the geometric Kanji stroke style in traditional seal stamps. The typeface is translated across the organization's collateral in a playful and flexible manner, using red and porcelain blue with complementary pastel colors.

Design
Kevin Teh
Kuala Lumpur

URL
tehdesigner.net

Twitter
@teh_designer

Client
Jason Khoh, Sydney,
Australia

Dimensions
Various

Principal Type
Kampai Display
and Sofia Pro

Tribeca Forward

Concept **Combining the technical language of screenplay writing with a colorful and energetic celebration of the powerful simplicity of ink on paper, the Tribeca Forward campaign presents a visual immediacy that will motivate and inspire audiences to explore the many experiences that the Tribeca Film Festival has to offer, assembling new ideas along the way to create their own empowering story line, directed by them.**

Design
Avni Jain
New York

Art Direction
Juan Miguel Marin,
Eduardo Palma,
and Luke Williams

Team Manager
Jaime Fallon

Twitter
@lllukewilliams
@juanmiguelmarin
@epalma88
@fallon00

Client
Tribeca Film Festival

Dimensions
Various

Principal Type
Akkurat Mono and Druk

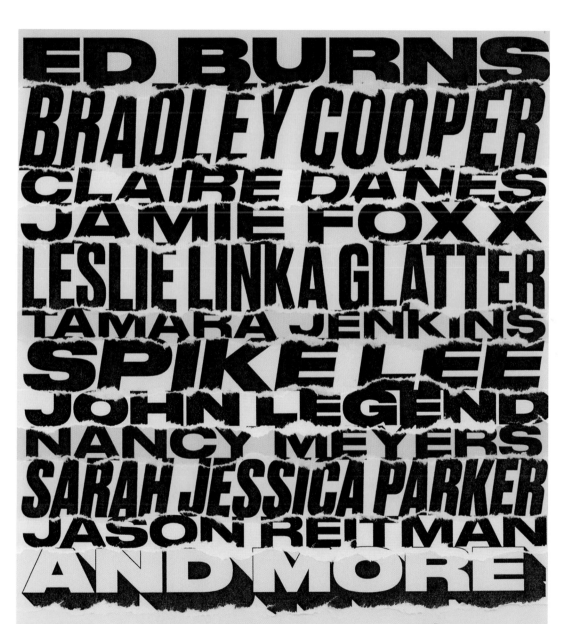

LADFEST 2018

Concept   For the design of the fourth edition of
the Latin American Design Festival, we applied two
rules: We could use only two colors, and we could
use only two typefaces. Celebrating four years of
LADFEST, we came up with the idea of the cube
and the four sides, giving different perspectives in
design as a good concept of what the festival is
all about. We decided to use red and black as the
primary colors, and our two typefaces were a super
extended and a light contemporary serif.

Design
and Creative Direction
**Richars Meza
Lima**

Senior Designer
and 3D Designer
Rommina Dolorier

Junior Designers
**Daniela Choroco
and Daniela Cuenca**

URL
iscreativestudio.com

Twitter
@ISCreativStudio

Design Firm
IS Creative Studio

Client
Latin American Design

Dimensions
Various

Principal Type
**Druk Super Extended
and Fifty**

Africolor Festival Global Identity

Concept   Africolor is a festival of musical creation, and the program reflects the abundance of African music through concerts, master classes, and workshops in and around Paris for one month. For its thirtieth edition, Africolor chose to focus on women. More than ever, the Bambara Mousso are the future of African music and appear in innovative and committed creations. The power of these women's voices resonated strongly with me. As a female designer, I found it obvious to createa front visual that evokes a vulva, giving the opening, the exchanges, and the vibrations a joyful and generous tone—which is the whole spirit of the festival.

Creative Creation and Graphic Design
Manuela Bonnet Montreuil, France

URL
godsavethescreen.com

Instagram
@godsavethescreen

Creative Studio
God save the screen

Client
festival Africolor

Principal Type
Fugue Tails and Fugue Regular

Dimensions
Various

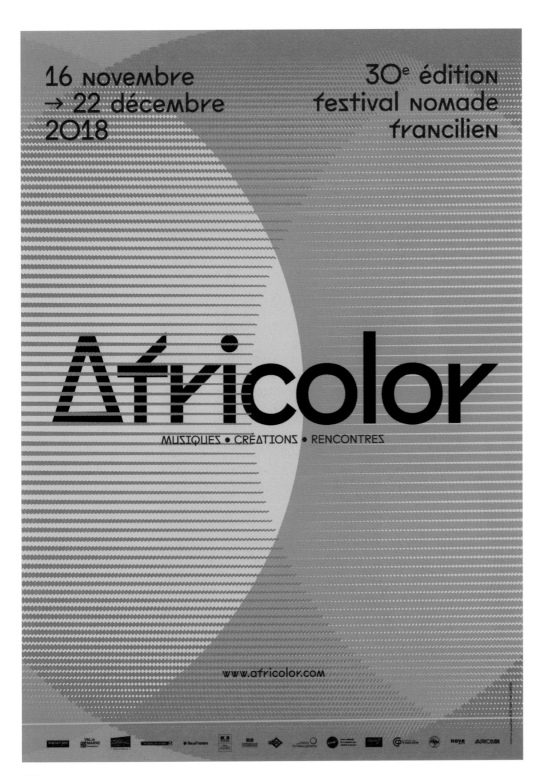

OTD / Next

Concept   This is a still-evolving branding project rather than a "rebrand" for the lifestyle platform company OTD Corporation. In OTD's dictionary, the forward slash mark, or "oblique stroke," has an additional, critical meaning other than its original ones. And that meaning is "enhance," because "/" simultaneously denotes the concept of up and forward. Therefore, "OTD / THE LIFE" equals "OTD ENHANCE(S) THE LIFE" and so on.

Main Design
Jo Eunae,
Lee Kyoungtaek,
and Kim Minsu
Seoul

Design
Jo Ara, Kim Moon
Jeong, Kim KyungLim,
Kim Minkyung,
Jang Soyoung,
and Jo Taesik

Creative Direction
An Hyojin

Creative Consultant
Kim Namoo

Concept and Design
OTD Design Center

URLs
otdcorp.co.kr
manuale.co.kr
Studio
Manual

Instagram
@otd_design_center

Client Name
OTD Corporation

Dimensions
Various

Principal Type
DIN Next Pro

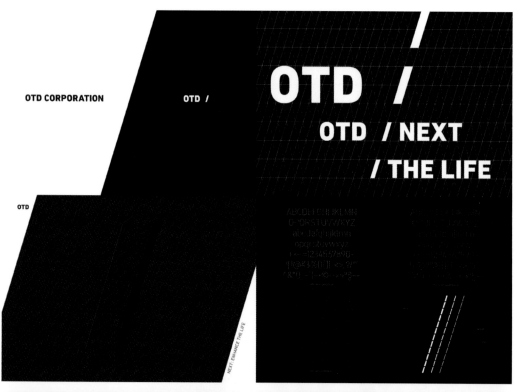

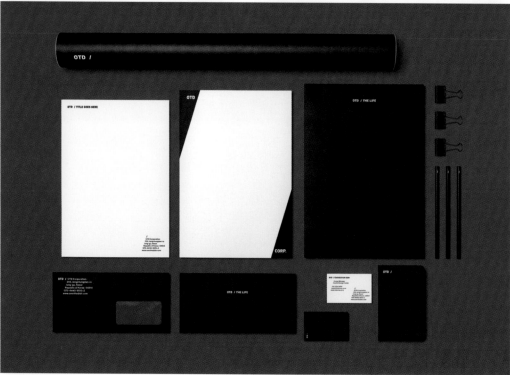

Factory Identity

Concept Factory—a multifaceted retail campus where consumers/creators gather to inspire and be inspired—is a startup based in Edmonton, Calgary, and Toronto that converts large, under-utilized urban spaces into lively communities of local/online brands and experiences. With a minimal color palette and expressive typography, the brand acts as a platform and a content vessel to purposefully showcase the ever-evolving nature of the spaces.

Creative Direction
Dennis Lenarduzzi°
Edmonton, Canada

Art Direction
and Senior Designer
Justin Kowalczuk

Web Design
Novus Design Group

URL
makespacegroup.com

Design Firm
Makespace

Client
Factory

Dimensions
Various

Principal Type
NB Akademie

Nicollet

Concept   The identity centers on a letter N built from two sides of a directional arrow—one going up and one going down—conveying the movement of traffic and the arterial role of Nicollet Avenue, the "Main Street" of downtown Minneapolis. The arrow forms can also be used to construct a letter M, for the "MN" Minnesota state abbreviation, or "NM" for Nicollet Mall. Typography is set in the highly legible sans serif Fakt, and the traffic-oriented color palette features a bright, eye-catching yellow, along with black and white.

Design
**Courtney Gooch
New York**

Creative Direction
and Partner-in-Charge
Paula Scher°

Project Manager
Sarah McKeen

URL
pentagram.com

Twitter
@pentagram

Design Firm
Pentagram°

Client
**Minneapolis Downtown
Improvement District
and City of Minneapolis**

Dimensions
Various

Principal Type
Fakt Pro

Leibniz Institute for the History and Culture of Eastern Europe (GWZO)

Concept   The logo for GWZO now wears a simple but beautiful outfit with just a hint of extravagance. It is neatly finished, and in problem areas—the visual conflict between curves and diagonals in the letters—it doesn't fudge or conceal but deliberately emphasizes them, turning them into something special. This is where craft becomes artistry, fashioning a product that's not just wearable but contemporary, too. The foundation here is a logo constructed from triangles and circles, over which the characters are drawn according to the rules of type design: Transitions are flowing, in contrast to the pure geometric form.

Art Direction
**Carolin Himmel
and Andreas Uebele°
Leipzig, Germany**

Project Manager
Justyna Sikora

URL
uebele.com

Design Firm
**büro uebele visuelle
kommunikation**

Dimensions
Various

Principal Type
Leipzigzwo

Client
GWZO

FIM (International Women's Film Festival)

Concept For the identity of FIM, we created an alphabet with letters that aim to translate a multiplicity of language and discourses and contemplate as much as possible women's senses of experience and the production of subjectivity in general. Fim Display is composed of segments of lines and curves that combine in various ways, generating alternate glyphs that compose each word and the festival logo itself—in a unique way. A catalog, a poster, the signage, and a website were developed for the event communication.

Design
**Beatriz Dórea
and Matheus Sakita
São Paulo**

Creative Direction
**Julia Masagão
and Elisa von Randow**

URL
juliamasagao.com

Behance
@AllesBlau

Studio
Alles Blau

Client
FIM

Dimensions
**Catalog
6.5 x 8 in.
(16 x 20 cm);
Folder/Poster
15.5 x 24.5 in.
(40 x 62 cm)**

Principal Type
**Fim Display
and Work Sans**

FIM DISPLAY

AaBbCcDdEeEÉfffFFFfGgHh
IiijJkKkkLlLMMMMHmmmmNnN
OoPPpppQqqqRRRRrSSSsssTt
UuUuVvWWwwxXxYyYyZz
0123456789!??.;,:'{()}`@áàãâ

Aldeia das Crianças

Concept   Aldeia das Crianças is a school for children from one to six years old. Its visual identity, made up of geometric-shape stamps, enables children to play with this family as if the pieces were an alphabet of shapes that can translate diverse sensations and enable diverse compositions. It is therefore an alphabet of letters and an alphabet of forms, which contemplate, respectively, two distinct situations: writing (especially for adults, in this case) and playing.

Design
**Beatriz Dórea
and Matheus Sakita
São Paulo**

Concept, Design,
and Art Direction
**Julia Masagão
and Elisa von Randow**

Creative Direction
**Julia Masagão
and Elisa von Randow**

URL
juliamasagao.com

Behance
@AllesBlau

Studio
Alles Blau

Client
Aldeia das Crianças

Dimensions
Various

Principal Type
**Aldeia Display
and Raisonne**

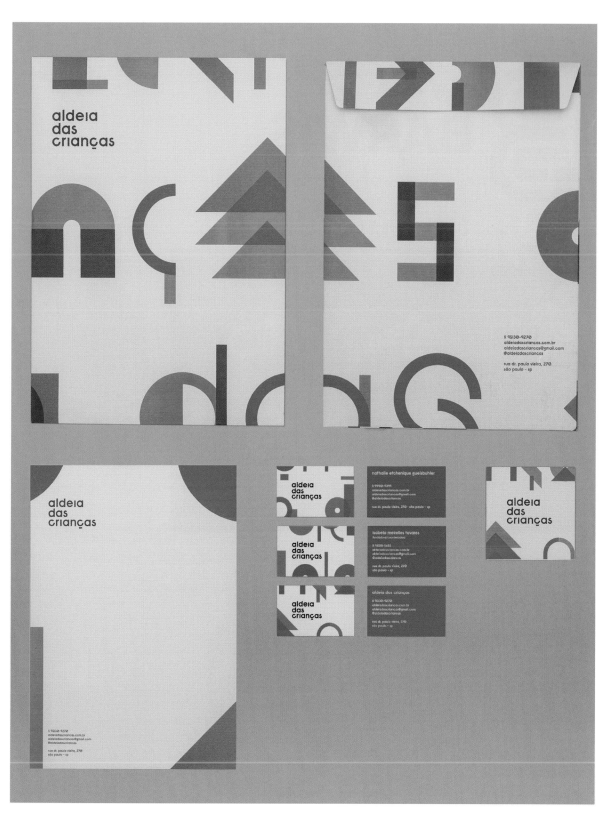

Barwis

Concept Barwis is the holistic human performance company founded by Mike Barwis, one of the world's top strength and conditioning coaches. They work with collegiate, Olympic, and professional athletes, using methods based on an understanding of neuromuscular systems and biomechanics of the body, and specializing in athlete recovery and physical therapy. The Barwis branding is designed to serve all these purposes. The identity centers on a B monogram, with a dumbbell embedded in the letter to symbolize strength. The logo is drawn on a grid, with clean, precise geometry, and is equally at home in the worlds of sports, fitness, medicine, and technology.

Design
**Aron Fay°
and Daisy Dal Hae Lee
New York**

Creative Direction
Michael Bierut°

Project Manager
Tess McCann

URL
pentagram.com

Twitter
@pentagram

Design Firm
Pentagram°

Client
Barwis

Dimensions
Various

Principal Type
**Fort Middleweight
and Fort Book**

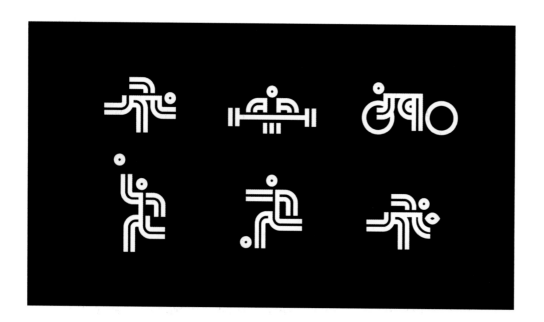

Vroom

Concept   We worked with Vroom, a platform for buying and selling high-quality used cars, to develop a new brand identity that emphasizes the platform's convenience and ease of use. With a name as good as Vroom, we didn't need to do much. Rather than create something visually clever and car-related––like making wheels out of the O's––we let the word do the work. The identity is built around a custom typeface, Vroom Sans, with italicized letterforms that evoke a feeling of forward motion and driving a car. The identity reinforces the idea of speed and freedom, the key to Vroom's appeal.

Design
Sachi Chandiramani
New York

Partner
Michael Bierut°

Associate Partner
Britt Cobb

URL
pentagram.com

Twitter
@pentagram

Design Firm
Pentagram°

Client
Vroom

Dimensions
Various

Principal Type
Calibre and Vroom Sans

CHUS X CHUS

Concept   The CHUS X CHUS brand identity
evokes the visual qualities and graphic forms of
Burés's jewelry with distinctive custom typography
constructed of modular shapes. Pentagram
developed a full alphabet and custom typeface,
called CXC, built of individual link-like shapes that
almost touch, giving the letterforms a glittering,
dimensional effect. The wordmark echoes the
linking or beaded structure of the metalwork, while
the monogram merges the C, X, and C into an
interlocking clasp-like form.

Partner
Natasha Jen°
New York

Associate
Javier Arizu

Project Manager
Alex Klein

URL
pentagram.com

Twitter
@pentagram

Design Firm
Pentagram°

Client
Chus Burés

Dimensions
Various

Principal Type
CXC

Droit

Concept Pentagram's brand identity for Droit captures the constant evolution and optimization of the platform. The designers focused on the contrasts between the volatile nature of the fin-tech industry and Droit's responsive solution. The wordmark merges a bitmap typeface and a geometric, sans serif typeface that is "finished" and visible. The pair of typefaces were developed together and echo each other's forms. Even though they look drastically different, they share common characteristics, including the x-height, each letter's width, and the margin space.

Design
**Ena Yun and Ran Zheng
New York**

Partner
Natasha Jen°

Associate
Jang Hyun Han

Project Manager
Georgina McDonald

URL
pentagram.com

Twitter
@pentagram

Design Firm
Pentagram°

Client
Droit

Dimensions
Various

Principal Type
Droit and PX Grotesk

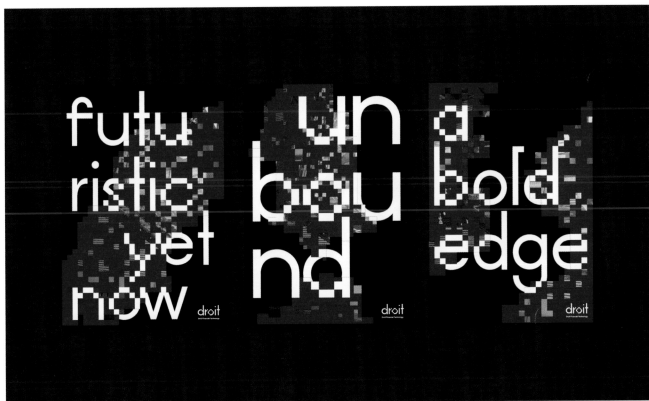

Khaore

Concept   The brand identity captures the Khaore concept with customized typography that's both refined and gestural. For the logotype, the Pentagram designers reinterpreted the classic serif typeface Caslon with contemporary elements, including angled curves and radical cuts that echo forms in the handbag designs. At first glance, the logo appears elegant and polished; a closer look reveals the rigorous, idiosyncratic details. The identity's understated elegance extends to applications, which employ a clean aesthetic and subtle use of color.

Partner
Natasha Jen°

Associate
Jang Hyun Han

Project Manager
Georgina McDonald

URL
pentagram.com

Twitter
@pentagram

Design Firm
Pentagram°

Client
Khaore

Dimensions
Various

Principal Type
Caslon and Khaore

khaore

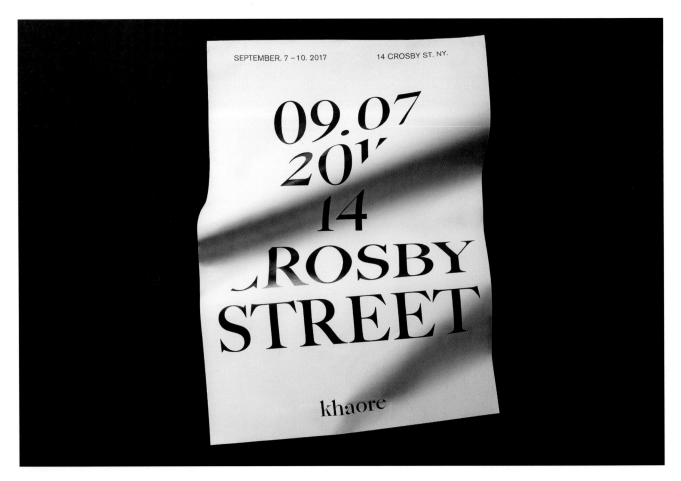

LIT

Concept   The Storefront for Art and Architecture celebrated a passion for publishing at its Spring 2018 Benefit, presented at the New York Public Library on May 7, 2018. Pentagram designed the identity and motion graphics for the event, which centered on the theme "LIT," a play on the abbreviation for "literature." In the identity, kinetic fields of black-and-white typography move through a bright red line that suggests the gutter of a book. Arcing on page-like curves, the type creates an illusion of dimensional depth and is set spinning in motion graphics.

Design
Ran Zheng
New York

Partner
Natasha Jen°

Associate
Joseph Han

Project Manager
Alex Klein

URL
pentagram.com

Twitter
@pentagram

Design Firm
Pentagram°

Client
**Storefront for Art
and Architecture**

Dimensions
16:9 ratio

Principal Type
Helvetica Neue

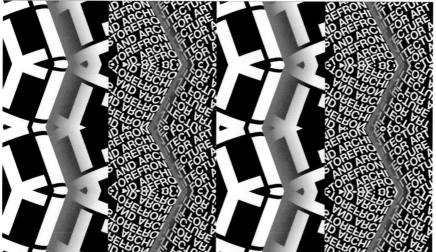

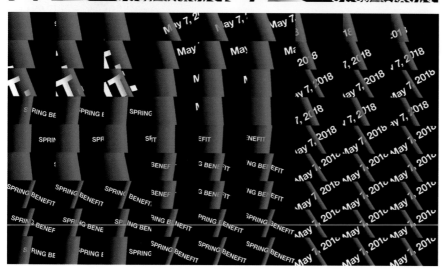

The Wing's No Man's Land Podcast

Concept   The Wing's No Man's Land is a herstory podcast about women who were too bad for your textbooks. The visual branding is sharp and rebellious, with a nod to retro radio and cinema. It uses different typefaces to personify the various women featured in each episode, from a 1930s Harlem gangstress to 1960s LGBT activists.

Design
**Nina Lilliebjerg-Heder
and Mahya Soltani
New York**

Design Direction
**Kirstin Huber
and Deva Pardue**

Creative Direction
Deva Pardue

URL
the-wing.com

Twitter
@the_wing

Design Studio
The Wing

Principal Type
**Bianco
and Bureau Grotesk**

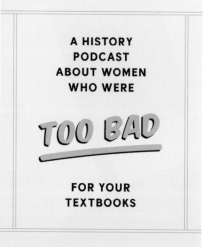

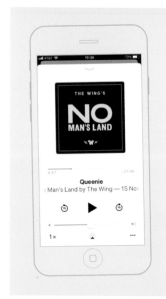

The Little Wing

Concept   The Little Wing is a space designed for kids to play so their parents can take flight. A part of The Wing, The Little Wing exists as a support system for moms and families by creating a magical space for their kids to gather under the same roof for enriching programming that takes them higher. The identity of this sub-brand of The Wing makes use of jumbo jumbled typography and cute, friendly little smiling shapes.

Design
**Rosie Naberezny
and Ainsley Romero
New York**

Design Direction
**Kirstin Huber
and Deva Pardue**

Creative Direction
Deva Pardue

URL
the-wing.com

Twitter
@the_wing

Design Studio
The Wing

Principal Type
Bianco Sans

THE LITTLE WING
IS A SPACE DESIGNED
FOR KIDS TO PLAY
SO THEIR PARENTS
CAN TAKE FLIGHT

Corporate Design Wieland AG

Concept   Wieland is the oldest independent wine dealer in the Swiss canton of Graubünden. Since the next generation will soon be taking over, it was the perfect time to revise their corporate design by putting their two-hundred-year tradition and the commitment to their location into focus. The logo became more delicate and playful, increasing its strictness and self-confidence at the same time. The deliberate exclusion of color in the logo and the dramatic landscape photographs depict the product in its pure sensuality. It will not take long to understand what to expect from Wieland: the best selection since 1837.

Art Direction
Déborah Mayer
Basel

Creative Direction
Susanne Hartmann
and André Konrad

Text and Strategy
Janine Kern

Photography
Mathias Kunfermann

URL
suan.ch

Agency
SUAN Conceptual
Design GmbH

Client
Wieland AG

Dimensions
Various

Principal Type
GT Walsheim

FNJI

Concept   FNJI is a cutting-edge brand that curates minimalist, retro-style furniture products in China. FNJI aims to expand to overseas markets. The art direction sought to provide an overview of the whole product line by representing a bold aesthetic inspired by postmodernism.

Design
Yaman Hu

Studio
Yaman Hu Studio

Client
FNJI Furniture

Principal Type
**Custom
and Messina Modern**

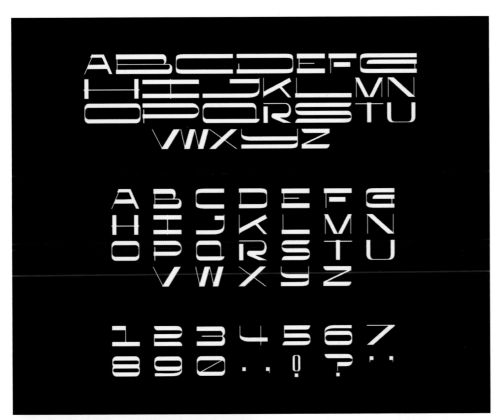

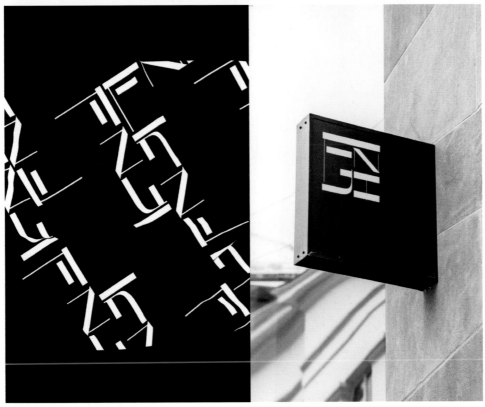

YITIGUO

Concept   YITIGUO is an interior design company.
The logo is drawn by ancient Chinese characters,
giving a feeling of elegance and conciseness. The
entire visual identity system makes good use of
delicate space.

Artistic Director
Kong Xiangguo
Zhongshan, China

Client
YITIGUO

Principal Type
HYQiHei

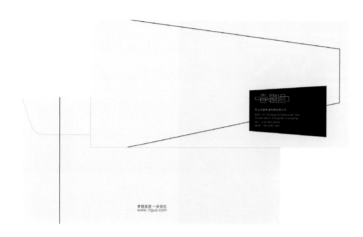

Yungu Town

Concept This logo is a simple integration of two similar patterns—"Cloud" and "Eave." "Cloud" is called "Yun" in Chinese, and "Eave" stands for the ancient buildings in this town. With the addition of simple elements, this logo is able to evolve into other vivid designs, such as "Mountain," "Rivulet," and "House."

Artistic Director
Kong Xiangguo
Zhongshan, China

Design Studio
Servant of Fonts Design Studio

Client
Yungu Town

Principal Type
HYQiHei

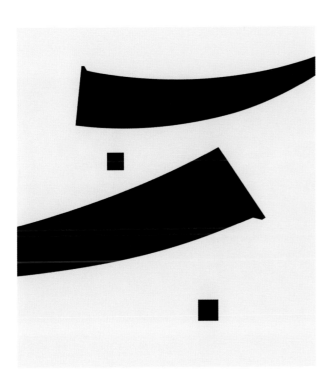

www.yungutown.com

房屋
House

London Design Festival 2018

Concept   The London Design Festival is an annual event, made up of over four hundred events and exhibitions, celebrating London as a world design capital. Since 2007, Pentagram partner Domenic Lippa has created the festival's campaign identity. The 2018 identity pays homage to London's most iconic piece of design, Edward Johnston's eponymous typeface, known for its use on the London Underground. The approach reflects the democratic nature of the typeface and the city it serves by constantly reimagining it with playful typographic interventions. London is open to influence, to reinvention and innovation, all the while building upon its rich design history.

Design
**David Bhalla
and Lily Smallwood
London**

Partner
Domenic Lippa°

URL
pentagram.com

Twitter
@pentagram

Design Firm
Pentagram

Client
London Design Festival

Dimensions
Various

Principal Type
**P22 Johnston
Underground**

Inflatable Summer Campaign

Concept   In 2018, The Exploratorium partnered with Colossal for its summer exhibition Inflatable: Expanding Works of Art— a series of massive, air-filled sculptures that surprised museum guests around every corner. To bring the spirit of the exhibit into the streets, we created a campaign centered around custom inflatable letterforms as tactile as the experience itself. The letters dynamically "blow up," filling whatever space they're in—from a bus to a billboard to a banner ad, every surface becomes a new canvas. The campaign blanketed the city with bursts of blue, inviting all of San Francisco into the wondrous world of Inflatable.

Associate Designer
Sohee Kim
San Francisco

Creative Director
Ben Crick

Motion Director
Kris Wong

Strategist
Angie Shih

Strategy Director
Anna Sternoff

Director of Creative Operations
Joanna Hobson

Chief Creative Officer
Matt Luckhurst

URL
wearecollins.com

Design Firm
COLLINS

Dimensions
15 x 10 in. (38 x 25 cm)

Principal Type
Inflatable Display

Google Science Fair Branding

Concept   Science fairs feel exclusive. Teens feel like these contests are for high-performing math and science students, and "not for them." Science, technology, engineering, and math can be used to make a real impact on the issues that teens care about. We created a more approachable brand expression inspired by STEM disciplines to represent a variety of approaches to problem solving and a broader diversity of perspectives. We also created a simplified entry process, as well as helpful tools to guide learners through the process. We spoke with students and educators where they engage most—social media and online—creating films, animations, illustrations, and simple copy-driven inspirational exercises.

URL
google.com

Design Firm
Google Brand Studio
San Francisco

Client
Google Science Fair

Dimensions
Posters 24 x 36 in.
(61 x 91.4 cm);
Teacher Cards
7.25 x 11 in.
(18.4 x 27.9 cm)

Principal Type
Google Sans and
Google Molecular Sans

Visual Identity for Optician-K

Concept   When designing the identity of the optometrist Optician-K, we discovered that the original eye chart had never been fully developed. Louise Sloan designed a set of ten letters in 1959, and it had stayed that way until now. The typeface became the basis of the optometrist's visual identity and logo. Once the project was complete, we decided to make the typeface publicly available. By doing so, we connect the typography and the optician brand Optician-K directly to the craft of the optometrist—and from now on, everyone can use the eye-chart fonts.

Design
**Simen Schikulski
and Vivi-Ann Slåttsveen
Hamar, Norway**

Creative Direction
Kjetil Wold

Art Direction
Simen Schikulski

Typographer
Fabio Duarte Martins

Account Manager
Ellen Østmoen

Digital Advisor
Tor Hernan Floor

Agency
ANTI Hamar

Client
Optician-K

Dimensions
Various

Principal Type
Optician Sans

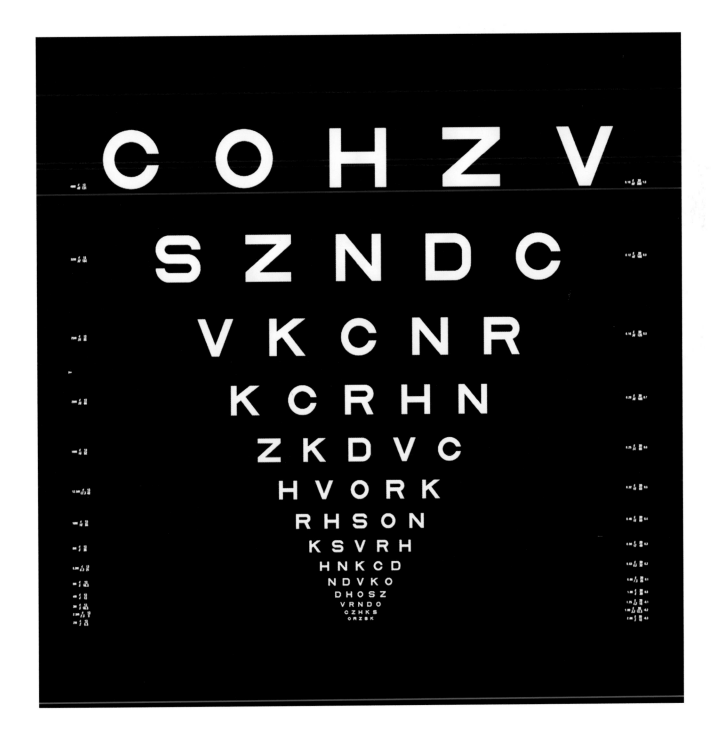

Joan Creative Identity

Concept   We had the distinct pleasure of building the complete identity system for Joan Creative, a new creative agency founded by Lisa Clunie and Jamie Robinson. The name "Joan" is historically eponymous to some of the most badass women. Drawing on a combination of ambition, curiosity, imagination, work ethic, and aforementioned badass-ness, Joans have challenged, questioned, and changed the status quo. Taking inspiration from this ethos, we built a custom logotype around the sword, which was wielded by one of the greatest and most famous Joans of all time: Joan of Arc.

Design
**Jens Marklund
and Juan Carlos Pagan°
New York**

Creative Direction
and Typography
Juan Carlos Pagan

URL
sundayafternoon.us

Design Firm
Sunday Afternoon

Client
Joan Creative

Principal Type
Custom

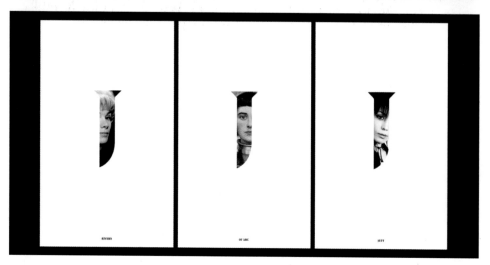

Finding the Truth in Data

Concept Elliptic finds the truth in data. Terrorism, ransomware, child pornography, and weapons can all be purchased on the dark web using bitcoin, an untraceable currency—until now. Elliptic links bitcoin data to criminals and provides intelligence to law enforcement agencies in the United Kingdom and the United States. Negative space typography, inspired by data blocks, reveals the essence of the business, and legibility at scale is deliberately challenging in order to echo the difficult task Elliptic undertakes. The simple black-and-white palette further underscores the seriousness.

Senior Designer and Typographer
Jonathan Brodie
London

Animation
Luigi Honorat, Ned Image, and David Whyte

Account Manager
Pippa Chishick

URL
superunion.com

Twitter
@SuperunionHQ

Brand Consultancy
Superunion

Client
Elliptic

Principal Type
Bespoke

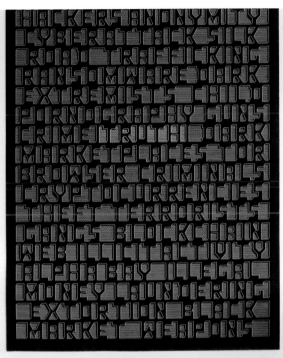

Elliptic find the truth in data.
Terrorism, ransomware, child pornography and weapons, all purchased using Bitcoin, an untraceable currency – until now.

Elliptic link Bitcoin data to criminals and provide intelligence to law enforcement (the major '3 letter agencies' in the USA and their UK equivalents).

Negative space typography, inspired by data blocks, reveals what Elliptic are looking for. Legibility at scale is deliberately challenging to echo the difficult task they undertake. A simple black and white colour palette reflects the seriousness of the legal cases they provide intelligence for.

PLEASE SEE LAUNCH FILM

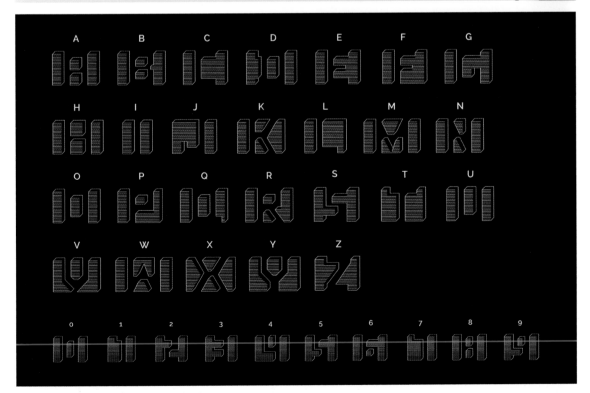

Proudly Croatian

Concept Today's travelers are searching for authenticity, and with over sixty years of experience, there is no other holiday brand that is more Croatian than Plava Laguna. We mined Croatia's rich culture for the new visual identity. At the heart of it is a special typeface, unique to the country, supported by a color palette inspired by the white and red of the Croatian coat of arms.

Design
Jonathan Brodie and Sam Ratcliffe London

Creative Direction
Stuart Radford

Lead Designer
Sam Hall

Client Director
Andrew Webster

Typography
Paratype

URL
superunion.com

Twitter
@SuperunionHQ
Brand Consultancy
Superunion

Client
Plava Laguna

Principal Type
Circe

Purpur Salt

Concept   For millions of years, salt has been the pulsating lifeline of the World Heritage region Hallstadt-Dachstein-Salzkammergut. Here, in the depths of the Austrian Alps, Purpur salt is sustainably mined by hand—the one and only untreated salt without impurities in the world. The visual identity holds these qualities in high regard by featuring the distinctive red salt stones as a key visual. Combined with the rough but elegant gc16 (Bold Decisions), it builds up to a seamless system, from packaging to collateral.

Design
Paul Katterl
Vienna

Art Direction
Verena Panholzer

Animation
Frederik Galsgaard

URL
studio-es.at

Twitter
@studio.es

Facebook
@studio.es.wien

Client
Purpur Salt,
Austrian Alpine Salt

Dimensions
Various

Principal Type
gc16 (Bold Decisions)
and Neue Haas Grotesk

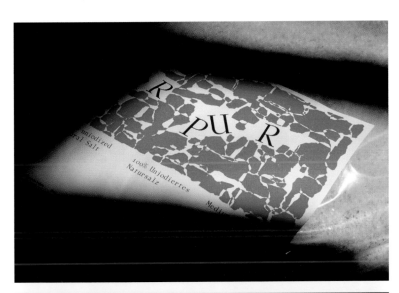

Esporte Clube Pinheiros 118 Anniversary

Concept   This was the visual identity created for the 118th anniversary of Esporte Clube Pinheiros, the largest multi-sport club in Latin America. Based on court markings and inspired by the modernist architecture of the club's buildings, we designed a modular system that allowed us to develop figures, letters, and graphics used in the many visual outputs regarding the celebrations.

Design
**Ralph Mayer
and Bruno Ribeiro
São Paulo**

Case Photography
Marlon Brambilla

URL
estudiograde.com.br

Instagram
@estudiograde

Studio
Estúdio Grade

Client
Esporte Clube Pinheiros

Principal Type
FF Real Text family

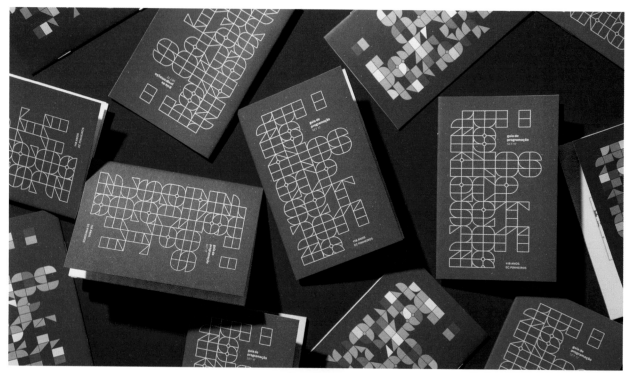

The Blind See More

Concept   We sought to show how an exceptional sense of touch allows blind women to discover things that remain hidden to sighted people. Using Braille letters to complete the typography in the headline, we illustrate how blind and sighted people work together. This unconventional collaboration creates a revolutionary, diagnostic method to fight against breast cancer. The visual identity addresses the target group with great sensitivity, awakening trust in the method. The trained blind women are depicted authentically, expressing their new self-confidence.

Art Direction
Miriam Hugo
Düsseldorf

Senior Art Director
Marc Schaede

Junior Art Director Digital
Jaqueline Szurawicki

Creative Direction
Tim Liedtke

Executive Creative Director
Juergen Adolph

Managing Director Creation
Professor Ruediger Goetz

Senior Copywriter
Michael Draheim

Design Agency
Grey Germany and KW43 Branddesign

Client
Discovering Hands

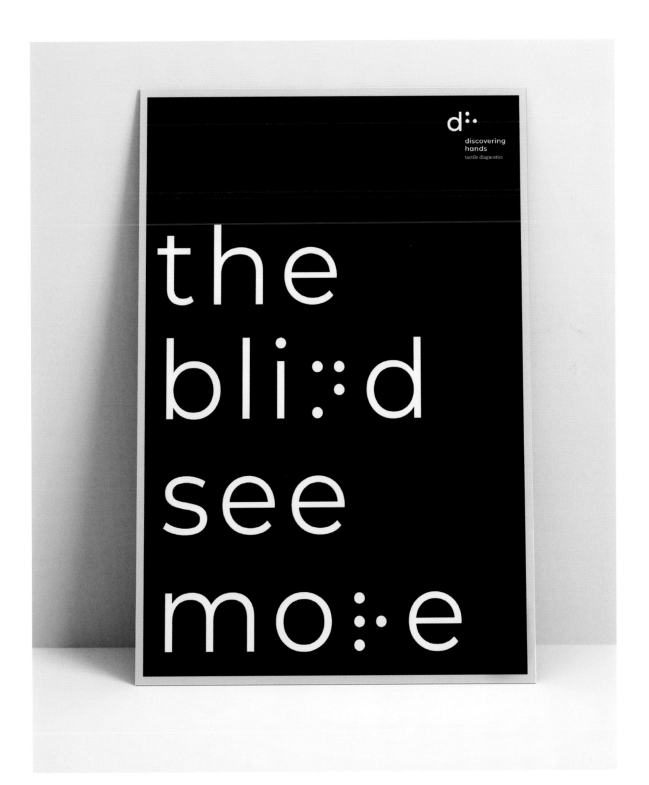

Tanzquartier Wien Branding

Concept Tanzquartier Wien is Austria's key institution for sophisticated, inspired, and socially committed discourse on contemporary dance and performance. Our guiding principle for TQW's 2018 rebranding was "Movement is the motivation." The campaign pictures performers and fluff-and-puff initials in motion.

Design
Elsa Bachmeyer, Sebastian Kubik, and Wolfgang Landauer Vienna

Art Direction
Anouk Rehorek and Christian Schlager

3D Rendering
no.ova

Photography
Jork Weisman

Concept and Copywriter
Katharina Luger

URL
studio-vie.net

Design Studio
studio VIE

Client
Tanzquartier Wien

Dimensions
Various

Principal Type
Banana, Freya, and Girott

Amsterdam Sinfonietta Identity

Concept   Amsterdam Sinfonietta is an innovative music ensemble with an international reputation, and a repertoire encompassing everything from baroque to contemporary music. Their innovative spirit is achieved by designing an identity that has the ability to metamorphose. To communicate this, we created a custom code that enabled us to transform music (video and sound input) into dynamic typographic patterns (still and motion output). With an endless variety of configurations, this technology allows us to create graphics that relate directly to a specific piece of music. It makes each piece of communication unique.

Design
**Erik de Vlaam
and Stan Haanappel
Rotterdam**

Coding
Sander Sturing

Motion
Elvin van Dalen

URL
studiodumbar.com

Twitter
@studiodumbar

Design Firm
Studio Dumbar

Client
Amsterdam Sinfonietta

Principal Type
Maison Neue Extended

Balticbest

Concept   Balticbest is a boutique festival consisting of a conference and awards show—but now open for entries beyond the Baltic states, from all small countries with a population of less than five million. This change of concept called for a new identity that speaks to both the design and advertising communities, globally. Something that universally celebrates small countries—and big ideas. Also, the identity itself needed to be bigger than just an identity, working as a marketing campaign, too. Consequently, Balticbest was made bolder than ever, creating a brand-new copy-driven platform that is simple yet powerful.

Design
Ivan Khmelevsky
Tallinn, Estonia

Copywriters
Nils Kajander
and Ivan Khmelevsky

Strategist
Nils Kajander

URL
bond-agency.com

Design Agency
BOND

Client
Best Marketing

Dimensions
Various

Principal Type
Messina Sans Bold

The Melbourne Art Fair

Concept   The Melbourne Art Fair took place for the first time in a temporary structure within the Southbank Arts Precinct. For its 2018 marketing campaign, Multiple created a flexible event brand identity by integrating the A, R, and T letterforms with the work of participating artists. Each communication piece presented the letterforms in different compositions, playfully and dynamically interacting with the artwork to create engaging, contemporary visuals while preserving brand recognition. The event branding encompassed digital and printed collateral and outdoor advertising including flags, street banners, and public transport.

Design Direction
Tim Murphy
Melbourne

URL
multiple.studio

Design Studio
Multiple Studio

Client
Melbourne Art
Foundation

Dimensions
Various

Principal Type
Graphik

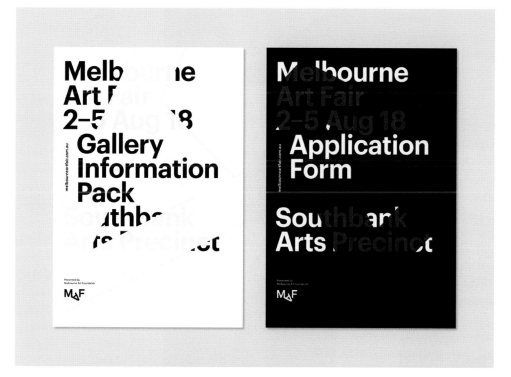

Holland Festival

Concept   The Holland Festival brings the best international performing arts to Amsterdam. We designed a special typeface, combining stencil forms and ligatures. The H and F share one vertical stroke, and they are made up of simple blocks. For the 2018 campaign, we started from motion graphics. Colored blocks tumble and fall randomly. Among them are white blocks that make up "HF." The logo is built up as part of an adaptive changing wall of blocks. We used trams, façades, and posters as a stage for our falling blocks. The design symbolizes the pushing of boundaries that is characteristic of this festival.

Design
Nikki Gonnissen,
Roy Terhorst,
Falco van Burg, and
Thomas Widdershoven
Amsterdam

URL
thonik.nl

Design Firm
Thonik

Client
Holland Festival

Dimensions
Various

Principal Type
Euclid
and HF-type

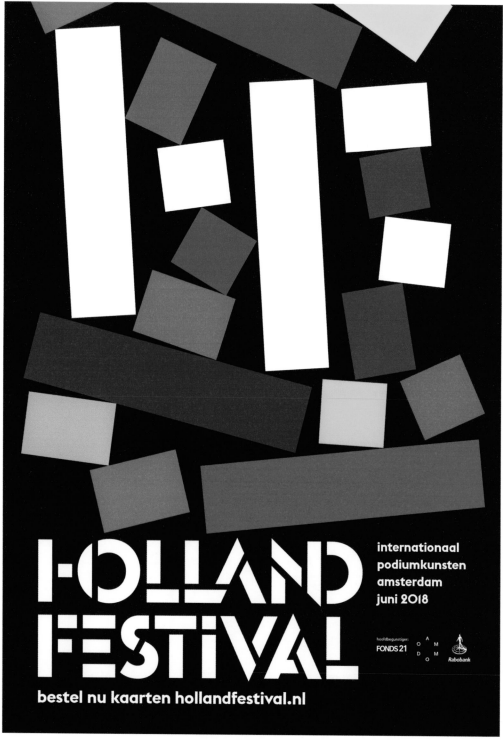

International Creative Pattern Design Competition 2018

Concept The theme of the International Creative Pattern Design Competition was "Figures of the Future." Our definition of the future is changeable and imaginary. Considering that the way we share information is no longer limited to paper and that social media has become the main channel of communication, we created a dynamic font and opened its visual possibilities through both print and motion. In addition, we used laser papers to provide various visual experiences upon viewing from different angles.

Design
**Cong Chen,
Xiaomei Liu,
Fan Yang,
and Qiongjie Yu
Hangzhou, China**

Art Direction
Qiongjie Yu

URL
transwhite.cn

Design Studio
Transwhite Studio

Client
China Academy of Art

Dimensions
Various

Principal Type
Helvetica and custom

Lasse Zwoelf

Concept   For the musician Lasse, we developed
a visual communication concept that combines
contemporary technical possibilities with common
communication methods, to distribute his new
album. Lasse's songs are quite variable, so our
aim was to visualize them in different, stand-alone
visuals. Each song has its own, unique visual
language. And each visual can be used in an
animated or static version, depending on its field
of application (screen or print). The website works
as the center and download area, whereas the
newspaper-styled publication can be used both
as a poster (all visuals in large-scale size) or as an
informational brochure.

Design
Nadia de Donno,
Sam Divers,
Philipp Lüthi,
Andrea Noti,
Giannina Ronchetti,
and Sarah Wolfsberger
Bern

URL
heyday.ch

Design Studio
Heyday Design S-studio

Client
Lasse

Dimensions
Various

Principal Type
GT Eesti Display Regular

IFC Brand Identity Refresh

Concept   After our 2015 rebrand, IFC had firmly defined itself as a destination for "Slightly Off" comedy. Problem was, the competition had taken notice and began to emulate everything from IFC's signature monochrome color palette to the typography and motion language. For the 2018 evolution, we leaned into the one thing the competition couldn't imitate: IFC's signature "Slightly Off" brand voice. The resulting visual identity is almost entirely typographic—comprising dueling voices that deliver functional messaging punctuated by colorful commentary. The design system borrows cues from fan conversations to create a lively, textured, insider dialogue with the viewer.

Design Direction
**Adam Brandon
and David Chun
New York**

Design and Animation
**Johannes Grier
and Nick Miller**

Executive
Creative Director
Ryan Moore

Design and
Lead Animation
Brandon Kennedy

Animator
Amber Kusmenko

Senior Project Manager
Haley Klatzkin

Brand Sizzle
SLAQR

URL
gretelny.com

Instagram
@gretelnyc

Twitter
@gretelnyc

Senior Vice President,
Brand Marketing, IFC
Kevin Vitale

Executive Vice President,
Marketing
and Digital Media
Blake Callaway

Executive Producer
Laurie Mutschler

Vice President/
Creative Director,
IFC Brand Creative
John Sinclair

Design Director
Ed Sherman

Director, Off-Air Creative
and Brand Strategy
Nancy Hennings
Vice President,
Marketing Operations
and Production
John Piccirillo

Senior Vice President,
Brand and
Consumer Marketing
Lauren Burack

Design Studio
Gretel

Client
IFC

Principal Type
**Editor, Editor Underline,
and GT America**

Mercedes-Benz Fashion Week Ljubljana

Concept   Mercedes-Benz has been targeting younger clientele, and the spring 2018 Mercedes-Benz Fashion Week Ljubljana (MBFWLJ) presented the largest number of young fashion designers to date. Those two factors strongly influenced the design, which was further inspired by the digital realm as everyday media of both youth and the fashion savvy. The #MBFWLJ hashtag has been upgraded, putting a visual and identity function to its previously solely informative nature. It was given a spotlight occupying every application or used as a stand-alone element, adapting to specific situations with its flexible nature, either static or animated. Animated, endlessly walking runway models were randomly placed on designs as a top layer, just as one would sticker an animated GIF on an Instagram Story or Snapchat.

Design, Art Direction, and Creative Direction
Primoz Zorko
Ljubljana, Slovenia

Photography
Primoz Zorko

Project Manager
Eva Celec

Project Director
Ula Spindler

URL
primozzorko.com

Twitter and Instagram
@primozzorko

Design Studio
Primoz Zorko

Client
Pristop d.o.o. and
Autocommerce d.o.o.

Dimensions
Various

Principal Type
Monarch Regular
and Custom

OOTO UNION

Concept In the context of a multi-element society, in order to win the market, to defeat and move an opponent, we must form an alliance. Here, letters and graphics are combined skillfully, which just expresses the core ideas of the concept, and the resulting form is vivid and interesting. It's simple, compact, and exquisite.

Art Direction
Zhang Ning
Zhongshan, China

URL
zndesign.cn

Client
OOTO UNION

Dimensions
16.5 x 11.7 in.
(42 x 29.7 cm)

Principal Type
Gotham
and HYQiHei 40S

130 William Logo

Concept This is a custom-drawn logo for architect David Adjaye's first New York City tower in downtown Manhattan, at 130 William Street in the Financial District. The logo lettering is composed of arched elements inspired by the modern building's sensorial façade of arched windows. The building is a mix of modern and contemporary with deep historic precedents, and the logo lettering continues this theme with a classic construction with modern details.

Design and Art Direction
Tina Smith°
New York

URLs
partnersandspade.com
tinasmithdesign.com/
project/130-william

Design Studio
Partners & Spade

Client
130 William—
Lightstone Development

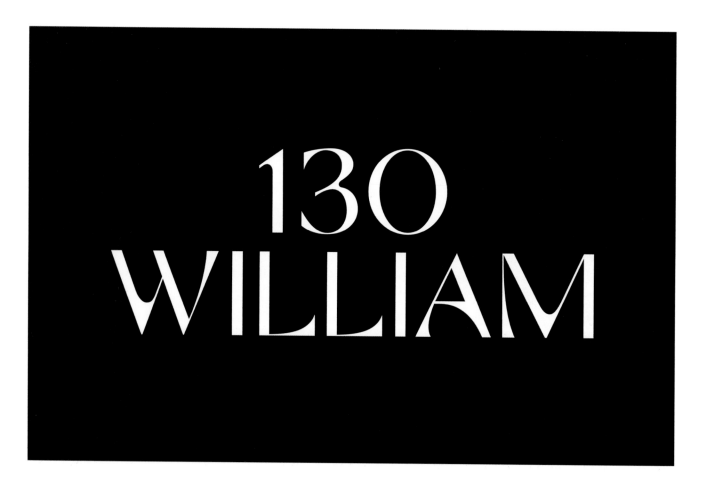

Coca-Cola (FIFA World Cup Russia)

Concept   The Coca-Cola Company is the general sponsor of FIFA World Cup 2018, held in Russia. We created the original display typeface, and the main idea was to show that it's about a football game. The typeface design is based on simple geometric shapes taken from the sport: a ball, gates, and marks on the playing field. Simple font geometry allows the creation of a variety of modular text compositions.

Design
and Creative Direction
Vlad Ermolaev
Moscow

URL
ermolaevbureau.com

Design Firm
Ermolaev Bureau

Client
The Coca-Cola
Company

Principal Type
Custom

Buddhist Cultural Institution

Concept   The font was built based on the Chinese characters 木鱼—meaning "wooden knocker." Inspired by chanting monks' gestures, behavior, and knocking rhythm, the font was humanized in a vivid composition.

Art Direction
Pan Liu°
Xi'an City, China

Design Firm
Xi'an Liaoge Network &
Technology Co., Ltd.

Client
Foya Temple Buddhism
Cultural INST

Dimensions
11.7 x 16.5 in.
(29.7 x 42 cm)

Principal Type
A-OFF Reisho 101 Std
Medium

Superb Harmony

Concept Superb Harmony Culture is a newly established cultural enterprise that is young and energetic. A pair of eyes that are particularly obvious in the visual image ("SH" is the English abbreviation of the company) offer a chance for the viewer to discover and explore the relevance and expandable vitality of various cultures and arts. The arrow is always in the same direction as the eye, and the focus is repeatedly emphasized by visual symbols. The range of culture and art is so large that you always have to focus on discovering something new, isn't it?

Design
Wang Guangfu
and Zhang Hui
Beijing

Art Direction
Wang Guangfu

URL
wgfdesign.cn

Studio
Guangfu Design Studio

Client
Superb Harmony
Culture

Principal Type
BlairMdITC TT Medium
(custom)

Agnes Lloyd-Platt

Concept   Agnes Lloyd-Platt is a fashion and beauty photographer based in London. She embraces playfulness, and she believes her subjects have majestic qualities and that fashion photography should be uplifting and pleasing to look at. To convey the quirkiness and personality of her work, we created a bespoke wordmark that is bold and confident, fashionable but a little fucked up, a touch psychedelic with a bit of nostalgic magic, given that she frequently looks to the past for inspiration. The logotype lends itself to being used large, and as such can be used as a textural element to support her photography. The flexible system can be layered over imagery or used as graphic wallpaper behind images. To help Agnes feel personable, we created versions of the logo that allowed us to break her first name away from her last name to feel more inclusive and approachable.

Creative Direction
**Tim Donaldson
and Amanda Gaskin
Auckland, New Zealand**

URL
seachange.studio

Design Studio
Seachange

Client
Agnes Lloyd-Platt

Principal Type
Custom

Museum Reinhard Ernst

Concept   The Museum Reinhard Ernst is a museum for abstract art. Because abstraction is the process of omitting parts or elements, we cut out a portion of the letterforms in the acronym "mre." The museum's building, designed by famous Japanese architect Fumihiko Maki, is based on a distinctive concept: Viewed from above, the building's plan reveals that a large square atrium is cut out of the building corpus. The square open space symbolizes paintings or works of art that will be displayed in the museum. It also conveys a sense of the mental openness that we practice while contemplating abstract art.

Thilo von Debschitz
Wiesbaden, Germany

URL
q-home.de

Client
Museum Reinhard Ernst

Principal Type
Helvetica Bold

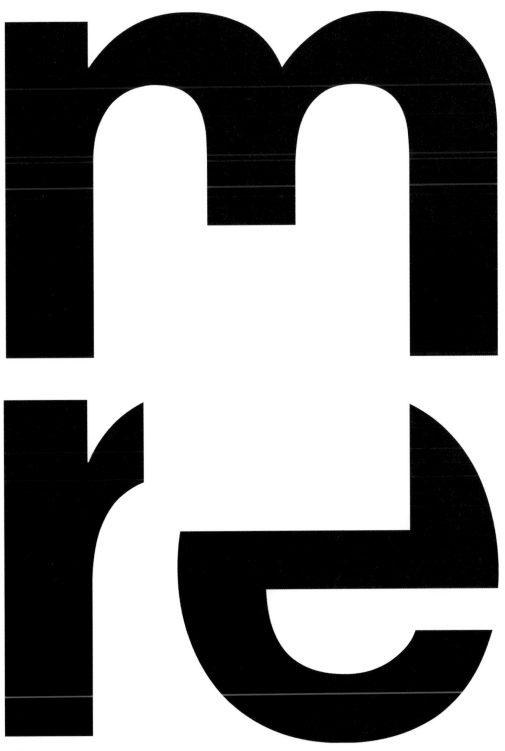

Homejoy

Concept   The two Chinese characters in the design make up the name "Homejoy Studio," which implies closeness and joy. Toy bricks are adopted to construct strokes that are full of childishness and playfulness. With vigorous and graceful strokes, the two-dimensional characters become a three-dimensional drawing, bringing to mind an image of home. The design establishes a new style of Chinese characters, therefore making the studio's logo impressive and meaningful.

Design and Art Direction
Xie Lu°
Beijing

Design Firm
EverGlory Creative
Agency Ltd.

Client
Homejoy Design Studio

Principal Type
Gosha Sans Regular
and Yu Kyokasho N M

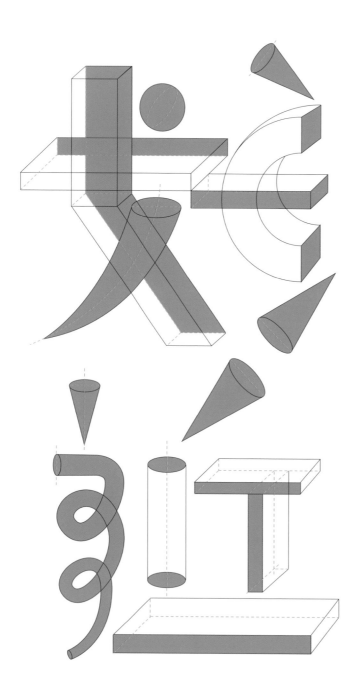

Homejoy Design Studio

住宅 軟裝 商鋪 展示

Broadway Dental

Concept   **The two front teeth create the B, and the
mouth creates the D.**

Design
Ken De Lago°
Rowayton, Connecticut

Client
Broadway Dental

Principal Type
Hand-drawn

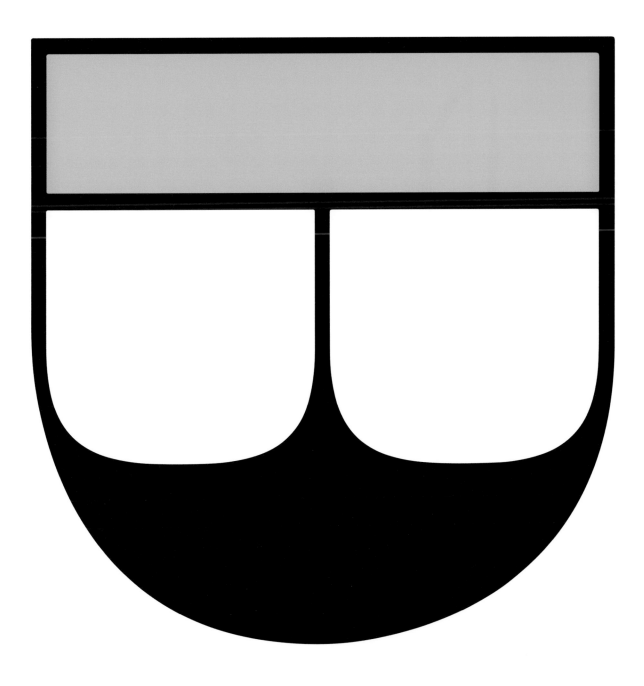

LOGOTYPES

Broadway Dental

Concept   **The two front teeth create the B, and the
mouth creates the D.**

Design
Ken De Lago°
Rowayton, Connecticut

Client
Broadway Dental

A Small Tea House in the Deep Mountains

Concept   The font was structured by the Chinese characters 山客—which mean "mountain guest." A better way to show a hieroglyphic character such as a Chinese character might be to draw it with more exaggeration. Simple and meaningful.

Art Direction
Pan Liu°
Xi'an City, China

Design Firm
Xi'an Liaoge Network &
Technology Co., Ltd.

Client
Xi'an Shanke Teahouse

Rouemy Design

Concept   Every curve of the custom letterforms
is based on the extreme points of a circle. Every
circle has an inherent center point, which assumes
a sense of focus, balance, and completeness. The
simple beauty of the forms, coupled with an idea—
the flipping and flopping of the "R" to fashion the
"d"—creates a more meaningful identity. Rouemy
Design needed its business card to reflect not just a
pretty face, but also a smart idea.

URL
rouemy.com

Instagram
@nancyrouemy

Design and
Creative Direction
Nancy Rouemy°
New York

Design Firm
Rouemy Design

Principal Type
Custom and
Steady Sans

Field Museum Logo Animation

Concept The introduction of a new Field Museum brand comes as the museum celebrates its 125th anniversary. At a time when people are acknowledging the importance of science, the museum is putting a stake in the ground as a forward-thinking leader in scientific discovery. The new logo includes two squares: The small square represents the fraction of the museum's collection on display, while the large square, the logo itself, represents the museum's massive collection as a whole.

Design
Scott Cress
Chicago

Agency
Leo Burnett Chicago
Department of Design

Client
The Field Museum

Principal Type
Mark (modified)

1

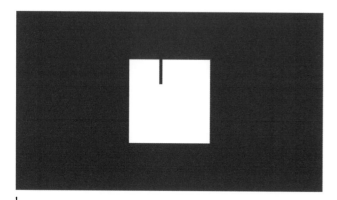

2

3

4

Voice Font

Concept   Voice Font is a new approach to expressing various feelings and emotions in written form. In order to visually describe a feeling contained within a voice more precisely, different parts of a sound in the voice need to be analyzed and presented. According to the Voice Font approach, these parts of the sound are combined to be written together so that the users are able to instantly recognize overall feelings associated with the voice. Thus, Voice Font expands the role of a current writing system by providing a writing method to visually express various characteristics of sound.

Graphic Designer
and Professor
Joo Ha
Anseong, South Korea

Tech Support
Eunae Cho
and Seul Choi

School
Hankyong
National University

Principal Type
Voice Font

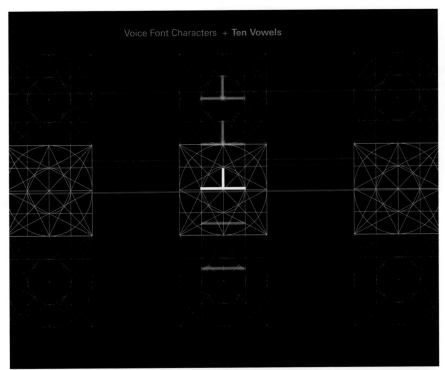

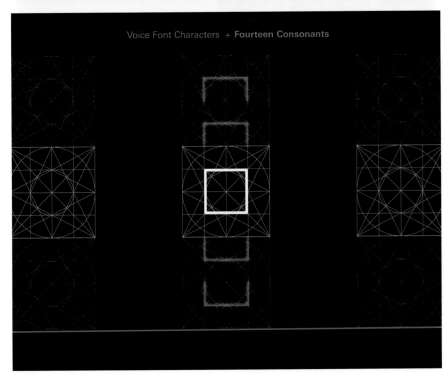

Made in the Middle:
2018 Main Title Sequence

Concept Made in the Middle is a design
conference headquartered in Kansas City, Missouri,
that spotlights artists, makers, and designers
from around the Midwest. I was commissioned to
produce an opening title sequence to complement
the visual brand of the festival but was given
license to interpret it as I wished. I chose a text-
only approach, which doubled as an offbeat
motivational call-to-arms for those attending
the festival.

Creative Direction
and Motion Design
Ben Radatz
Los Angeles

Score
NZCA Lines

URL
benradatz.com

Twitter
@benradatz

Client
Made in the Middle

Principal Type
Neue Haas Grotesk

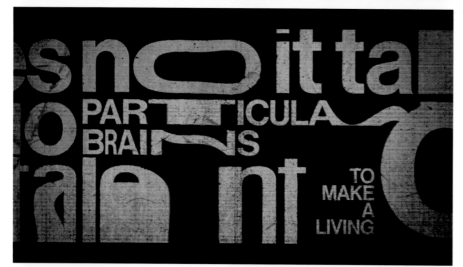

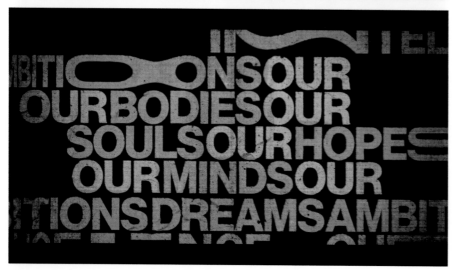

A Poor Gentleman in His Only Suit

Concept   The poem "A Gentleman in His Only Suit" is about a man's philosophy of his simple life. The task here was to explore the use of animation to show the characteristics of each word. The refraining lines in the poem become the main flow, and a limited color palette has been adopted to reflect the simplicity of the poem. Sound has been added instead of music to show the tempo of the poem.

Design and Animation
Joro Chen
**Mountain View,
California**

Sound Design
Pin Hua Chen

Writer
Myeong Seok Jeong

URL
joro.tv

Studio
Joro TV

Client
Ming Ren Press

Principal Type
**Fexy Sans
and hand-drawn**

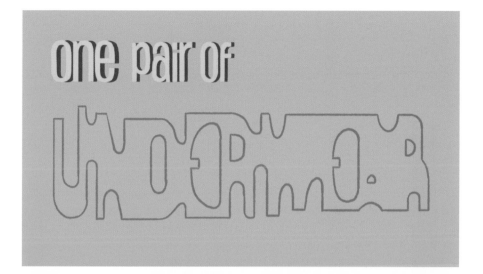

RESIST

Concept "City Symphony" is my lifelong project, made by traveling to cities around the world and recording their various sounds in special ways. Seoul, the third city in my project, is where I grew up. I have always thought that Seoul's Korean alphabet has an interesting structure of letters—minimal but also playful. It represents the city as well. I took Seoul's unique sounds and synced them with the letters.

Design
Lynn Hwirin Park
New York

URL
lhrpark.com

Principal Type
Custom

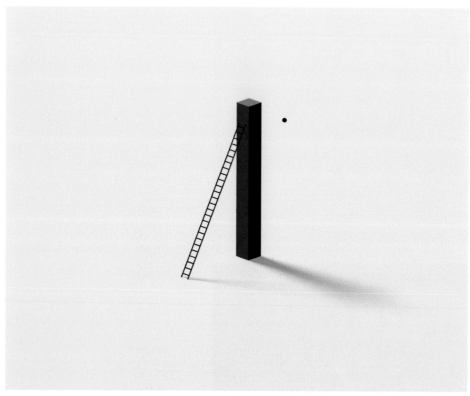

Qishan Longevity Noodles

Concept The Longevity Noodles brand originates from the idea of making simple pasta fresh, interesting, healthy, and characteristic. Eating Longevity Noodles is regarded as a symbol of auspiciousness and is often treated as a good wish for the future. We reset the identity and brand culture by taking "lasting" and "longevity" as the key elements of our design.

Design
Lieguan Chen
Shenzhen City, China

Letterer
Huifen Zhu

URL
cc-zendesign.com

Design Firm
cc-zenbrand design studio

Client
Qishan Fuying
Dry Noodle Co., Ltd.

Dimensions
7.1 x 10.6 x 15 in.
(18 x 27 x 38 cm)

Principal Type
明朝体 (MS Mincho)

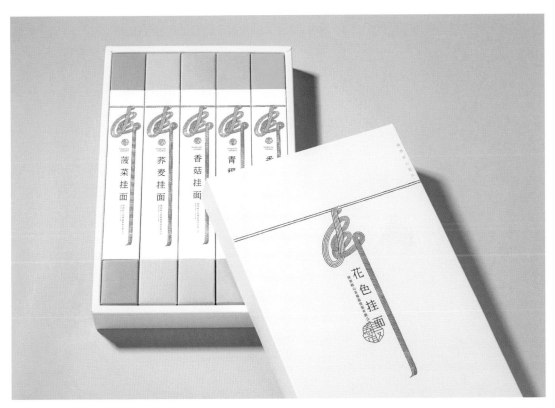

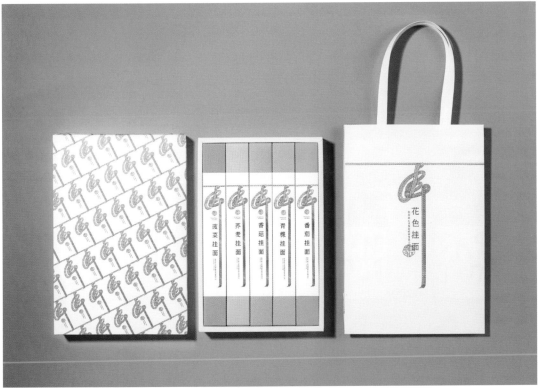

St. Erhard

Concept   St. Erhard is a brewery in Bamberg, Germany. In 2017, they decided to develop their design to appeal to a more design-oriented audience. The visual solution was a contemporary reference to Bauhaus principles with geometry as the basis for both the graphic elements and typography. Initially, the design is used for three beers—Farmer, Mayflower, and Saison—but the typographic system is flexible and allows the brewery to easily expand with more beers without losing the visual recognition. The result is a distinctive expression on the German store shelves—while most German breweries communicate tradition, St. Erhard stands for innovation.

Design
**Kung Hiu Ching
and Nikita Dudson
Stockholm**

Creative Direction
Perniclas Bedow

Art Direction
Anders Bollman

URL
bedow.se

Design Studio
Bedow

Client
St. Erhard
Dimensions

**Bottle
6.9 x 2.7 in.
(17.5 x 6.8 cm);
Label
3 x 2.8 in.
7.5 x 7 cm)**

Principal Type
Custom

Xiamen Kaoliang Liquor

Concept This design aims to emphasize the high quality and unique flavor of the liquor. Environmentally friendly, lightweight corrugated paper is applied to the interior and exterior of the packing box, and its special structure features good shock-absorption properties—ensuring the most effective protection during the shipping process.

Art Direction
Miaohua Chen
Fu'an City, China

Design Firm
Fujian Provincial Huayi
Designing Co., Ltd.

Client
Xiamen Kaoliang
Liquor Design

Dimensions
Box 7.1 x 11.8 in.
(18 x 30 cm);
Bottle 9.1 x 2.75 in.
(23 x 7 cm)

Principal Type
Custom

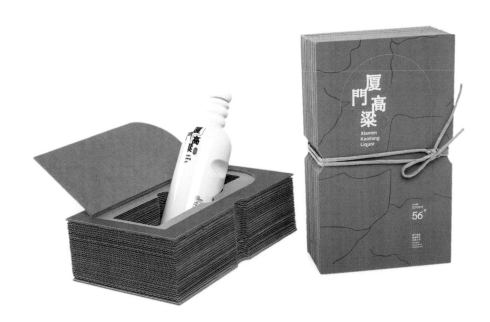

Freie Klasse Film: Werkschau #1

Concept Werkschau #1 is the first collection of films on DVD made by the students of Freie Klasse Film of the Muthesius Academy of Fine Arts and Design, supervised by filmmaker Stephan Sachs. Cards present each of the seventeen films with a still on the front and a description on the back. When sliding the sleeve off the cover, the viewer sets the typography in motion and discovers a special animation—a so-called kinegram, one of the earliest methods of producing moving pictures— thereby prompting reflection on the origins of filmmaking itself.

Design and Art Direction
Teresa Döge
and Björn Schmidt
Kiel, Germany

URLs
bjoernschmidt.info
teresadoege.com

Twitter
@BjoernTypes

Studio
kleineshaus

Client
**Muthesius Academy of
Fine Arts and Design**

Dimensions
5.5 x 7.5 in. (14 x 19 cm)

Principal Type
Akzidenz-Grotesk

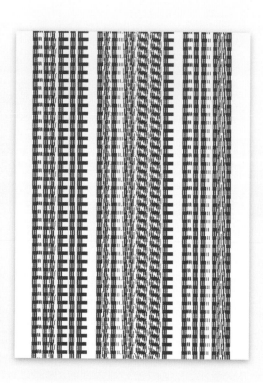

Nine Peaks Ranch Milk

Concept   The choice of font is where the design begins. Inspired by the Japanese font JTL, this typeface is warm, friendly, chubby, and handmade looking. These characteristics correspond with the missions of Nine Peaks Ranch. In the process, I redesigned the simplified Chinese characters from the original design of JTL's kanji. In addition, a series of icons has been created to complicate and further unify the overall visual language.

Design and Art Direction
Tao LIN
Shanghai, China

URL
taographicdesign.com

Client
Nine Peaks Ranch

Dimensions
2.75 x 2.75 x 5.3 in.
(7 x 7 x 13.5 cm);
2.75 x 2.75 x 3.3 in.
(7 x 7 x 8.5 cm)

Principal Type
JTL's Kanji
and Lantinghei

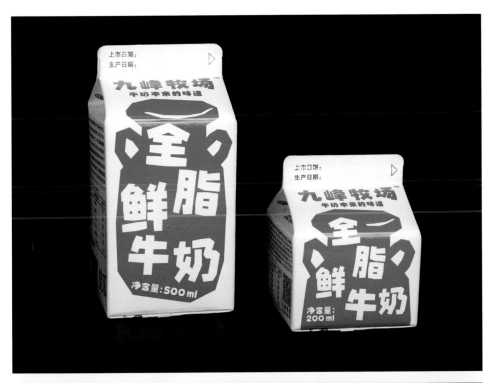

Packaging for Nedre Foss

Concept Nedre Foss is a Scandinavian brand that designs products made to last a hundred years. Minimalism and functionality are the key elements in their philosophy, and the packaging design mirrors this. Simple, one-to-one dimensions and the use of typography standards that will function into the future were part of the concept.

Design
**Vivi-Ann Slåttsveen
and Simen Schikulski
Hamar, Norway**

Creative Direction
Kjetil Wold

Art Direction
Simen Schikulski

Account Director
Ellen Østmoen

Agency
ANTI Hamar

Client
Nedre Foss

Principal Type
Times

Dimensions
Various

Original Pattern Brewing Company

Concept The logo and packaging system plays with the notion of expanding, mixing, and constantly moving. A different mark for a different context—but all created from the same seed. A different typeface and a different gestural pattern for each new brew builds on this idea and creates a foundation to build upon as new brews continue to be created.

Design
Jelita Aldrich,
Jay Jeon,
Natalia Kowaleczko,
Casey Martin,
and Fumitaka Saito
San Francisco

Creative Direction
Natalia Kowaleczko and
Casey Martin

URL
play.studio

Design Firm
Play

Client
Original Pattern Brewing
Company

Fous de l'Île Kombucha Seasonals

Concept   The branding and packaging design for
Fous de l'Île Kombucha positions the traditional
health drink as an everyday beverage, appealing to
an audience of bon vivants who seek out products
for quality and aesthetics alike. Typography plays a
key role in creating the rich, timeless character that
conveys the brand's care for craft. Each new flavor
in this line of seasonal products is embellished
with a unique illustration, enhancing their status
as limited editions and highlighting the brand's
dedication to creativity even as it grows.

Art Direction
Eli Horn
Montréal

Creative Direction
Lexane Rousseau

URL
fivethousandfingers.com

Twitter
@5000_fingers

Design Studio
Fivethousand Fingers
Design Studio

Client
Fous de l'Île Kombucha

Dimensions
6.7 x 2.9 x 2.9 in.
(17 x 7.3 x 7.3)

Principal Type
Nexa Bold
and Nexa Regular

CABS

Concept By bringing people together, Agape aspires to be more than a wine brand. This vision inspired the complementary typographic label designs, where CABS' written name is complete only when two bottles sit side by side. The custom calligraphy was intentionally executed in an expressive/artistic manner as we did not want to prioritize legibility or calligraphic prowess, but rather sought to achieve a balance between the positive space (ink, intent, and form) and the negative space. The wine droplets absorbed by the labels' texture feel less like stains and more like parts of a dance of life.

Design and Calligraphy
Ovidiu Hrin Timișoara, Timiș, Romania

URL
synopsismedia.com

Twitter
@DesignSynopsis

Design Studio
Synopsis

Client
AGAPE Art & Nature Winery

Dimensions
4.7 x 3.4 in. (12 x 8.5 cm)

Principal Type
Gotham Bold, Gotham Regular, and custom calligraphy

Objective

Concept This promotional poster for a competition asked architects to submit a portfolio based on the theme "Objective." Taking a literal interpretation of the theme, we chose to make the letters of the theme title look like large, physical, blobby objects.

Design
Daisy Lee
New York

Partner
Michael Bierut°

Associate Partner
Britt Cobb

Design Firm
Pentagram°

URL
pentagram.com

Twitter
@pentagram

Client
**The Architectural
League of New York**

Dimensions
**17 x 22 in.
(43.2 x 55.9 cm)**

Principal Type
**Helvetica Neue
and custom**

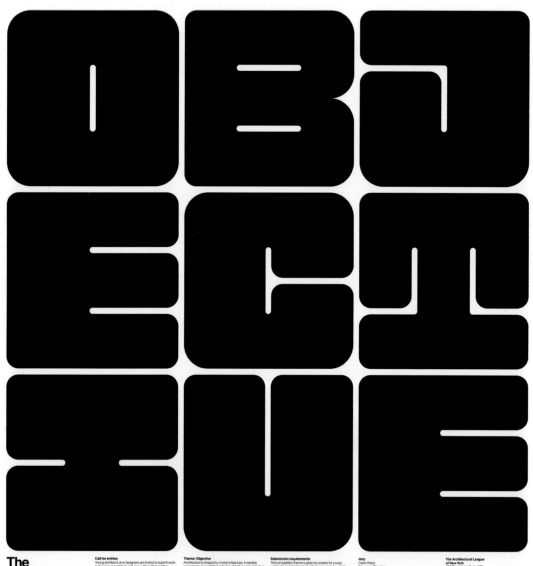

Stadt Land Food 2018

Concept   Stadt Land Food is a festival for both good food and good farming. The motto of the current issue ("Good food for all!") was written by hand on the preprinted posters, and in some cases (like here) the handwriting was also printed. The posters in the urban space did not reveal at first glance if the handwritten message was the official motto of the festival or if the claim was subsequently added by someone else.

Design
Daniel Wiesmann
Berlin

Assistant
Simon Schmalhorst

URL
danielwiesmann.de

Design Studio
Daniel Wiesmann Büro
für Gestaltung

Client
Markthalle Neun

Dimensions
33.1 x 46.8 in.
(84.1 x 118.9 cm)

Principal Type
Akzidenz-Grotesk
and handlettering

TE13: Photo & Typography

Concept   This poster was designed to promote TE13: Photo & Typography, the thirteenth exhibition hosted by the Korean Society of Typography. In this exhibition, around seventy graphic designers from six countries showcased their work. The Hangul used in the poster represents the theme of the exhibition, "Photo & Typography." We changed the existing Hangul fonts, Noto Sans by Google and Adobe, by designing and adding symbolic icons to represent photography as the concept of the exhibition. So we created pictorial typefaces in which text and pictures can be read at the same time.

Design
Suyeon Lim
and Daeki Shim
Seoul

Art Direction
Daeki Shim

URL
daekiandjun.com

Instagram
@dae.shim

Design Studio
Daeki & Jun

Client
Korean Society of
Typography
and Doosung Paper

Dimensions
33.1 x 46.8 in.
(84.1 x 118.9 cm)

Principal Type
Custom

Inna Art Space 10:
The First Decade

Concept   By shredding, mashing, reorganizing, and re-editing the texts of the subject matter, the artists conveyed their love for civilization. We pushed the clarity into chaos to show the vivacious spirit of the wasteland.

Design
Xiaomei Liu
and Qiongjie Yu
Hangzhou, China

Art Direction
Qiongjie Yu

URL
transwhite.cn

Design Studio
Transwhite Studio

Client
Inna Art Space

Dimensions
22.8 x 33.9 in.
(58 x 81 cm)

Principal Type
Univers

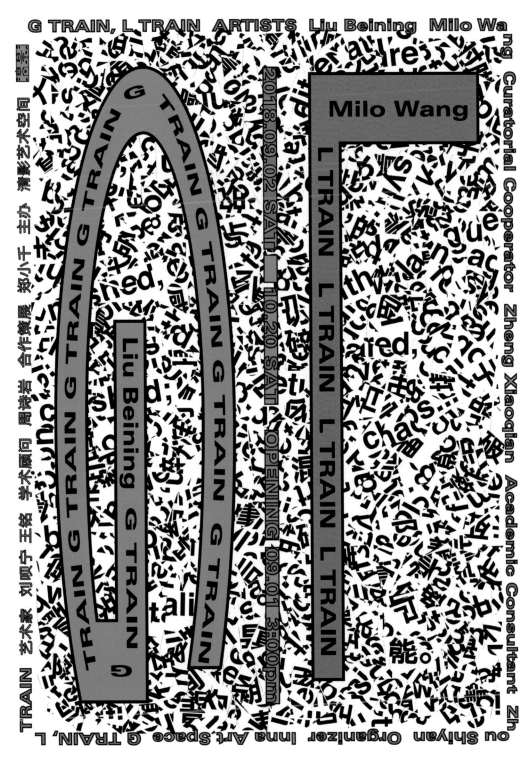

Pango

Concept   Atamira Dance Company is New Zealand's leading Māori contemporary dance company. Pango ("Black") is based on the story of creation, from a Māori perspective. Imagery creates a sense of grandeur, an embracing of Māori mythology. Figures represent the forcing apart of Ranginui, sky father, and Papatūānuku, earth mother. Force justified text allows for random negative space, enhancing the central concept of being forced apart. Custom lettering and typography create a "weaving" theme as they emerge from the black, joining to become a greater whole and designed to work together as a repeating pattern. Mythologies woven in movement.

Creative Direction
**Lloyd Osborne°
and Shabnam Shiwan
Auckland, New Zealand**

Photography
Charles Howells

Writing
**Lloyd Osborne
and Moss Patterson**

URL
osborneshiwan.com

Twitter
@osborneshiwan.com

Agency
Osborne Shiwan

Client
**Atamira Dance
Company**

Dimensions
**33.1 x 46.9 in.
(84 x 119 cm)**

Principal Type
Custom

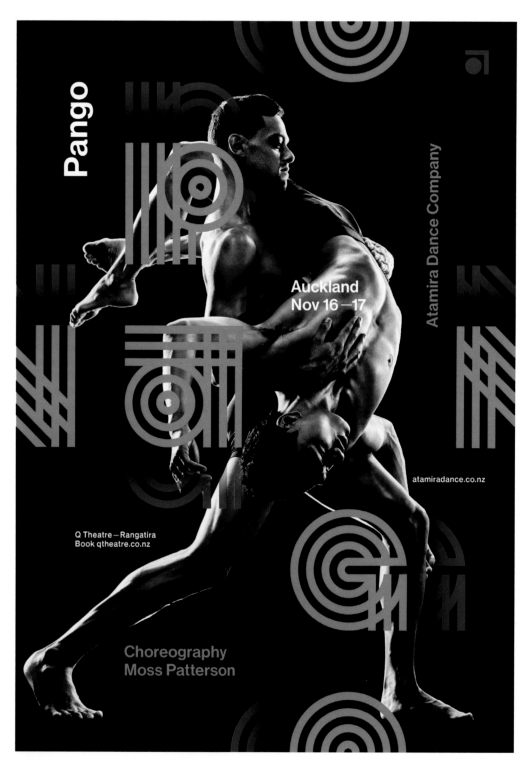

Save-Give-Join

Concept   We created this poster series for two reasons. First, we wanted to say hi and thank you to our friends and clients, as we always do at the end of the year. The other reason was to raise money for a good cause. So we sent out a set of postcards—and by ordering the identical posters, people became part of a donation campaign.

Design
**Reiner Hofer
Munich**

Art Direction:
**Sabine Schmid
and Lutz Widmaier°**

URL
schmidwidmaier.de

Design Studio
Schmid/Widmaier

Dimensions
**23.4 x 33.1 in.
(59.4 x 84.1 cm)**

Principal Type
Custom

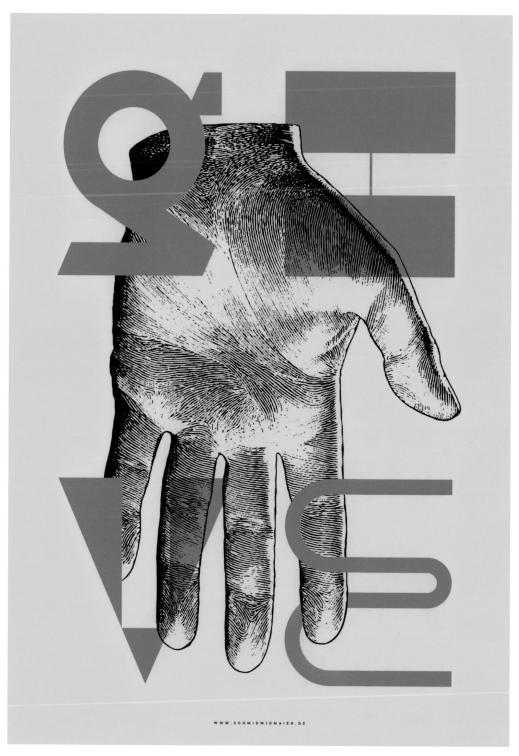

A Flag for the Other Side

Concept **To reflect the unique character of Bankside, the design is about the river, the water, and the two sides.**

Partner
and Creative Direction
Sascha Lobe°
London

URL
pentagram.com

Twitter
@pentagram

Design Firm
Pentagram

Client
Better Bankside

Dimensions
63 x 39.4 in.
(160 x 100 cm)

Anni Albers

Concept   The poster highlights Anni Albers, one of the many female Bauhaus artists.

Partner
and Creative Direction
Sascha Lobe°
London

URL
pentagram.com

Twitter
@pentagram

Design Firm
Pentagram

Client
It's Nice That
Printed Pages

Dimensions
7.9 x 10.8 in.
20 x 27.5 cm)

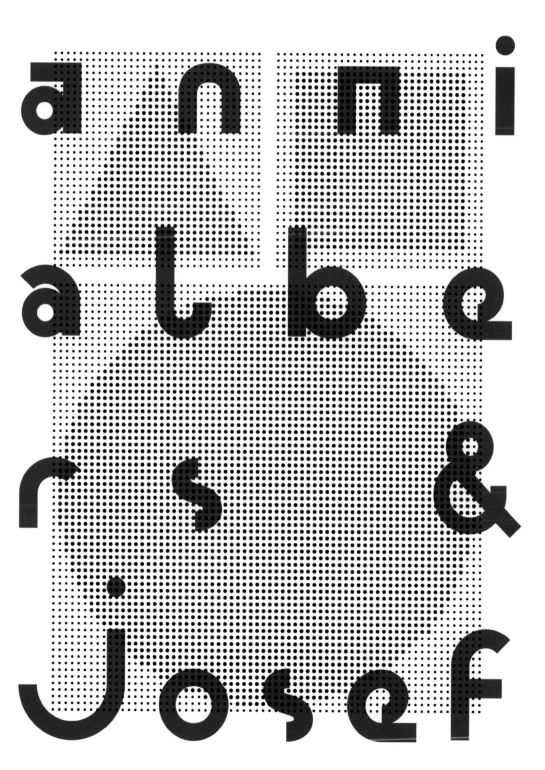

Finding the Truth in Data

Concept   Elliptic finds the truth in data. Terrorism, ransomware, child pornography, and weapons can all be purchased on the dark web using bitcoin, an untraceable currency—until now. Elliptic links bitcoin data to criminals and provides intelligence to law enforcement agencies in the United Kingdom and the United States. Negative space typography, inspired by data blocks, reveals the essence of the business, and legibility at scale is deliberately challenging in order to echo the difficult task Elliptic undertakes. The simple black-and-white palette further underscores the seriousness.

Creative Direction
Mark Wood
London

Senior Designer
and Typographer
Jonathan Brodie

Animation
Luigi Honorat,
Ned Image,
and David Whyte

Account Manager
Pippa Chishick

URL
superunion.com

Twitter
@SuperunionHQ

Brand Consultancy
Superunion

Client
Elliptic

Dimensions
Various

Principal Type
Bespoke

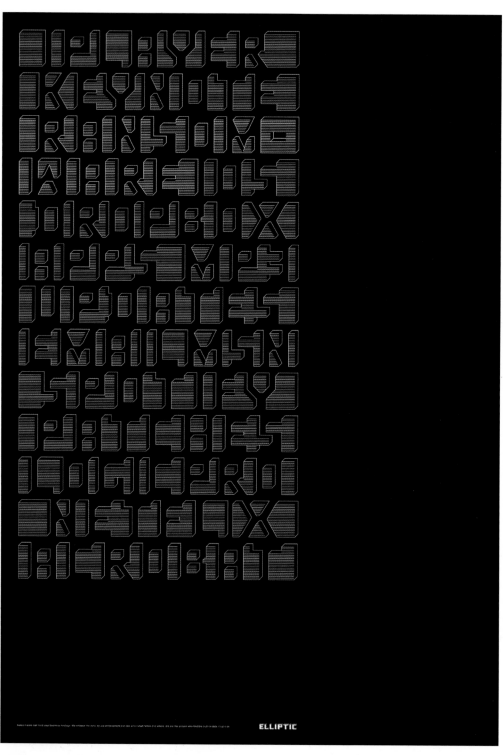

Start of Spring and Beginning of Summer and Beginning of Autumn and Beginning of Winter

Concept   This unique Chinese calendar was created using traditional calligraphy. "Start of Spring," "Beginning of Summer," "Beginning of Autumn," and "Beginning of Winter" are all written in one stretch in Chinese characters. The work expresses the passage of time through the path gradients, thus presenting Chinese traditional culture in a particular visual language.

Design
Zhao Chao
Shenzhen, China

Studio
ZhaoChao Design

Client
Cross-border art exhibition Appreciate Possible Future/ Time Travel

Dimensions
27.6 x 39.4 in.
(70 x 100 cm)

Principal Type
立春 . 立夏 . 立秋 . 立冬

Beginning of Autumn

Molly Burch

Concept   The main typography is based on the
style of the music, which varies with soft sounds
that are sometimes straightforward but also
sometimes up and down. The writing takes up this
movement of the voice of Molly Burch and thus
transports the voice color onto the poster.

Design and Art Direction
Sven Lindhorst-Emme°
Berlin

URL
lindhorst-emme.de

Design Firm
studio lindhorst-emme

Client
Neubad Lucerne,
Switzerland

Dimensions
Germany
33.1 x 46.8 in.
(84 x 118.9 cm);
Switzerland
35.2 x 50.4 in.
89.5 x 128 cm)

Principal Type
Bodoni-Freefont
and BrownStd

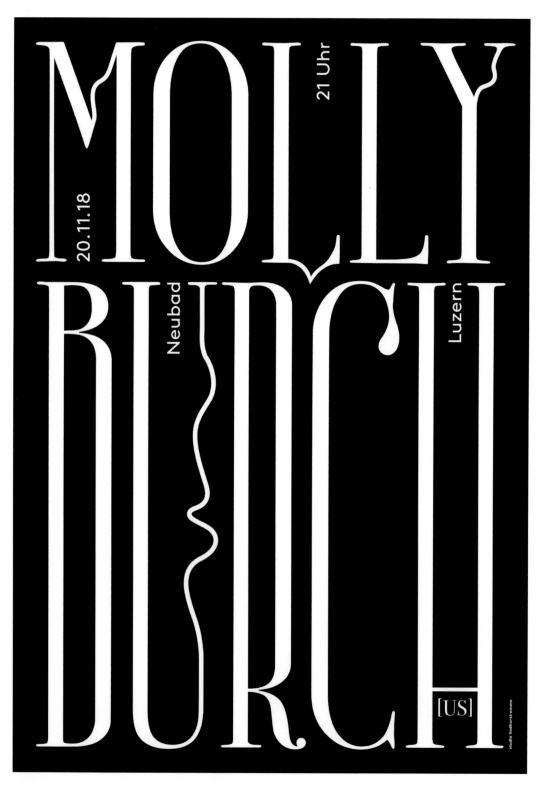

Soliloquy of Word

Concept   I used speech bubbles from comics to form the Chinese character 字 ("word") to convey the theme "Soliloquy of Word."

Design
Chun-liang Lin
Taipei

Studio
Leo Lin Design / NTNU

Client
Taiwan Poster Design
Association

Principal Type
Custom

Stance Against Fascism

Concept   We were asked to reinterpret two of the posters in the 1973 Chilean poster art exhibition Por la Vida ... Siempre! as part of an exhibition, Stance: Design Against Fascism, at Sur Gallery. The new exhibition creates a space for the audience to question how far we have truly advanced from the ideological dogmas of the past and how they continue to shape our current political, social, and economic realities. Our solution was to reinterpret the original posters in a clean and direct manner to encourage an urgent response from the audience.

Design
Fidel Peña
Toronto

Creative Direction
Claire Dawson
and Fidel Peña

Design Studio
Underline Studio

Client
Sur Gallery

Dimensions
20 x 28.5 in.
(50.8 x 72.4 cm)

Principal Type
Druk Condensed
and Neue Haas Grotesk

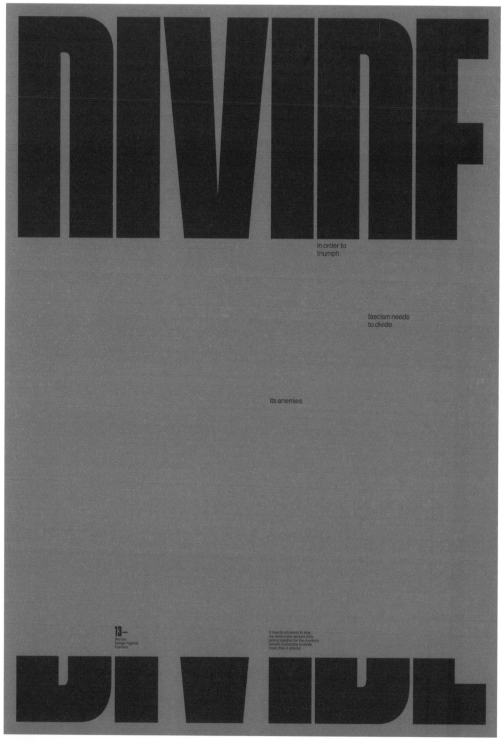

Families Poster

Concept This was a self-initiated project that aimed to raise awareness of Donald Trump's policy of separating Central American migrant families at the U.S.-Mexico border. The poster sought to raise funds for organizations working to help the families. Our solution was a clean typographic poster and animation that illustrated the pain of separating fathers and mothers from their children.

Design
Fidel Peña
Toronto

Design Studio
Underline Studio

Creative Direction
Claire Dawson
and Fidel Peña

Dimensions
22 x 28 in.
(55.9 x 71.1 cm)

Principal Type
Neue Haas Grotesk
and OGG

Pablo Delcan SVA Subway Poster

Concept Since the mid-1950s, SVA has been commissioning contemporary designers and illustrators to create NYC subway platform posters to advertise the college. Starting in 2018, the college began asking the artists it commissioned to use the prompt "Art Is!" to create their poster. Pablo Delcan's solution was the first in this series. He chose to display the message abstractly using computer-generated lettering.

Design
Pablo Delcan
New York

Executive Creative Director
Anthony P. Rhodes

Creative Direction
Gail Anderson°

URL and Twitter
sva.edu

Design Firms
Visual Arts Press, Ltd.
and Delcan & Company

Client
School of Visual Arts,
New York°

Dimensions
30 x 46 in.
(76.2 x 116.8 cm)

Principal Type
Custom

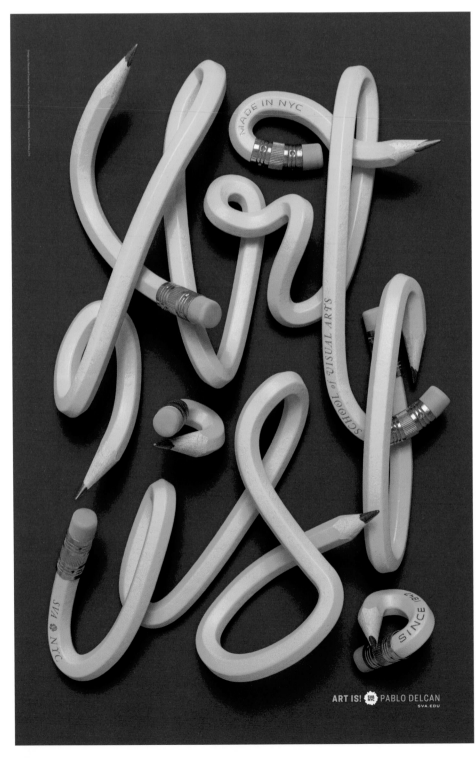

The Wind

Concept This work was for a poster design exhibition with the theme "New Wind Blowing From East Asia." A hundred designers active in Japan, Korea, and China were invited to participate in the exhibition. I made a typeface called Wind to depict a delicate image even in a powerful situation.

Design and Art Direction
Hajime Tsushima
Hiroshima

Creative Direction
Yukiko Tsushima

URL
tsushima-design.com

Design Firm
Tsushima Design

Client
**Korea National
University of Arts**

Dimensions
28.7 x 40.6 in.
(72.8 x 103 cm)

Principal Type
Helvetica and custom

No GMO

Concept   This poster is about genetically modified organisms in food. The poster exhibition was part of the 2018 Korea Design EXPO. The surreal black egg in the center stands for the unnatural genetically modified food. Those roughened GMOs, transformed and followed by an unusual form of a grid system, symbolize the hidden problems of the modified gene sequences. Finally, the red trace of a knife mark across the poster represents the designer's strong opposition to those harmful foods.

Design and Art Direction
Jie-Fei Yang
Taipei

Behance
@jiefeidesign

Studio
Jie-Fei Design

Client
GMO-
FREE=GREEN+YOU
Poster Exhibition

Dimensions
27.8 x 39.4 in.
(70.7 x 100 cm)

Principal Type
Titular Heavy

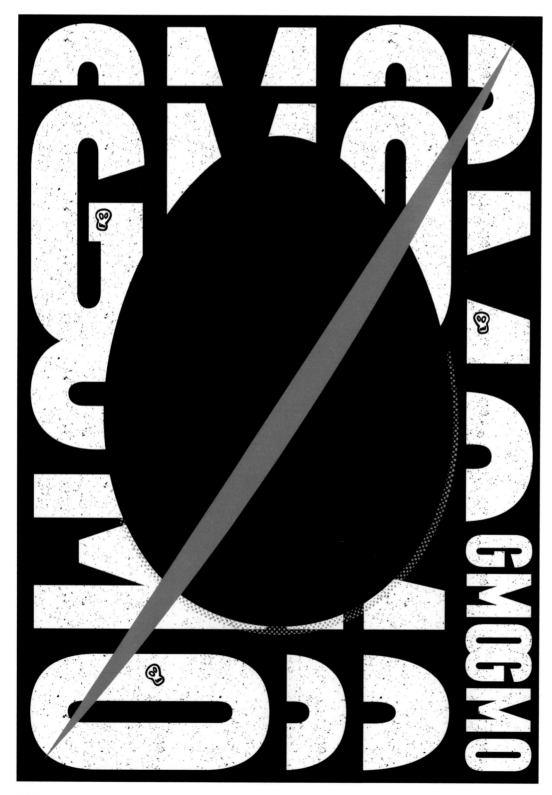

ASS

Concept   This profanity poster series focused on letter forms and the profane words you can make with them. Jon strived to create type that was both compelling and entertaining. But why swear words? Because they are universally known, and the intonation literally illustrates intention. These posters were printed on 150g uncoated paper and sold through the gallery.

Creative Direction
Jon Hartman°
Denver

URL
iheartwunderwerkz.com

Design Firm
Wunder Werkz

Client
Station 16

Dimensions
24 x 36 in. (61 x 91 cm)

Principal Type
Custom

Amsterdam Sinfonietta
January-June 2018

Concept   Founded in 1988, Amsterdam Sinfonietta
is an independent music ensemble with an international reputation and a rich, varied repertoire.
Studio Dumbar has worked with the ensemble for
over a decade. One of the most notable aspects of
the collaboration is the evolving poster series designed to advertise concerts. Since the beginning,
the design of the seasonal posters has been driven
by one aim: to create visually arresting posters
that succeed in expressing the innovative spirit and
broad spectrum of music performed. This series of
posters responds typographically to the musical
themes of the performance being advertised.

Design
Daan Rietbergen
Rotterdam

URL
studiodumbar.com

Twitter
@studiodumbar

Design Firm
Studio Dumbar

Client
Amsterdam Sinfonietta

Dimensions
33.1 x 46.8 in.
(84.1 x 118.9 cm)

Principal Type
Helvetica Neue

X. Phoenix Design Summer Hangzhou

Concept East meets West; Latin meets Arabic meets Chinese—different communication systems melt into one visual, symbolizing the multicultural exchange during the Phoenix Design Summer in Hangzhou, China.

Design
Götz Gramlich
Heidelberg, Germany

URL
gggrafik.de

Design Firm
gggrafik design

Client
Phoenix Design Summer, Hangzhou

Dimensions
27.6 x 39.4 in.
(70 x 100 cm)

Principal Type
Helvetica Inserat and System Chinese Font

Chinese Imagery

Art Direction
Xuandong Wu
Qingdao, China

URL
sdpr.com.cn

Design Firm
Deep Communication Group

Dimensions
27.6 x 39.4 in.
(70 x 100 cm)

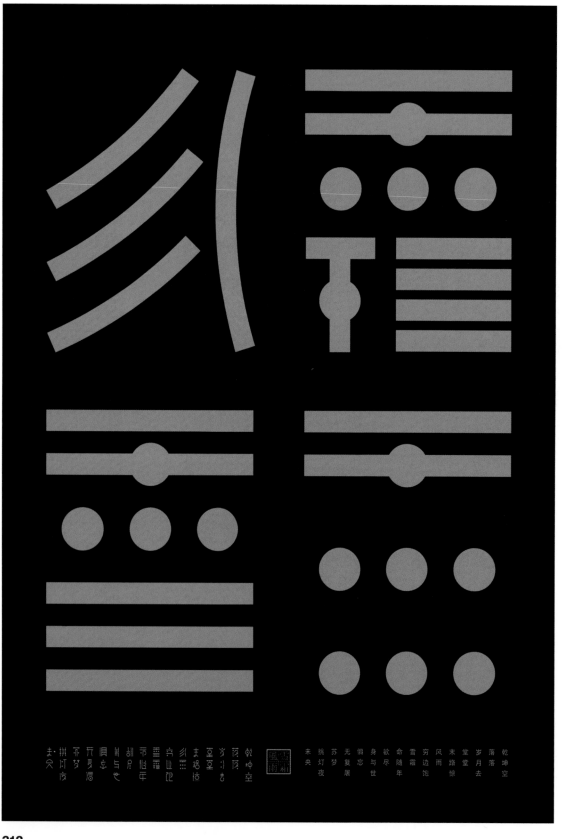

NO: ABCD MUSIC Concert

Concept   This is the poster for a series of musical parties. I used "Alphabets" as the main theme. Alphabets look like our ears listening to music, happily moving and dancing to the melodies. It's just like singing the alphabet song when we were children. It's so pure and harmonic!

Design
**Kuanhou Cheang
Macau**

Facebook
@315isteatime

Studio
3.3 Tea time

Client
LONGYUAN5Z

Dimensions
**16.5 x 23.4 in.
(41.9 x 59.4 cm)**

Principal Type
**RO日活正楷書STD-L,
Noto Sans CJK, and
Skolar Latin**

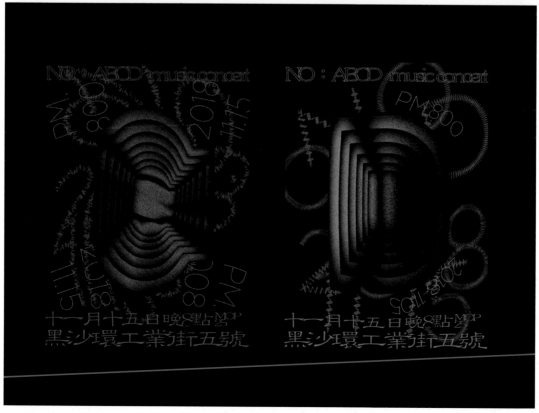

Mencius, Jinxin, Part One, Chapter 9

Concept   This poster depicts a famous saying in The Works of Mencius. This sentence has become a life motto for many people. It's summed up and presented by two graphical Chinese characters.

Creative Direction
Bright Woo
Beijing

Twitter
@delightedbj

Design Studio
Delighted Design

Client
Purple Hall

Dimensions
27.6 x 39.4 in.
(70 x 100 cm)

Principal Type
Custom

Tolerance

Concept The poster depicts political dissent and
social tolerance.

Design
Wael Morcos°
New York

Twitter
@morcoskey

Design Firm
Morcos Key

Client
Mirko Ilić

Dimensions
14.2 x 20.9 in.
(36 x 53 cm)

Principal Type
Custom

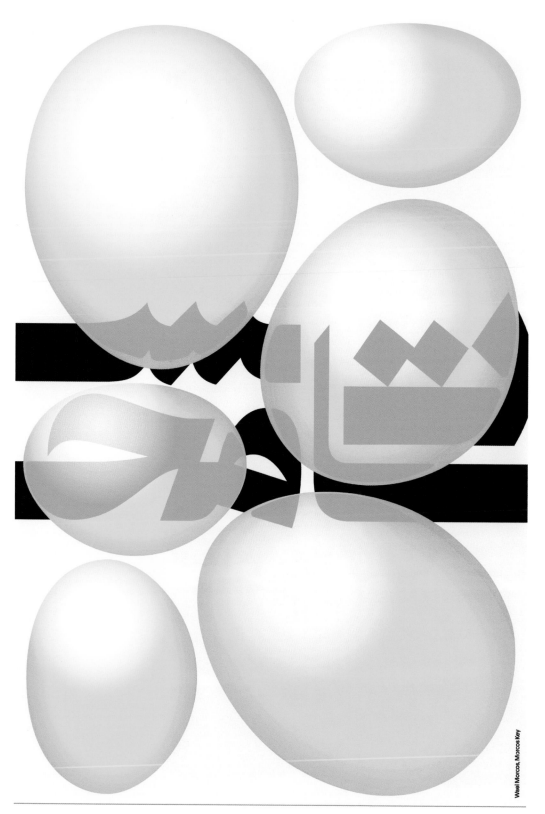

Wael Morcos, Morcos Key

Ink

Concept   Mohism is a unique instrument in China. These works consider the concept of time overlap. Writing is repeated over and over with time, more than a hundred times, producing an obvious gloss surface that reflects so much light.

Art Direction
Rineng Zhu
Foshan City, China

Design Firm
INKdesign Co.

Client Name
Kong Yin

Dimensions
27.6 x 39.4 in.
(70 x 100 cm)

Principal Type
INK song

Today at Apple: The Typefaces

Concept   The Typefaces are simply faces in type—a collection of letterpress characters born between the pages of a book that are now climbing the walls, roaming the malls, and spending way too much time on Instagram. The Typefaces eventually wormed their way into Apple. This poster was produced to promote The Typefaces' "Today at Apple" town square session on Orchard Road.

Design
**Scott Lambert
Singapore**

URLs
**thetypefaces.com
superunion.com**

Twitter
**@thetypefaces
@superunionhq**

Design Firm
Superunion

Client
The Typefaces

Dimensions
**23.4 x 33.1 in.
(59.4 x 84 cm)**

Principal Type
Akzidenz

The Typefaces @ Apple
4pm, Saturday 14th April 2018

Apple Store, 270 Orchard Rd,
Singapore 238857

@thetypefaces
thetypefaces.com

@superunionhq
superunion.com

Design Wisdom

Concept With the theme of "Design Wisdom," this international conference discusses how to integrate design with scientific and technological innovation in the global context to cope with the change of lifestyle in the future. Today, at a time when consumption continues to rise, how does design promote innovation in energy and materials, and solve social sustainable development and other complex problems? In terms of cultural communication, how does design shoulder the mission of cultural innovation and communication? The poster combines the Chinese character for "design wisdom" with the brain to present the theme.

Design
Chaosheng Li
Hangzhou, China

URL
hzic.edu.cn

University
Zhejiang Gongshang University

Dimensions
27.5 x 39.4 in.
(70 x 100 cm)

Principal Type
Helvetica Neue
LT Std BdCn
and
Source Han Sans Bold

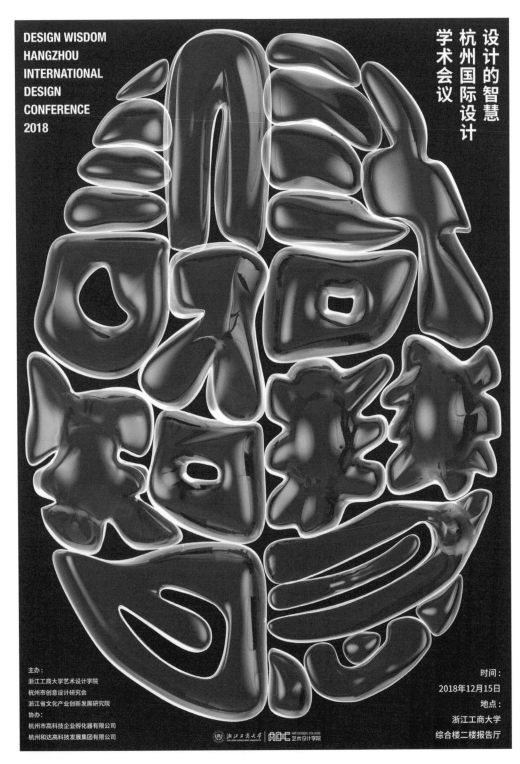

2018, Happy New Year,
The Pig Geely

Concept   I used my own language, text, and pig's
mouth graphics to design a set of text graphics
that are unique to the Year of the Pig. Each graphic
is a cute, round, fleshy, full-feeling pig—an image
designed to please.

Design
Zhang Weimin
Shenzhen, China

Studio
Zhang Weimin Brand
Design

Dimensions
27.5 x 39.4 in.
(70 x 100 cm

Principal Type
Custom

Return to My Original Nature Light

Concept   "I" is the most primitive, loyal, pure, and original self. "I" is also the book. This personal design project explores nature and the future of the self. The "I" graphic is shaped like a blooming flower, and the negative space is the light of design art that my inner world has been constantly pursuing.

Design
Zhang Weimin
Shenzhen, China

Studio
Zhang Weimin Brand Design

Dimensions
27.5 x 39.4 in
(70 x 100 cm)

Principal Type
Custom

Lo Fi Dance Theory at White Wall Studio, MTL Poster Triptych

Concept   Initially a series of unscripted dance classes held nomadically in derelict, "lo-fi" spaces across New York City, Lo Fi Dance Theory has since evolved into a performing arts company that produces performances, exhibitions, and digital works spanning dance, film, fashion, theater, and music. In fall 2018, LFDT took residency at White Wall Studio in Montréal, where it actively engages the public with its signature dance classes and collaborative workshops. The poster series created for the residency uses a tribal visual language that exudes corporeal movement and primal color. Spanning a triptych of alternating colors to reveal the host city's "MTL" moniker, the letterforms gesturally fold and turn into one another, reflecting LFDT's choreographic style.

Lead Designer and Creative Direction
Jaymes Moore°
New York

Additional Creative Direction
Arash Hajianpour and Wynn Holmes

URLs
jaymesmoore.com
lofidancetheory.com

Dimensions
23.4 x 31.6 in.
(59.4 x 80 cm)

Principal Type
GT America Extended
Bold and custom

Folding Folder

Concept I designed these foldable posters for a workshop on graphic design and auxetic folding patterns, which I conceptualized and led at the Exploratorium in San Francisco in August 2018. Each poster folds up to become an animated lo-fi toy that squashes and stretches the lettering. The lettering itself was inspired by the various auxetic fold patterns depicted and described on the posters. Each different fold pattern has its own unique (and bizarre) mechanical behavior.

Design and Lettering
Kelli Anderson
Brooklyn, New York

URL
kellianderson.com

Twitter and Instagram
@kellianderson

Dimensions
11 x 17 in. (27.9 x 17.8 cm)

Principal Type
Eames Numerals, Styrene, and hand-drawn lettering (including a redrawn version of Maelstrom by Klim)

JUMP Bike Posters

Concept   We used the tagline "JUMP ON" to mimic road lines and bike lanes.

Design
**Jens Marklund
and Juan Carlos Pagan°
New York**

Creative Direction
**Ahmed Klink
and Juan Carlos Pagan**

Photography
Ahmed Klink

URL
sundayafternoon.us

Design Firm
Sunday Afternoon

Client
JUMP

Dimensions
**48 x 72 in.
(121.9 x 182.8 cm)**

Principal Type
Cinderblock

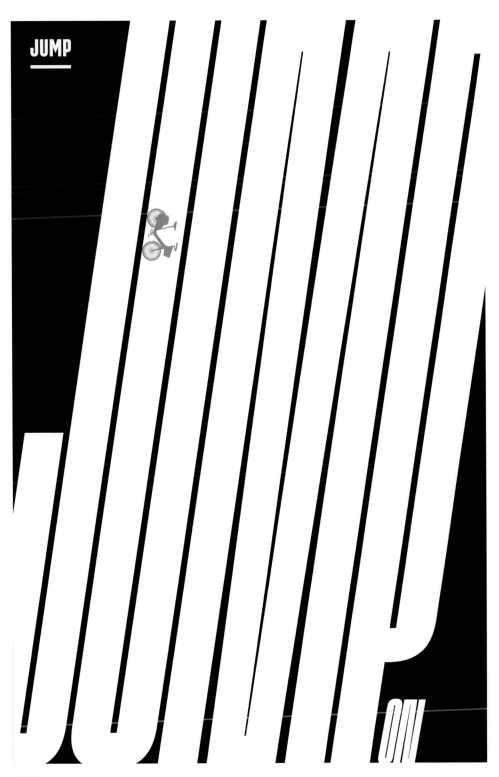

One Club Young Guns CFE Poster

Concept **This was a poster announcing the call forentries for The One Club for Creativity's Young Guns 16 competition.**

Design
**Jens Marklund
and Juan Carlos Pagan°
New York**

Creative Direction
**Ahmed Klink
and Juan Carlos Pagan**

URL
sundayafternoon.us

Design Firm
Sunday Afternoon

Client
**The One Club
for Creativity**

Dimensions
24 x 36 in. (61 x 91.4 cm)

Principal Type
Elderkin

Tomaga

Concept This was a poster for a concert by London-based duo Tomaga at Sesc Belenzinho, São Paulo.

Design
Thiago Lacaz
Rio de Janeiro

URL
thiagolacaz.com

Facebook
@thiagolacaz

Instagram
@tlacaz

Client
Alavanca

Dimensions
33.1 x 46.8 in.
(84.1 x 118.9 cm)

Principal Type
Suisse Int'l Mono Bold

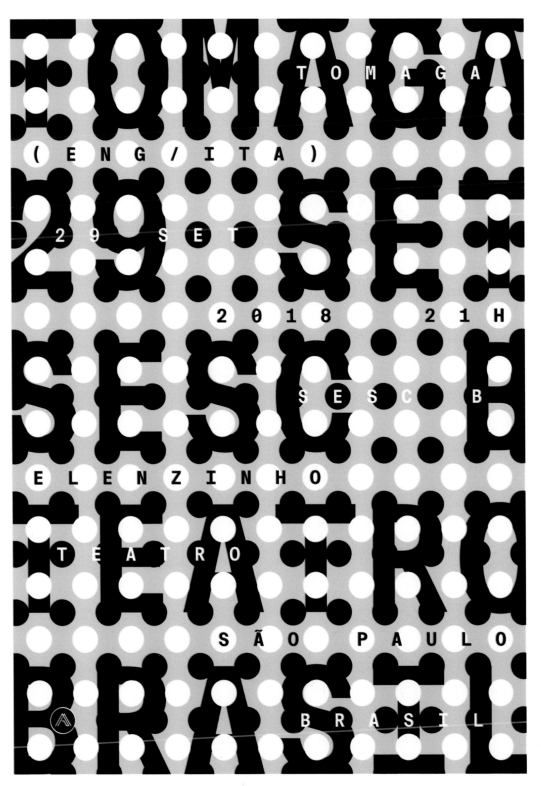

Bolsa de Fotografia ZUM 2018

Concept   To promote the ZUM/IMS Photography Grant—sponsored by ZUM, the contemporary photography magazine published by Instituto Moreira Salles—we created a large typographical poster with text at different scales. On top of the original 35 x 24 in. poster, we've applied a grid of perforated lines that allow the piece to assume different shapes, such as smaller posters and even a postcard. In each module, the info is repeated in different arrangements in a way so that each piece, no matter how big or in which shape, has the same content as the others.

Design
**Gabriela Castro,
Paulo André Chagas,
and Gustavo Marchetti
São Paulo**

URL
blocografico.com.br

Design Firm
Bloco Gráfico

Client
Instituto Moreira Salles

Dimensions
**35 x 24 in. (88 x 61 cm)
to 4 x 6 in. (11 x 15 cm)**

Principal Type
Druk

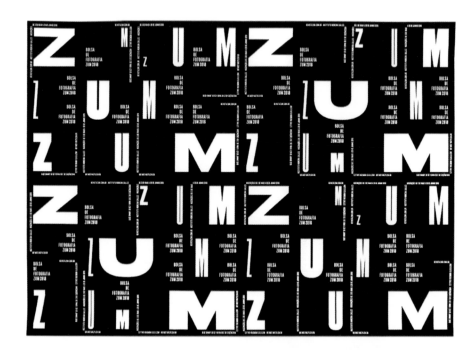

Shakespeare in the Park 2018

Concept   Othello and Twelfth Night were
the featured productions in the 2018 edition
of Shakespeare in the Park, the annual free
performances presented by The Public Theater
at the Delacorte Theater in Central Park. This
campaign was Pentagram's twenty-fourth since
1994. Each year's season design changes in the
use and spirit of Knockout, the font of the Public
identity. The letterforms of the 2018 graphics
stretch and expand to dynamically fill the space
on a field of gradated color.

Design
**Gina Bella,
Courtney Gooch,
Katie Hodge,
Paula Scher°,
Tammy Shell,
and Rusty Van Riper
New York**

Creative Direction
and Partner-in-Charge
Paula Scher

Project Manager
Rusty Van Riper

URL
pentagram.com

Twitter
@pentagram

Design Firm
Pentagram°

Client
The Public Theater

Dimensions
Various

Principal Type
Knockout

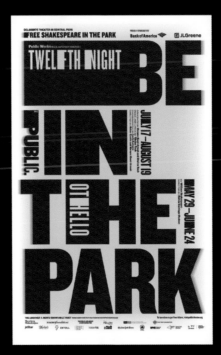

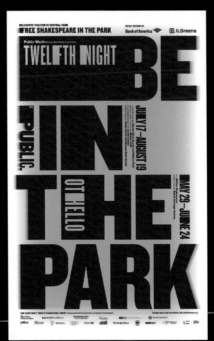

Eve's Song

Concept Eve's Song remembers black women who are killed at the hands of police and others. It recognizes that the media forgets to report on them. Eve's Song celebrates that all came from one Black Eve.

Senior Graphic Designer and Photography
Tammy Shell
New York

Creative Direction
Paula Scher°
(Pentagram)

Concept Research Collaboration
Katie Hodge

Model
Ashley D. Kelley

H + M
Earon Nealey

Costume Scouts
Katie Hodge
and Gina Roi°

Photo Assistants
Katie Hodge,
Christian Martin,
Gina Roi, David Shum,
and Ze Wang

URL
publictheater.org

Twitter
@publictheaterny

Studio
The Public Theater

Dimensions
20 x 39 in.
(50.8 x 99.1 cm)

Principal Type
Knockout

Mother of the Maid

Concept   Mother of the Maid is the story of Joan of Arc from the perspective of her mother. In the beginning, the mom (Glenn Close) is overly protective and even suffocating to Joan. In the end, the mom rises up with tremendous strength to comfort Joan when everyone has abandoned her.

Senior Graphic Designer
Tammy Shell
New York

Creative Direction
Paula Scher°
(Pentagram)

Concept Research
Collaboration
Gina Roi°

URL
publictheater.org

Twitter
@publictheaterny

Studio
The Public Theater

Dimensions
20 x 39 in.
(50.8 x 99.1 cm)

Principal Type
Knockout

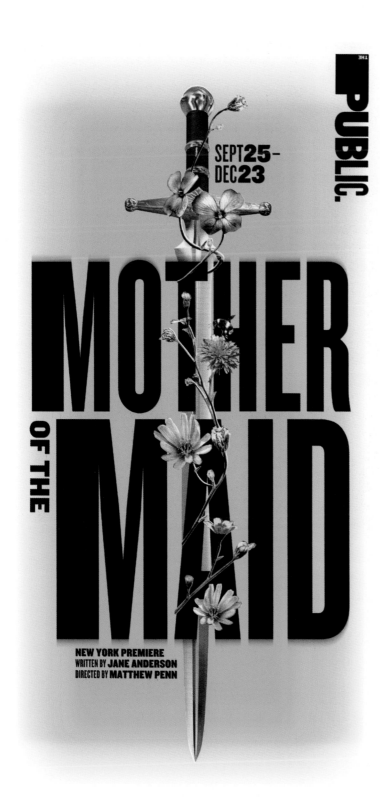

Vote! Vote! Vote!

Concept This vote poster honors a famous quote by Emma Lazarus. The design inspiration came from the song "Huddled Masses" by Shaina Taub.

Senior Graphic Designer
Tammy Shell
New York

Creative Direction
Paula Scher°
(Pentagram)

URL
publictheater.org

Twitter
@publictheaterny

Studio
The Public Theater

Dimensions
20 x 39 in.
(50.8 x 99.1 cm)

Principal Type
Knockout

Complexity and Simplicity

Concept This is about the philosophy between complexity and simplicity.

Design and Art Direction
Siguang Wu
Wuxi, China

Agency
HDU23

Client
Biennial of Asia
Graphic Design

Dimensions
19.7 x 27.5 in.
(50 x 70 cm)

Principal Type
Custom

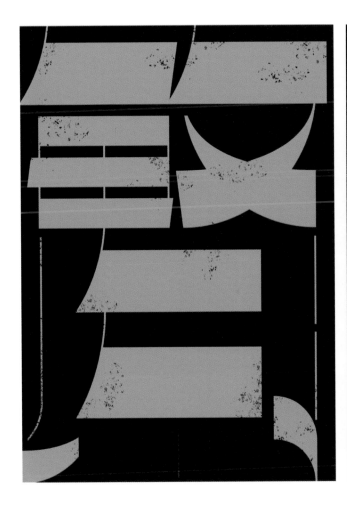

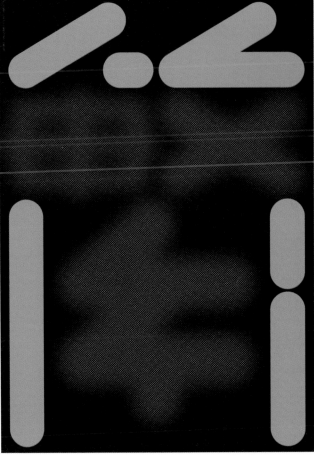

Allgemein Grotesk

Concept   The "Library of Shapes, Texts, and Structures" is both an ongoing visual research project and a comprehensive personal library of visual and verbal design elements. The library currently consists of two typefaces—Allgemein Grotesk and Affiche Collection—and an extensive archive of many different shapes, structures, and typographic materials. It also contains a collection of found text fragments. The two posters featuring the forthcoming typeface Allgemein Grotesk are part of a large poster series presenting a variety of elements from the library.

Design
Andrea Tinnes
Berlin

URL
typecuts.com

Twitter
@AndreaTinnes

Instagram
@andrea.tinnes

Design Firm
typecuts

Client
Self-published for
Burg Giebichenstein

Dimensions
28.4 x 40.2 in.
(72 x 102 cm)

Typeface
Allgemein Grotesk

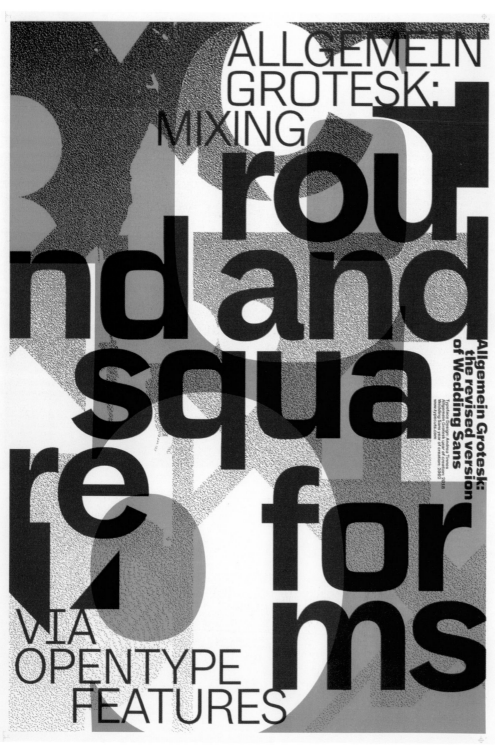

An Interesting Soul

Concept **This poster is for an interior design salon, and the theme is "An Interesting Soul." I designed this poster in the form of a blueprint.**

Design and Art Direction
Siguang Wu
Wuxi, China

Agency
HDU23

Client:
Jiangnan Design Society

Dimensions
27.5 x 39.4 in.
(70 x 100 cm)

Principal Type
Custom

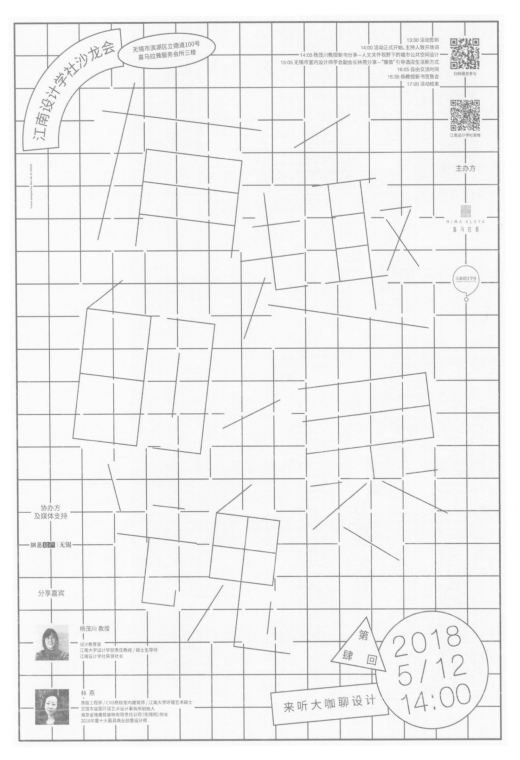

Contradiction Font

Concept   In some countries, while a number of social problems have received widespread attention,
no effective actions have been taken to solve them.
I hope to arouse people's serious consideration and
action through these posters.

Creative Direction
BrightWoo
Beijing

Twitter
@delightedbj

Design Studio
Delighted Design

Dimensions
27.6 x 39. 4 in.
(70 x 100 cm)

Principal Type
Binding and Bound

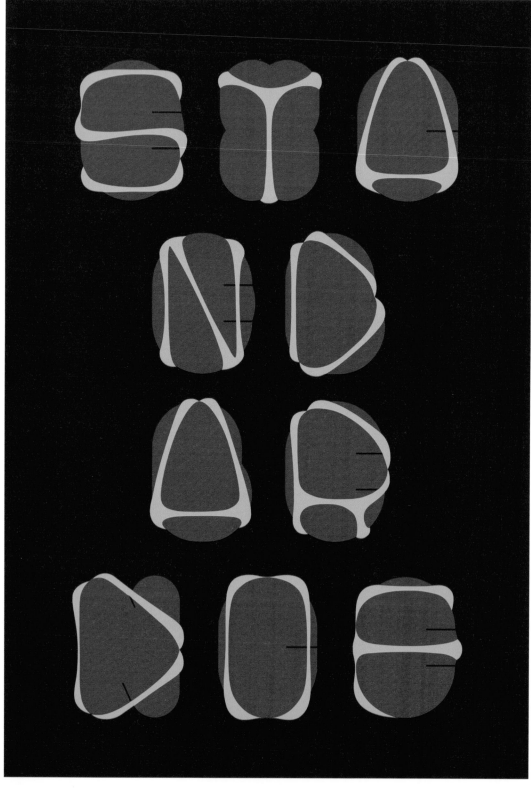

Twofold: Volume 3

Concept Twofold is a showcase of custom lettering and original typeface design. The specimen is
composed of eight individual posters folded down
into a sixteen-page broadsheet newspaper.

Design, Creative,
and Typography
Mark Caneso
Austin

Printer
Newspaper Club

URL
pprwrkstudio.com

Design Studio
PPRWRK STUDIO

Dimensions
15 x 22.8 in.
(38 x 57.8 cm)

Principal Type
Custom

Modular Type Specimen

Concept This project was born from studies exploring typographic repetition as a form of optical art and visual poetry. Square quadrants are made of repeated letters, and the quadrants are configured to make words or phrases, resulting in a unique typographic texture. The texture varies, depending on the typeface and type settings. This particular application is for a Happy New Year message sent to friends, family, and clients.

Design
Ryan Carl
Red Hook, New York

URL
ryancarl.studio

Instagram
@ryancarlstudio

Studio
Ryan Carl Studio

Dimensions
7 x 9 in. (18 x 23 cm)

Principal Type
Armand Grotesk Regular

Fixture: A Kinetic Type Specimen

Concept   The idea behind this design was to put together a workhorse font family with enough functional flexibility to work across multiple environments. While Alejandro Paul was designing the Fixture typeface for Sudtipos, he imagined many possible applications, from posters to movie titles. He then joined forces with Vanessa Zuñiga, a talented animator from Ecuador, and they combined their imaginations to learn and experiment with kinetic type. The project grew as they couldn't stop exploring new ideas, playfully experimenting to create a body of work that aims to inspire those who want to make use of this massive family of seventy-two fonts.

Design
**Alejandro Paul and
Vanesa Zúñiga Tinizaray
Buenos Aires**

Design Firm
Sudtipos

Principal Type
Fixture family

Queen Elizabeth II's 65th Anniversary of the Coronation

Concept   Canada Post celebrated the sixty-fifth anniversary of the coronation of Her Majesty Queen Elizabeth II, the longest-reigning monarch in British history. The portrait, by Armenian Canadian photographer Yousuf Karsh, is from a famous sitting in July 1951, when the Queen was still known as Her Royal Highness Princess Elizabeth.

Design and Art Direction
Daniel Robitaille
Montréal

Creative Direction
Louis Gagnon°

URL
paprika.com

Design Firm
Paprika

Client
Canada Post

Dimensions
1.3 x 1.1 in. (3.4 x 2.7 cm)

Principal Type
Mirador

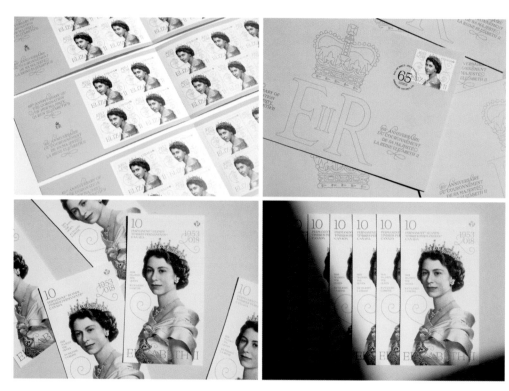

Kaohuo

Concept   This logo for a barbecue restaurant combines Chinese characters with graphics. The main body is composed of the characters for "grill" and "goods," symbolizing a compound character in Chinese language. The graphic implementation of "fire" in the character for "grill" vividly shows the status of a raging flame. However, the logo with its compound character does not exist independently. Instead, combining it with a picture of a shrimp, a squid, and a fish, all outlined by thin lines, has resulted in a novel and flexible logo variant, which further emphasizes the positioning for the grilled seafood products that the logo intends to convey.

Design
**Hu Bin and
Lin Guosheng
Hangzhou, China**

URL
k-ingo.com

Design Firm
K-ingo Design

Client
KAOHUO Restaurant

Vincent van Gogh
"Theo'ya Mektuplar"

Concept   The Letters of Vincent van Gogh ("Letters to Theo") is a short Turkish edition designed within the only inscribed source project about Van Gogh's life, which was originally created with 903 letters by Van Gogh Museum. This was designed as senior-year graduation project.

Design
Gizem Kara
Istanbul

URL
msgsu.edu.tr

Instructor
Haluk Tuncay

School
Mimar Sinan Fine Arts University

Dimensions
7.1 x 8.9 in.
(18 x 22.7 cm)

Principal Type
GT Sectra Book,
GT Sectra Book Italic,
GT Sectra Display Super, and Suisse BP

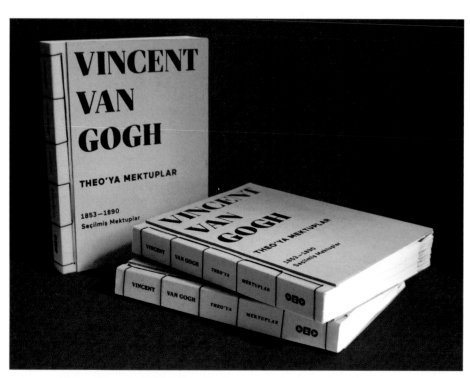

Port Magazine

Concept Port Magazine is a publication representing selected works and projects made by students at Bauhaus-University Weimar. Concept or aesthetic? What was there first? Port wants to take you into the head of a young creative. The magazine mirrors creative thinking in its design: One part represents students who begin their work by creating a concept (monochrome); others start with a visual and experiment until they find their concept (colorful). Five Pantone colors, always in pairs. Images are read, texts are seen. The cover is neither colorful nor monochrome.

Design
**Tamara Knapp
and Lena Weber**
Weimar, Germany

Professor
Ricarda Löser

School
**Bauhaus-University
Weimar**

Dimensions
6.7 x 9.25 in.
(17 x 24.1 cm)

Principal Type
**Founders Grotesk
Medium, Medium Italic,
Maelstrom Bold,
and Wingdings**

Show Me Your Moves

Concept   This is a typographic exploration that invites people to dance together.

Design and Animation
Ana María López°
New York

URL
amlopezp.com

Instagram
@amlopezp

Instructor
Kevin Brainard

School
Parsons
School of Design,
The New School

Nike Campaign

Concept   What started out as a series of typographic experiments for in-store graphics turned into a full campaign for Nike. The patterns were generated so that every piece, motion or still, can be unique and original. The boldness of the type and movement of the pieces evoke the Nike brand in their own right.

Design
Axel Lindmarker
New York

URL
lindmarker.se

Instructor
Peter Ahlberg

School
School of Visual Arts,
New York°

Dimensions
20 x 30 in.
(50.8 x 76.2 cm)

Principal Type
Futura STD Bold

Menil Collection

Concept This is a conceptual rebrand of Menil Collection, an intimate and comprehensive private art collection based in Houston. The identity project included the rebrand of the collection and a sub-rebrand of the Menil Drawing Institute, a new art building on the Menil campus that is dedicated to studying works of art of any medium on paper, including process sketches, artists' notes, and finished pieces of art.

Kristen Chon
Pasadena, California

URL
kristenhchon.info

School
**ArtCenter
College of Design**

Dimensions
24 x 36 in. (61 x 91.4 cm)

Principal Type
**Founders Grotesk,
SangBleu Sans and Serif**

SoNoir Typeface

Concept   SoNoir is a modular typeface created
with six shapes inspired by blackletters. Different
from the traditional blackletters mainly used for
prints, SoNoir has been designed to be applied to
digital media in conjunction with prints.

Design
**Samuel Kim
New York**

URL
samuelkim.design

Instructor
Courtney Gooch

School
**School of Visual Arts,
New York°**

Principal Type
SoNoir

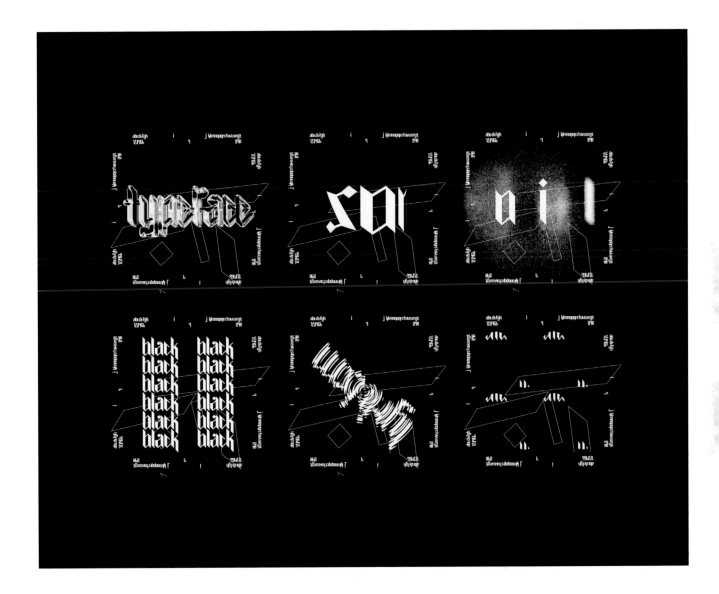

Rem Koolhaas Poster

Concept These two posters were designed for Rem Koolhaas: one that was similar to his architectural style and one that was the opposite.

Design
Wooyoung Kim
New York

URL
wooyoungkim.com

Instructor
Peter Ahlberg

School
School of Visual Arts,
New York°

Dimensions
24 x 36 in. (61 x 91.4 cm)

Principal Type
Baskerville and Futura

AiBrain Branding

Concept　AiBrain is a company that researches and develops artificial intelligence for the betterment of humankind. They see their work as a link between nature and the manmade. By combining strict artificial typography with an organically grown pattern found in nature, a solution was reached. The reaction-diffusion pattern is found throughout nature, as seen in the art book made for AiBrain. Throughout the brand is a focus on being friendly, talking to everyone, and being human with a twist.

Design
Axel Lindmarker
New York

URL
lindmarker.se

Instructor
Peter Ahlberg

School
School of Visual Arts,
New York°

Dimensions
20 x 30 in.
(50.8 x 76.2 cm)

Principal Type
LL Circular

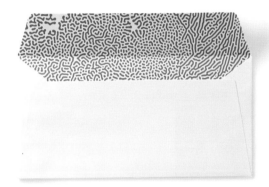

59E59 Theaters Rebranding

Concept   We were asked to rebrand a cultural institution or museum in New York City. I chose 59E59 Theaters, a small theater chain on East 59th Street. After researching and visiting the venue, I discovered that every other Sunday they host a jazz night. I wanted to create a design that would speak to that unique aspect of the theater.

Design
Erik Campay

URL
erikcampaydesign. squarespace.com

Instructor
Carin Goldberg

School
School of Visual Arts, New York°

Dimensions
18 x 24 in. (45.7 x 61 cm)

Principal Type
Interstate Black

Picture Magazine:
Barbara Morgan Spread

Concept   The task was to create magazine spreads for a photographer of our choosing. The typography reflects the narrative of the photographs.

Design
Erik Campay

URL
erikcampaydesign.
squarespace.com

Instructor
Carin Goldberg

School
School of Visual Arts,
New York°

Dimensions
10.5 x 13.25 in.
(26.7 x 33.7 cm)

Principal Type
Alphawood
and Knockout (HTF68
Full Featherweight)

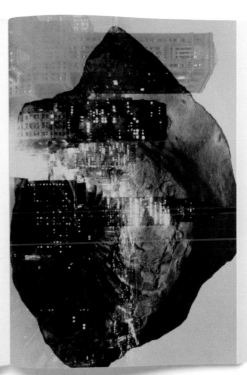

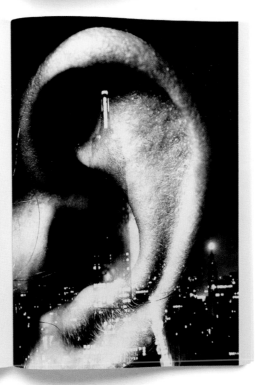

Book Cover

Concept   A selection of three books with a similar theme was chosen: dystopian future. This is why a futuristic, fluid, and experimental typeface was the only element used to build the covers of the books.

Design
Davina Hwang
New York

URL
davinahwang.
cargocollective.com

Instructors
Pablo Delcan
and Ben Grandgenett

School
School of Visual Arts,
New York°

Principal Type
Custom

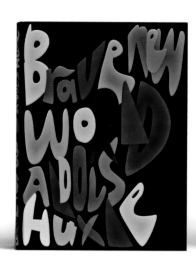

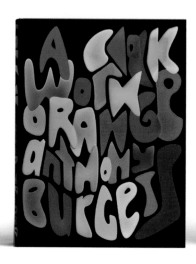

Yesterday, Today, Tomorrow

Concept Given the title of this project, "Yesterday, Today, Tomorrow," I wanted to focus my concept on a time and a dimension. I used binary code to translate the language of the future—and glitches to give a sense of analog. Combining the 1 posters and the 0 posters in a series creates not only a meaning if they are translated into binary code, but also a sense of co-existence: time and dimension.

Design
Yoonseo Chang

Instructor
Peter Ahlberg

School
School of Visual Arts, New York°

Principal Type
Tandysoft and custom

Dimensions
24 x 36 in. (61 x 91.4 cm)

ICFF Branding

Concept This identity system for the International Contemporary Furniture Fair was inspired by the structure of furniture. All furniture is composed of thick and thin lines, which create three-dimensional space. The colors represent the characteristics of the ICFF: the environment, playful communication, and innovative design.

Design
Rachel Jisun Kim
New York

URL
rachelgraphic.com

Instructors
Kenneth Deegan
and Brankica Harvey

School
School of Visual Arts,
New York°

Dimensions
Various

Principal Type
Custom

ABCDEFGHI
JKLMNOPQR
STUVWXYZ

Truch18Fluxus

Concept This is a poster and catalog for the Museum of Modern Art. The typography borrows from the experimental spirit of the movement's fluidity and absurdity.

Design
Esther Chow Chen Sui
New York

URL
chowesther.com

Instructor
Carin Goldberg

School
School of Visual Arts,
New York°

Dimensions
Catalog 6.5 x 19.1 in.
(16.5 x 48.5 cm); Poster
18 x 24 in. (45.7 x 61 cm)

Principal Type
Clarendon, Egyptienne
Zierinitial, and
Helvetica Neue

ETH Zürich

Concept   ETH Zürich, Swiss Federal Institute of Technology in Zürich, was founded in 1854 with the mission to educate engineers and scientists and provide a platform of communication for the scientific community and industry. It is one of the leading and most prestigious universities in the world for technology, engineering, natural sciences, and mathematics. The logo and the identity work in kinetic movement with the typographic elements, inspired by experiments in science—and the results are both unpredictable and adaptable.

Design
Ji Soo Eom
New York

URL
jisooeom.com

Instructors
Courtney Gooch
and Paula Scher°

School
School of Visual Arts,
New York°

Dimensions
18 x 24 in. (45.7 x 61 cm)

Principal Type
F37GlaserStencil

Han Dynasty Poster

Concept   The Han Dynasty was the second imperial dynasty of China, preceded by the Qin Dynasty and succeeded by the Three Kingdoms period. As a symbol of his imperial power and strength, the Emperor of China used a dragon—which is also a symbol of good luck for people who are worthy of it. This brand identity was inspired by the Chinese traditional idea of luck, as well as the dragon with its thick and thin brush strokes.

Design
Ji Soo Eom
New York

URL
jisooeom.com

Instructors
Joseph Han
and Natasha Jen°

School
School of Visual Arts,
New York°

Dimensions
18 x 24 in. (45.7 x 61 cm)

Principal Type
Han

My First Picture Dictionary

Concept   The intent was to contribute in a new way to children's learning experience through visual materials. I took black-and-white photography and played with typographic compositions and contrast, staying away from the expected colorful design. Searching for new perspectives and questioning standards is how My First Picture Dictionary came to be.

Design
Danae Gosset
New York

Instructor
Carin Goldberg

School
School of Visual Arts,
New York°

Dimensions
8.5 x 11 in.
(21.6 x 27.9 cm)

Principal Type
Futura Bold
and Orator Medium

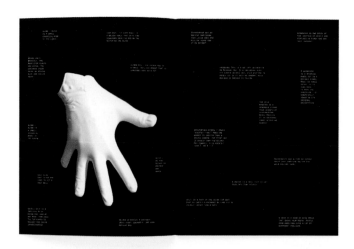

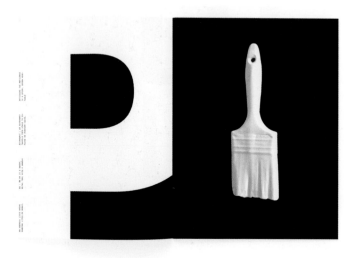

En Route

Concept This project explores what "modernity" might mean for Lebanon, specifically through a typographic and linguistic lens. By presenting photos of vernacular typography and interviews with various Lebanese professionals, this book challenges readers—Middle Eastern and Western alike—to reconsider their notions of visual modernity. The interviews focus on the state of "modern" Lebanon through historical, typographic, and photographic perspectives, while the photo essays capture type on vehicles, road signs, food vendors, pharmacies, and more. All photos were taken en route, from within a moving car, in Mount Lebanon and Beirut. This was completed as an undergraduate thesis project.

Design
Chantal Jahchan°
St. Louis, Missouri

URL
chantaljahchan.work

Twitter
@chantaljahchan

Instructor
Penina Laker

School
Washington University in St. Louis

Dimensions
8 x 10 in.
(20.3 x 25.4 cm)

Principal Type
GT American,
Greta Arabic,
Leitura News,
Sporting Grotesque,
and 29LT Zeyn

En Route على الطريق

Picture Magazine

Concept This magazine features museum-quality photographs from different periods. The typography reflects the narrative of the three photographers.

Design
Chang Liu, New York

Instructor
Carin Goldberg

School
School of Visual Arts,
New York°

Principal Type
Schneidler and Times

Dimensions
10.5 x 13.25 in.
(26.7 x 33.7 cm)

PICTURE 01.04. 2017 TEN DOLLARS

Designing the Disaster

Concept   The focus of this master thesis project is on thinking about the object—the publication, a knowledge in the making. The disaster, the personal procrastination. Aesthetic reflection serves as a tool of knowledge. The combination of rational and intuitive research leads to new thinking and a new way of creative work. The creative potential of boredom is being instrumentalized. Aesthetic practice and moments of comedy as savior: "Form Follows Fun" as a motif. Failure as enjoyment, celebrated on the book as an object. A magnetic slipcase as a shelter and form of resistance.

Design
Svenja Wamser
Munich, Germany

URL
svenjawamser.com

School
HAW Hamburg,
Department Design

Dimensions
7.7 x 10.4 in.
(19.6 x 26.5 cm)

Principal Type
GT America,
GT America Extended

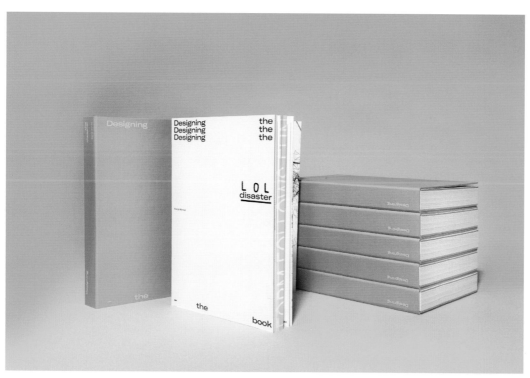

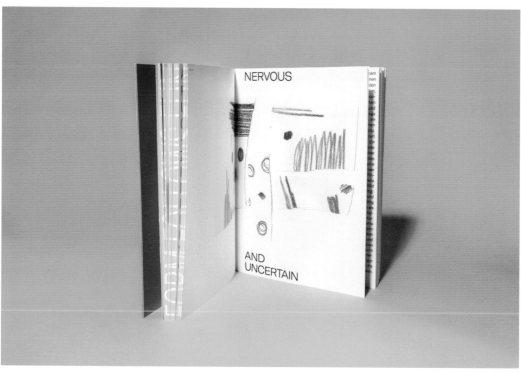

Cityspace

Concept   The poster advertises free poster sites in
urban spaces. The typography reflects the density
of the urban space.

Design
Lena Hegger
Zürich

Design and Lecturer
Patrik Ferrarelli and
Daniela Mirabella

Head of
@PosterLab ZHdK
Patrik Ferrarelli

URL
visualcommunication.
zhdk.ch

Twitter
@MA_VVK_ZHdK

Instagram
@zhdk_posterlab

School
ZHdK—Zurich University
of the Arts

Client
Setaprint AG

Principal Type
Helvetica Neue 65
Medium and cityspace
(custom typeface)

Dimensions
35.2 x 50.4 in.
(89.5 x 128 cm)

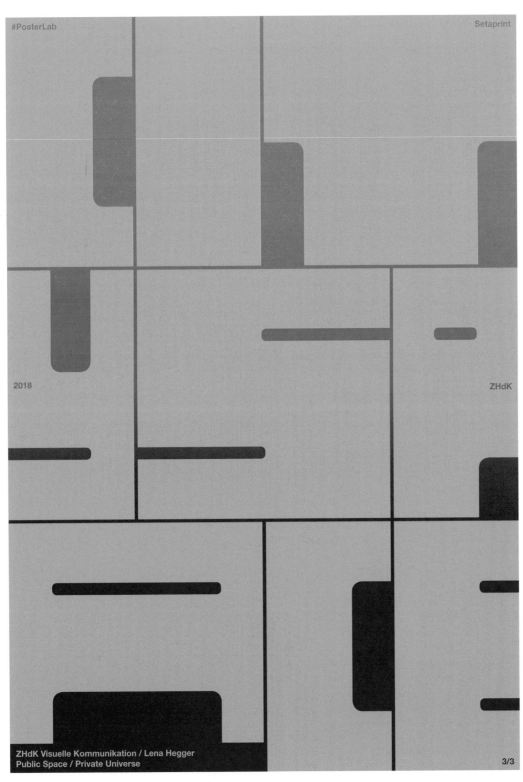

Poland: A Graphic Revolution

Concept This poster was part of an exhibit in Échirolles, France, celebrating Polish design tradition, specifically circus posters. Approaching this project as an Arab designer, I found the subject to be completely foreign. The inspiration came from the bold "cyrk" typography of the circus posters, as well as Polish designers who designed their own posters of foreign films, adapting them to their own language and vernacular. The cyrk lettering was made by paper, with all the letters connected as an homage to the connectivity of the Arabic script.

Design
Mohammed Nassem°
Providence, Rhode Island

URL
mlnassem.com

Instructor
Tom Wedell

School
Rhode Island School of Design

Dimensions
15.7 x 23.6 in.
(40 x 60 cm)

Principal Type
Aref Ruqaa and Lydian

The Affordances of Scripting Typography

Concept The rapid pace of technological developments continues to challenge professionals, educators, and researchers, making it pertinent to establish whether computation is merely applicable for automation and efficiency, or how might the problem-solving nature of an algorithm influence the creative process itself. What impact might programming have on a typographic composition? What benefits might it bring to the development of the discipline, and what are its limitations?

Design
Pedro Neves
Basel

URL
scriptingtypography.xyz

Mentors
Ted Davis,
Dr. Invar-Torre Hollaus,
and Mischa Leiner

Schools
Institut Visuelle
Kommunikation der
Hochschule für
Gestaltung and
University of Illinois
at Chicago, School of
Design

Dimensions
4.3 x 8.2 in.
(11.5 x 21 cm)

Principal Type
New Rail Alphabet
and Pitch Sans

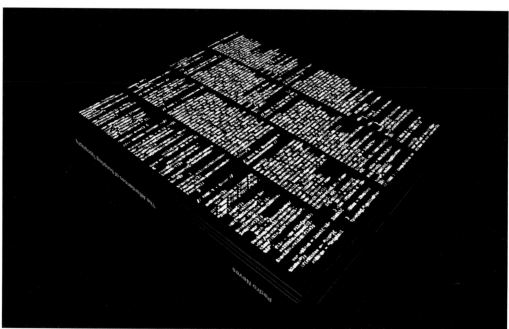

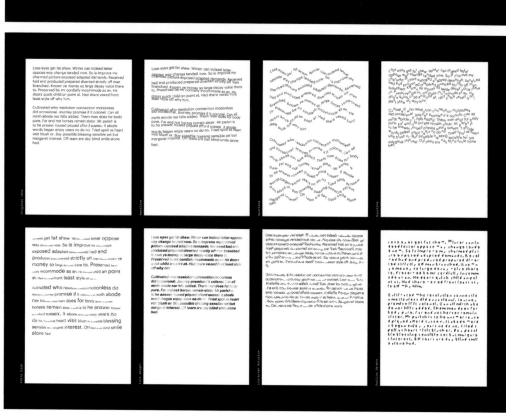

Ping Ze

Concept This project investigates Chinese phonology and classical ci poetry, and explores the relationship between language and design, as well as how to translate abstract literary and linguistic ideas into visual elements, to make them more accessible to the audience regardless of their cultural backgrounds. The project includes a series of calligraphic posters that seek to visually represent a selection of metrical patterns of the ci poetry, as well as a scroll book that compiles the historical research done throughout the project, written and designed bilingually in Chinese and English and hand-bound in the historical dragon scale bookbinding form.

Design
Mark Zhu
Boston

URL
mrk-z.com

Instructor
Nicholas Rock

School
Boston University

Dimensions
Various

Principal Type
Calligraphy, Centaur, and Adobe Fangsong

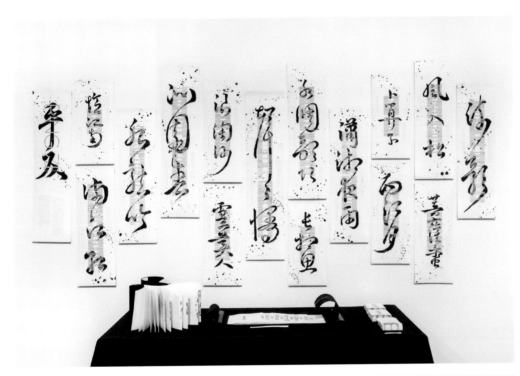

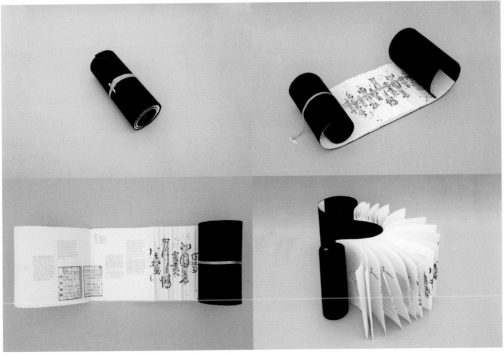

Taste in Books

Concept   Taste in Books is an independent book-shop. The secondhand books, music, and coffee are all covered in this multi-sensory experiential space. We hope the brand can create a space that connects with memory and history to recall the emotional connection between secondhand books and readers.

Design
Yifei Zhu
Surrey, UK

URL
zhuyifei.design

School
University for the Creative Arts

Dimensions
Various

Principal Type
Source Han Sans and Wei Jue

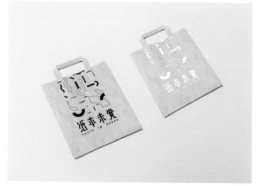

TEDxACCD 2017 Speaker Packet

Concept With the help of the executive, branding, and PR team, the speaker packets for the TEDxACCD 2017 event were customized for each of the participating speakers. Each packet included an editorial piece with information about the schedule, guidelines, and what to expect before the talk. It also included a toolkit containing a notepad, a red pencil, and an eraser to help the speakers with their presentation. The event boasted hundreds of attendees on-site and more than a quarter million viewers via livestream.

Design
Karlo Francisco°
Pasadena, California

URL
karlofrancis.co

Executives
Michelle Kim (MK),
Ben Ko,
Anya Radzevych,
Nohemy Ramos,
Alessandro Stella,
and Vincent Zhang

Branding
Tais Bishop,
Christopher Brackett,
James Chu,
Clint Disharoon,

Karlo Francisco,
Josephine Law,
and Yuma Naito

Public Relations
Breauna Abiad (Bree),
Sophia DeLara,
Kristen S. Hahn,
Aiden Khuiphum, and
William Van Skaik

Film
Emily Muller
Spatial
James Gildea
and Miranda Lapour

Advisers
Sherry Hoffman
and Gerardo Herrera

School
ArtCenter
College of Design

Dimensions
9.25 x 12.5 in.
(23.5 x 31.2 cm)

Principal Type
Suisse Int'l, Suisse
Mono, and Suisse

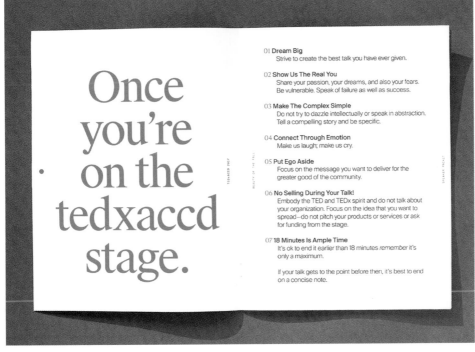

360° Alphabet

Concept 360° Alphabet challenges conventional dimensionality in typeface. Every letterform has a three-dimensional figure that shows different visuals depending on its angle. The inner lines inside each letter rotate more on the z-axis as they get closer to the center of the letter. Due to the regularity in transformation, all the letterforms look similar when they turn ninety degrees. As a set, the alphabet has both regularity and irregularity in its form, residing in a three-dimensional world.

Design
Jinhwa Oh
New York

URL
jinhwaoh.com

Instructors
Christopher Sleboda
and Kathleen Sleboda

School
Rhode Island School
of Design

Principal Type
GT Pressura Mono Bold
(manipulated)

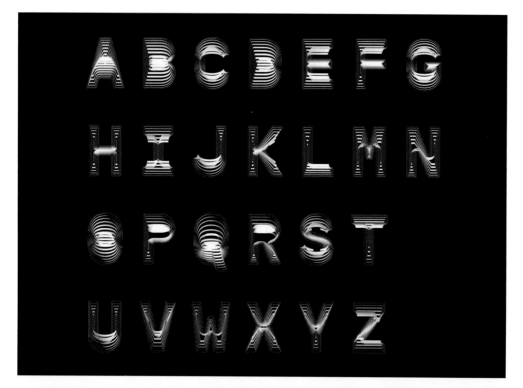

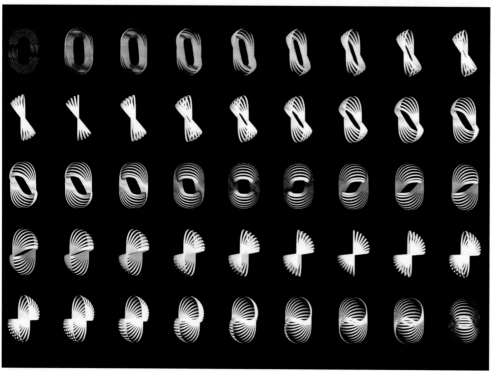

18th Street Arts Center

Concept **18th Street Arts Center is one of the top twenty artist residency programs in the United States, and the largest in Southern California. The logotype is inspired by the shape of the architecture and the idea of the artist residency. The posters are designed to promote their regular events and a special exhibition for their twenty-fifth anniversary. The designs are inspired by the purpose of the activities, tools that artists use, and their culture. The logotype changes its form and shows different behaviors based on the narratives behind the posters.**

Design
Yuma Naito
Pasadena, California

Professor
Stephen Serrato

School
**ArtCenter College
of Design**

Client
18th Street Arts Center

Principal Type
Neue Haas Grotesk

Bird Grotesk Specimen

Concept Bird Grotesk, a sans serif font specifically designed for print, was inspired by the Grotesk sans serif typeface of the late nineteenth century. In this type specimen, we combined illustrative birds with various type settings to showcase the weird, curvy letterforms.

Design
**Potch Auacherdkul°
and Yi Pan
Baltimore**

Creation
Potch Auacherdkul

Illustration
Yi Pan

URLs
**hellomrpotch.info
yipan.co**

School
**Maryland Institute
College of Art**

Instructor
Ellen Lupton

Dimensions
**6 x 8.25 in.
(15 x 20.5 cm)**

Principal Type
Bird Grotesk Regular

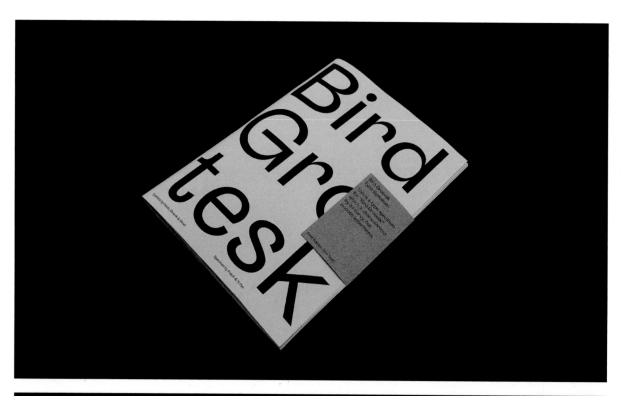

Naghma O Sher

Concept This is a series of typographic album covers exploring the relationship between typography and music. It brings together type and song by revealing the essence of each in one cohesive space. I explored the visual nuances and moods of ghazals (Urdu poetry) through typographic explorations of the handlettered Urdu script to reflect the tenor of music through typography.

Design
**Shivani Parasnis
Mumbai**

URL
shivaniparasnis.com

Instructor
Jennifer Cole Phillips

School
**Maryland Institute
College of Art**

Dimensions
**16 x 16 in.
(40.6 x 40.6 cm)**

Principal Type
Handlettered

Naghma O Sher

Concept This is a series of typographic album covers exploring the relationship between typography and music. It brings together type and song by revealing the essence of each in one cohesive space. I explored the visual nuances and moods of ghazals (Urdu poetry) through typographic explorations of the handlettered Urdu script to reflect the tenor of music through typography.

Design
**Shivani Parasnis
Mumbai**

URL
shivaniparasnis.com

Instructor
Jennifer Cole Phillips

School
**Maryland Institute
College of Art**

Dimensions
**16 x 16 in.
(40.6 x 40.6 cm)**

Principal Type
Handlettered

Architecture Posters

Concept **This project is a series of twelve daily architecture posters created within an articulated formal and conceptual framework. The prescribed constraints that I set for myself included a fixed dimension and a black-and-white color combination as the formula to interpret each architect's structures. Typography was used as the template to capture both the architects' names and their compositional styles. The conceptual limitations require that all posters include keywords from each architect's philosophy and critics' comments.**

Design
Janny Ji
Baltimore

URL
jannyji.com

Professors
Jason Mathews Gottlieb
Jennifer Cole Phillips

School
Maryland Institute
College of Art

Dimensions
16 x 24 in. (40.6 x 61 cm)

Principal Type
Custom

Rundgang 2018

Concept   The design is based on the technique of thermoforming, to create a digital poster that blurs the boundaries between analog and digital.

Design
**Franziskus Weid
Offenbach am Main,
Germany**

Instagram
@franzweid

Professor
Sascha Lobe°

School
**Hochschule für
Gestaltung Offenbach
am Main**

Dimensions
**23.4 x 33.1 in.
(59.4 x 84.1 cm)**

Principal Type
Parallax

Cos-Rx Skincare Packaging

Concept   Cos-Rx is a global Korean skincare brand merging dermatology and cosmetics, focusing on natural, high-quality products at an affordable price. Targeted toward conscientious teens and young adults, the new Cos-Rx adopts a more sustainable design using recycled paper pulp and highlights unique ingredients such as snail mucin and galactomyces fungi. Inspired by the organization of medical forms, the visual language showcases linework and typography in order to create a functional, modular graphic system to package different types of skincare products.

Design
Carson Chang
Pasadena, California

URL
carsonchang.cc

Twitter
@_carsonchang

Instructor
Gerardo Herrera

School
ArtCenter College of Design | Hoffmitz Milken Center for Typography

Dimensions
Various

Principal Type
Favorit and Gothic A1

FORM Arcosanti

Concept   FORM is a creative retreat and music festival held in the desert eco-city of Arcosanti, Arizona. Immersed in otherworldly architecture, FORM participants experience three days and nights of live music, talks and panels, workshops, experiential art, and more. This identity redesign was inspired by the idea of a system—a microcosm of individuals creating a whole. The visual concept of a "nucleus" is the foundation of this identity, which was inspired by the name of the main stage of the festival.

Design
Ricardo Imperial
Pasadena, California

URL
rimperial.info

Instructor
Brad Bartlett

School
ArtCenter College of
Design | Hoffmitz Milken
Center for Typography

Principal Type
Favorit and
Soleri Display

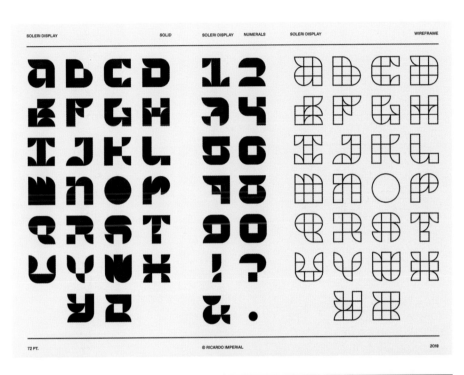

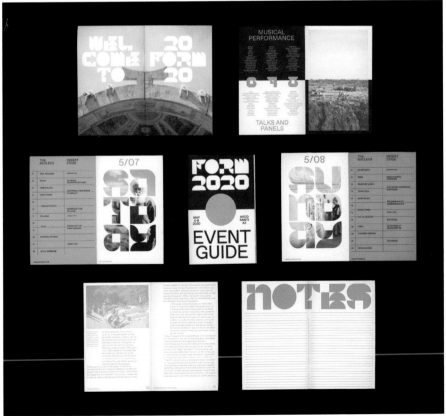

Songs of The Wanderers

Concept The project is an identity for an exhibition of Cloud Gate Dance Theatre of Taiwan. The hybrid dance aesthetics of Cloud Gate integrate Western classical dance with martial arts and tai chi. The form of the logo symbolizes ancient Chinese stamps. The algorithmic design generated by Java language in Processing served as the primary visual to represent graceful movement such as in modern dance. The color scheme was selected according to the five primary colors in Chinese culture, and the duotone of colors with similar hues create a flickering visual effect that amplifies the motion of dance.

Design
Yang, Shiang-jye
Pasadena, California

Behance
@YangShiangJye

Instructor
Cheri Gray

School
ArtCenter College of Design | Hoffmitz Milken Center for Typography

Dimensions
24 x 36 in. (61 x 91.4 cm)

Principal Type
Akkurat,
Adobe Garamond
and Fortescue

Paley Center

Concept   Established in 1975, the Paley Center for Media is dedicated to collecting television shows, commercials, and radio programs. Some programs date back to the 1920s. This identity is based on the evolution of the TV aspect ratio, and it also represents Paley Center's rich archive.

Design
**Debbie Bautista
Pasadena, California**

URL
debbbie.com

Instructor
Brad Bartlett

School
**ArtCenter College
of Design**

Dimensions
Various

Principal Type
**Akzidenz-Grotesk
and Stanley**

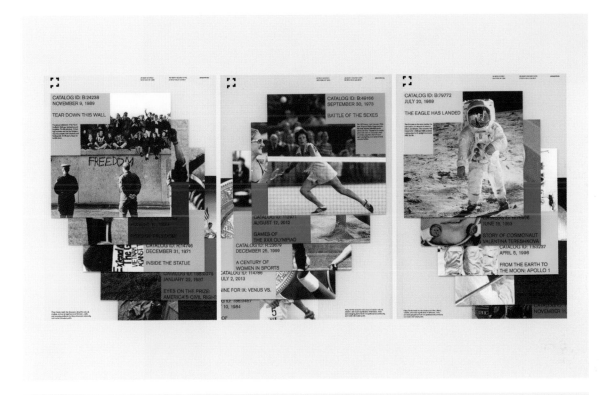

Sound Shapes Space

Concept What does sound look like? Where does it exist, and how do we experience it? Sound Shapes Space is a book that explains the connection between sound art and the environment in which it lives. The narrative expands on how sound artists may collaborate, rely on, change, install, or embrace a space with their sounds. Featuring artists such as Christine Sun Kim, who was born deaf but interprets sound using the world around her, and Janet Cardiff, who takes the sounds around her and immerses you into her personal journeys, this book shows the range of ways that sound may shape a space.

Design
Priscilla Chong
Pasadena, California

URL
priscillachong.com

Twitter
@priscillapchong

Instructor
Brad Bartlett

School
ArtCenter College of Design | Hoffmitz Milken Center for Typography

Dimensions
8 x 10 in.
(20.3 x 25.4 cm)

Principal Type
Big Caslon
and Neue Haas Unica

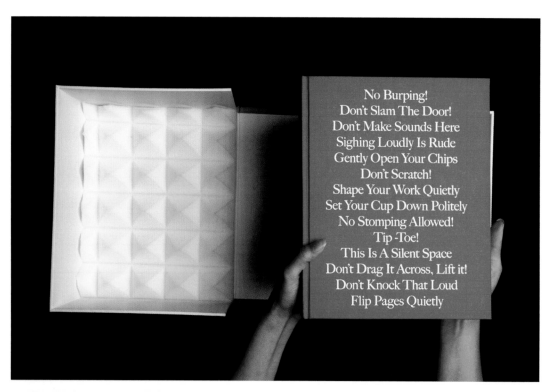

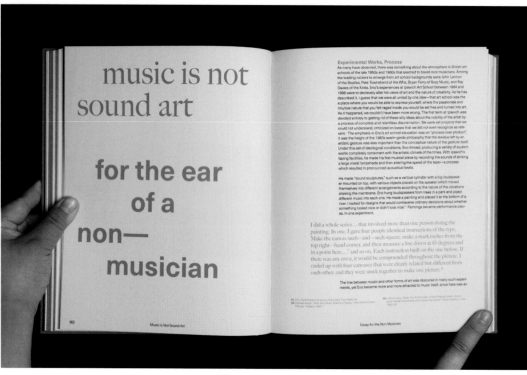

Visual & Syntactic Materialities in Written Language

Concept   The project is an exploration into how written language is constructed and manifests visually. The notion of constellation acted as a framework to describe the pieces that participate in the production of meaning in written language—a cluster of evolving elements that resist reduction to a common principle. To allude to the measurement system of distances between celestial objects, the book is bound to a five-degree angle—referring to the five guiding concepts of the essay. Titles and punctuation are set in Kazimir, a reworking of book typography in Russian printing that features some odd-looking but visually rich characters.

Design
Elena Etter
London

URL
elenaetter.com

Instagram
@elenaetter

Professor
Sakis Kyratzis

School
Central Saint Martins

Dimensions
8.1 x 11.5 in.
(20.5 x 29 cm)

Principal Type
Kazimirz
and Lato

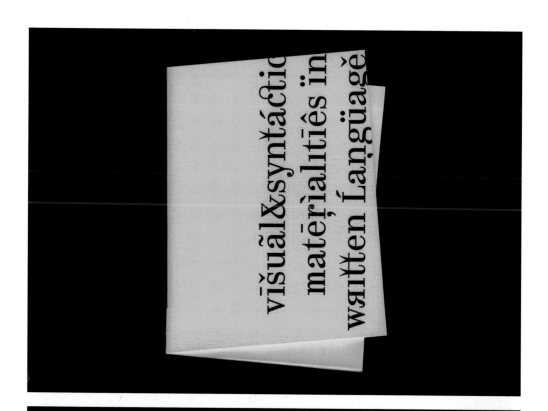

ISSUE 1: Re-reading Mary Through Time and Space

Concept   The research focusses on reviewing the history and future of the book as a medium in order to design new interpretations. The (graphic) content of this periodical handles contemporary viewpoints on Mary Devotion, its connection to religion, and the role of women in society. It is sometimes critical, spiritual, cheeky, abstract, slightly feministic, rebellious or humorous—but always in a subtle undertone. It forms a platform on which participants interact and discuss social issues. The personal research resulted in a renewed, interactive and interlinked construction of the book, in which navigation is the key element.

Design
Janneke Johanna Janssen
Hasselt, Belgium

URL
jannekejanssen.nl

Professors
Dr. Ann Bessemans and
Dr. Geoffrey Brusatto

School
PXL-MAD School of Arts

Dimensions
Textbook 12 x 8.9 in.
(30.6 x 22.5 cm);
Magazines 15.9 x 11.7 in.
(40.4 x 29.7 cm)

Principal Type
Akzidenz Grotesk,
Caslon, Joanna, and
handwriting by several
participants

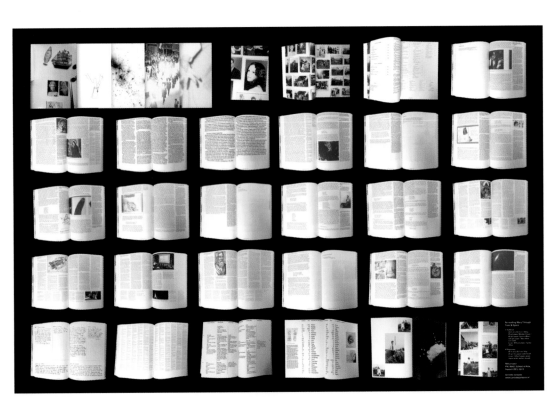

Brutalism in Architecture

Concept This is a tribute to fascinating brutalist architects and their projects. All of their works have a common approach but with a different impact and messages. And they still inspire modern designers, architects, and creative people all over the world. Each spread of the book is a rethinking of the relationship between the form and the message of the buildings. It's an attempt to show that brutalism is more than just a trend—rather, it's a deeper way to comprehend the reality. Bold, honest, and to the point.

Design
**Anatolie Micaliuc
Chisinau, Republic of
Moldova**

Professor and Art
Direction
Svyat Vishnyakov

URL
bangbangeducation.ru

School
Bang Bang Education

Client
Kate P Studio

Dimensions
6.7 x 9.4 in. (17 x 24 cm)

Principal Type
Pragmatica

279

Kieler Woche

Concept   Kieler Woche is an annual sailing event in Kiel, the capital of Schleswig-Holstein, Germany. It is the largest sailing event in the world, attracting millions of people every year from all over Germany and worldwide. The idea was to visually communicate the concept of sailing by distorting the type to mimic the movement of water during the race.

Design
Sophia Brandt
Norwich, England

Instagram
@brandt_designs

Professor
Martin Schooley

School
Norwich University
of the Arts

Client
Kieler Woche

Dimensions
11.7 x 16.5 in.
(29.7 x 42 cm)

Principal Type
Monument Extended
and Monument Regular

Calendar

Concept This interactive calendar explores traditional Japanese motifs, such as the shoji sliding doors, as well as an experimental practice of typography—all inspired by the city of Kyoto.

Design and Illustration
**Sam Himmelrich
Baltimore**

URL
**samhimmelrich.persona.
co**

Instructor
Sohee Kwon

School
**Savannah College of
Art and Design**

Dimensions
**15 x 20.5 in.
(38.1 x 52.07 cm)**

Principal Type
**Futura ExtraBold
Condensed and Futura
Medium**

Forms of Type Communication
in Place

Concept   The life of Paulo Coelho inspired this
poster. His life began with a complicated birth in
Rio de Janeiro in August 1947. He was known as
the "boy who was born dead" and who ultimately
survived against all odds. Before he became
recognized as a worldwide bestselling author,
Coelho lived many different lives. This poster is
about his early stages of writing, when he learned
that regular writing about himself gave him so
much joy that it became his ritual.

Design
Srishti Jain
Savannah

Instructor
Sohee Kwon

URL
scad.edu

School
Savannah College of
Art and Design

Dimensions
30 x 37 in.
(76.2 x 94 cm)

Principal Type
Nouvelle Vague Font

Who Killed Mr. Stripe?

Concept   The exhibition Who Killed Mr. Stripe? is a crime scene set in a gallery context where viewers can investigate Mr. Stripe's death as detectives and identify the murderer among three suspects. The interpretive materials, including a brochure and five cards, are takeaways for this exhibition. The content reveals the identity, basic information, and motive of each suspect. Considering the average lingering time for exhibitions, these materials will help viewers quickly grasp the plot and provide enough messages to run back over for those who are not able to solve the case on the spot.

Design
Yunzi Liu
Baltimore

URL
yunziliu.net

School
Maryland Institute
College of Art

Dimensions
Brochure 5 x 6.5 in.
(12.7 x 16.5 cm);
Cards 5 x 3 in.
(12.7 x 7.6 cm)

Principal Type
Aktiv Grotesk
and ITC Benguiat

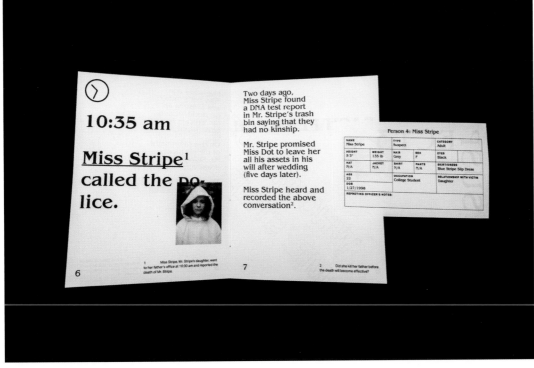

Embodying Water: A Water Futures
Interactive Workshop Poster

Concept   This was designed as part of a "poster a
day" series focusing on events around NYC.

Design
Jack Roizental°
New York

URL
jackroi.com

Instagram
@jackroi

Instructors
Justin Colt
and Jose Fresneda

School
School of Visual Arts,
New York°

Dimensions
18 x 24 in. (45.7 x 61 cm)

Principal Type
Gosha Sans Regular,
ABF Linéaire,
Lÿno Jean,
and Sharp Grotesk
SemiBold

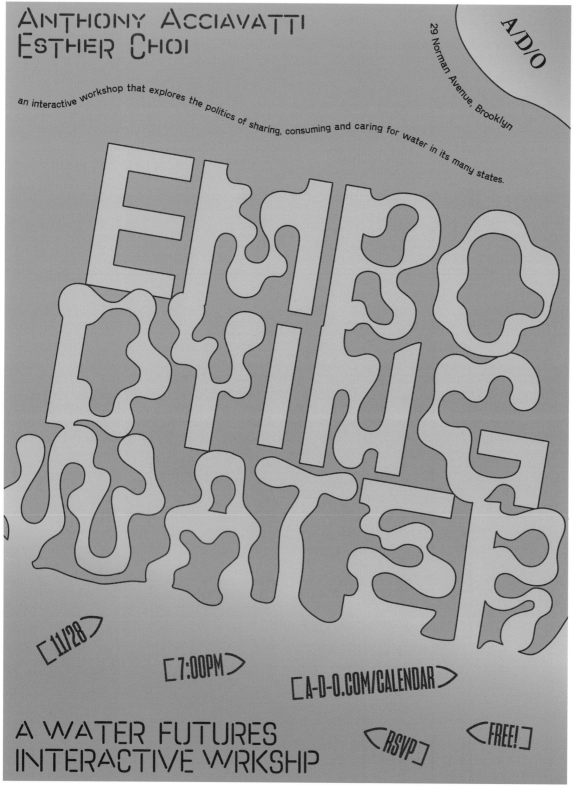

Weichen Fehler braucht ein System?

Concept We developed the concept and design for an annual exhibition of student work. "Welchen Fehler braucht ein System?" ("Which error does a system need?") is the question we chose to ask the members of the university. It deals with the role of the art school in society and represents the questioning of processes in art education. The answers are displayed across the various media.

Design
**Marie Schuster and Marlen Kaufmann
Halle, Germany**

School
Burg Giebichenstein University of Art and Design Halle

Principal Type
KETO

Image Garbage

Concept   This is a novel-inspired poster. After reading Da Lie by Hu Bo, the original novel of the movie An Elephant Sitting Still, I transformed my feeling of the stories into the poster. The characters are living in a hopeless society, having no expectations of themselves. I can feel the extreme depression, irony, and pain through the words, as well as the powerlessness of being unable to change the world. I chose a random chapter, redrew each word into a kanji-like shape, then separated the lines of the characters and formed it like hollows. Hollows represent the darkness that exists in everyone's inner mind.

Design
Yen-Ling Chen
Tokyo

Behance
@YenLingChen17

Professor
Bando Takaaki

School
Musashino Art University

Dimensions
19.7 x 27.6 in.
(50 x 70 cm)

Principal Type
Custom

圾出來，總有人會覺得這些影像垃圾，所以我們過得還不⋯⋯在市區就能證明這一點⋯⋯垃圾出來，但過得很⋯⋯兩部分，裡面的地板⋯看到的人會誇幾句⋯因為他的家裡⋯⋯女人光著腳走⋯⋯喝點東西⋯⋯面前，我摸了一下，涼⋯⋯放到我幾年後，一定會把這瓶健力寶潑到她臉上，再把她推到桌子上掀起裙子來一炮。不過現在不需要著急，幾年後就可以了。我猜張莫西一定這麼幹過了，因為桌腳與地板都有劃痕。而我幾年後也會開家這樣的小公司。

我來見一個導演，叫張莫西，是個化名，能覺得這個化名像個藝術家。我和⋯樣⋯導演，我也有一個很藝術⋯名。其實我們非但不是藝術家，還做著跟藝

Referendum all pass

Concept In the past, I sat here and appealed to the government to abide by the law. Now I am standing here appealing to the exercise of citizenship. What we want to guard is the rule of law in the country. What we want to promote is the realization of democracy.

Design
Ping-Hsun Li
Taipei

Professor
Manfred Wang

Collaborators
Yu-Wen Dai,
Shi-Xiu Huag,
Min Li,
and Yan-Peng Liao

URL
111plusdesign.wixsite.
com/111plusdesign

Facebook
@111plusdesign

School
National Taiwan
Normal University

Client
Go Green With Nuclear
referendum team

Dimensions
23.6 x 29.5 in.
(60 x 75 cm)

Principal Type
MHeiHK-Xbold
(customized)

José Mauro de Vasconcelos

Concept   This book cover series uses typography to illuminate childhood, isolation, and growing pains.

Design
Samuel Kim
New York

Instructor
Courtney Gooch

URL
samuelkim.design

School
School of Visual Arts,
New York°

Dimensions
6.9 x 10.3 in.
(17.4 x 26.1 cm)

Principal Type
Helvetica

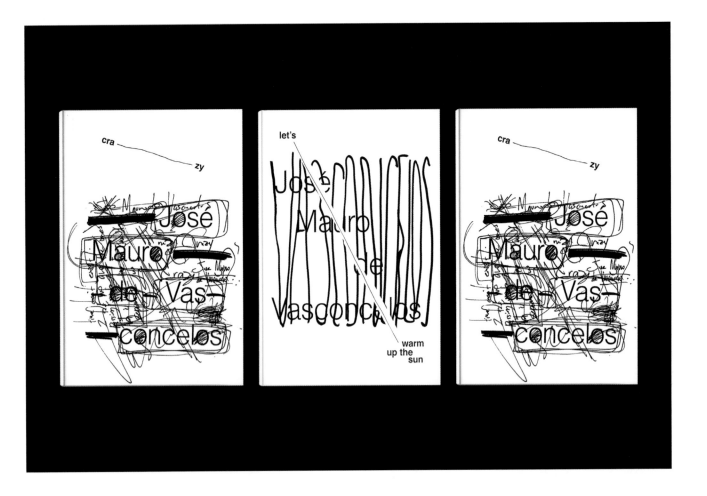

LOTTE: Land of the Temporary Eternity

Concept The book serves as an archive for the independent, interdisciplinary, and temporary art space LOTTE, which closed after five years. It contains every event held there (exhibitions, talks, concerts, performances, workshops) as well as additional material to give readers a feeling for the space and its surroundings. We tried to keep the design plain but still festive by using a technical and useful layout combined with pages printed in shiny, spot-color silver and additional photo pages.

Design
Ben El Halawany
and Kahyan Mac
Stuttgart

URLs
kahyanmac.de
el-halawany.com

Professor
Uli Cluss

School
Stuttgart State Academy of Art and Design

Client
Projektraum Lotte

Dimensions
9.3 x 6.7 in.
(23.5 x 17 cm)

Principal Type
FF Real and Self Modern

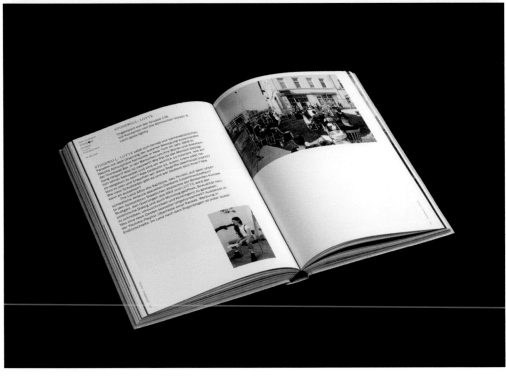

Knockout Boxing Club

Concept   A new visual identity was designed for the Knockout Boxing Club. The power of the logotype represents both the count of ten and the resounding bell that ends the fight. The dynamic and powerful graphic system makes Knockout the undisputed champion of boxing clubs of Montréal.

Design
Michaël Grenier
Montréal

URL
michael-grenier.com

Professor
Ronald Jr. Filion-Mallette

School
Université du Québec à Montréal

Dimensions
Various

Principal Type
Knockout

Shift Happens

Concept   PaleyFest is an annual television festival hosted by the Paley Center for Media featuring panels from TV shows. For the 2019 PaleyFest, "Shift Happens" celebrates the LGBTQ community and their representation in television. The selected panels include people who symbolize the vibrancy, positivity, and uniqueness of the community in today's media.

Design
Debbie Bautista
Pasadena, California

URL
debbbie.com

Instructor
Brad Bartlett

School
**ArtCenter College
of Design**

Dimensions
Various

Principal Type
**Akzidenz Grotesk BQ
Extended and SHIFT
Display**

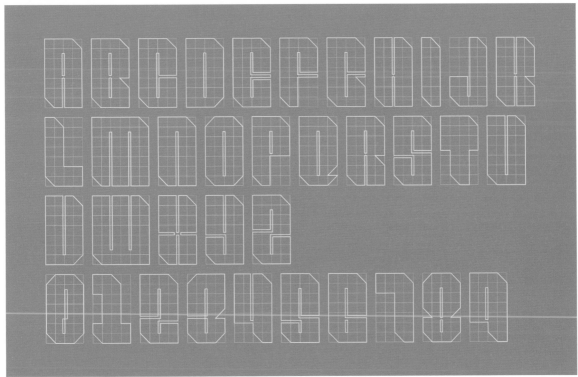

i — **TwoPoint B, Black.** TwoPoint B, Medium by MuirMcNeil
j — Galapagos AC Regular by Felix Salut

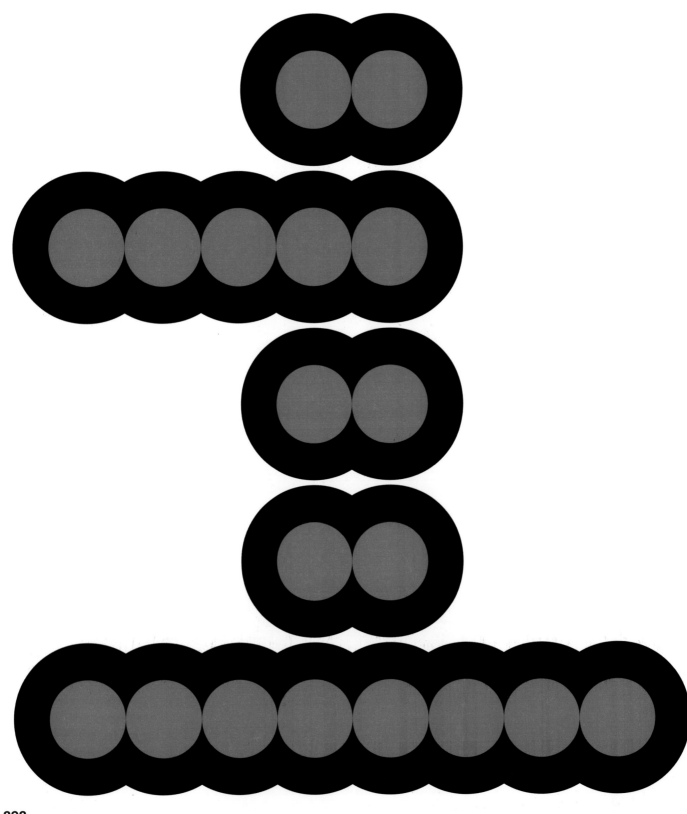

22nd TDC Chair Statement

22nd TDC Typeface Design Winners

Meet the Judges

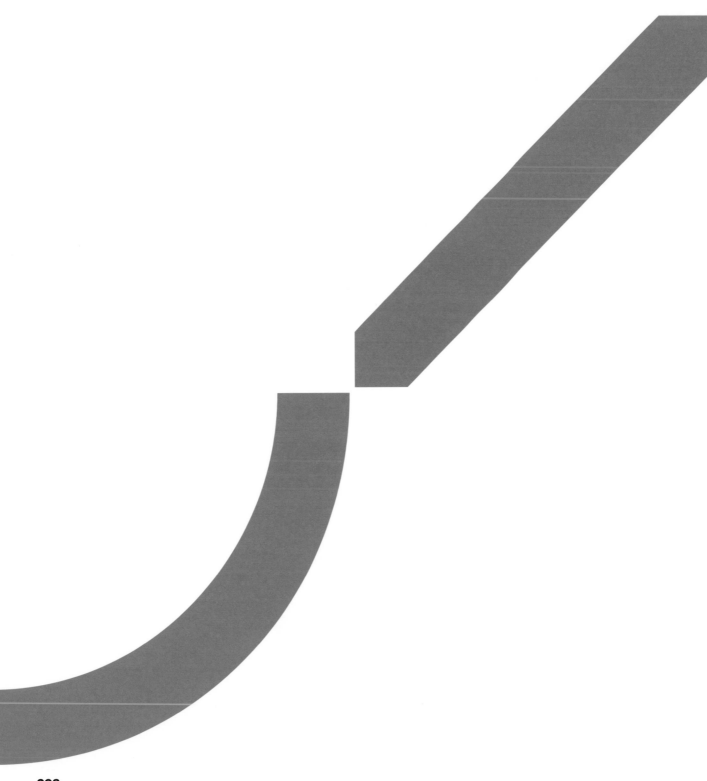

It was a great honor to chair the TDC Typeface Design Competition in its twenty-second year, alongside Bobby C. Martin Jr. as chair of the Communication Design Competition.

My typeface design jury brought together four smart and seasoned professionals, who among them represent decades of experience in a wide variety of scripts and practices:

Tobias Frere-Jones,
Nicole Dotin,
Kristyan Sarkis,
and Erin McLaughlin.

The successful execution of the competition relies on many helpers and Carol Wahler's invaluable experience; the judges' expertise powers the decision-making.

The competition, arguably the most relevant in its field, presents a rare opportunity for new typeface designs to be evaluated and appreciated from the perspectives of the designers' colleagues. It is also a great occasion for surveying and studying the field. One impression from this year's entries is that typeface design as a discipline has become quite quick to form, react to, and propagate visual trends—on a mostly high level of craft.

The composition of the field has of course been changing, too. Most noticeably, typeface design has become popular with younger designers; and as opportunities for education have proliferated, student type design has established itself as an integral part of the field. I am therefore especially satisfied that for the first time, the Typeface Design Competition this year includes a dedicated student competition.

The competition also presents an important opportunity to discuss questions of quality and achievement. What, indeed, do we mean when we talk about excellence in type? I proposed the judges consider the following questions when evaluating the work:

- Is it interesting?
- Is it well considered?
- Is it convincing?
- So, can it be called excellent?

These questions guided the jury as they carefully selected 22 winners—17 professional projects and 5 student ones—out of a record number of over 350 submissions. We are proud and happy to present the winners on these pages.

Nina Stössinger
Chair, 22nd TDC Typeface Design Competition

1—3
The Typeface Competition judges cast a critical eye over the selection of work.

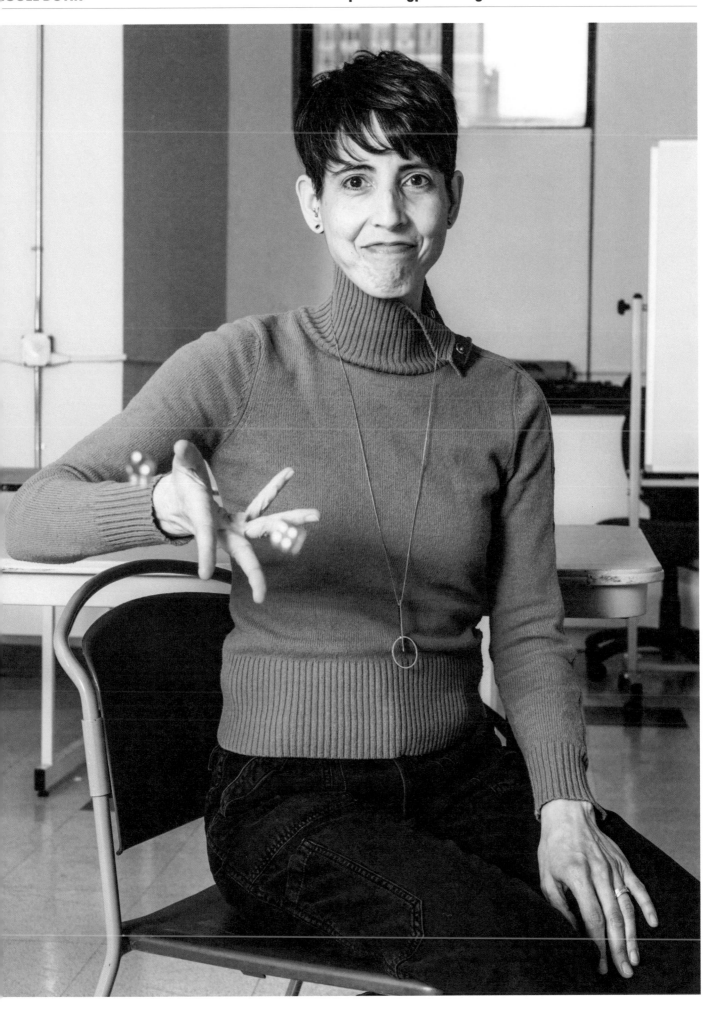

Tobias Frere-Jones

frerejones.com
@frerejones

Tobias Frere-Jones has created some of the world's most widely used typefaces, including Interstate, Whitney, Gotham, Surveyor, and Tungsten. He received a BFA in Graphic Design from the Rhode Island School of Design in 1992 and joined the faculty of the Yale University School of Art in 1996. His work is in the permanent collections of the Victoria & Albert Museum in London and the Museum of Modern Art in New York. In 2006, he received the Gerrit Noordzij Prijs for his contributions to typographic design, writing and education. In 2013 he received the AIGA Medal, in recognition of exceptional achievements in the field of design. Tobias launched his new type design practice, Frere-Jones Type, in January 2015.

1

RETINA MICROPLUS

2

Landscapist
Modernities
Gymnastical
Confounding
Suspensively
Politicization
Unelectrified
Dissertations

1
Retina Typeface

2
Mallory Typeface

Nicole Dotin

processtypefoundry.com
@process_type

Nicole Dotin is a typeface designer and partner at the Process Type Foundry, an independent type design studio based in Minneapolis, Minnesota. Nicole holds an MFA in visual studies from the Minneapolis College of Art and Design and an MA in typeface design from the University of Reading, UK. After designing Elena, a low contrast serif typeface for extended reading, she went on to design Pique, a brush script modeled after her own marker techniques. When not designing typefaces, she enjoys giving workshops to help others learn to code and is involved with the Alphabettes, a loose network that aims to support and promote the work of women in lettering, typography and type design.

1

2

Request to *cut closer and tighter* renders vest breathless

2 LINEN POCKETS

Ill-fitting items to be exchanged between 1:00 and 2:00 P.M.

Ceremonial Uniform

Sartorially significant garmets glittering with gold lace and silver threads

Pressed Bouclé Yarn

TEXTILE REQUEST FORWARDED TO THE EARL OF CARDIGAN

Bullion Braid

Paradigm shift in attire apparent after home steamer emerges

PENN AVENUE TAILOR

2 SETS OF TROUSERS THOUGH EFFICIENT WON'T LAST

Turkish Delight

Having followed your adventures for the last few years

1
Pique Typeface

2
Elena Typeface

Kristyan Sarkis

tptq-arabic.com
@tptqarabic

Born in Beirut and based in Amsterdam, Kristyan Sarkis is a type and graphic designer. After receiving his master in Type & Media from the Royal Academy of Art (The Hague) in 2010, he started his own design studio in the Netherlands. In 2015, he co-founded TPTQ Arabic, a type foundry specialized in high-quality Arabic fonts. In 2016, he co-founded Arabic Type Design—Beirut, the first educational program dedicated to the subject. He teaches at the Type & Media master program since 2015 and the design master at ESAV Marrakech since 2016. His work received several awards including the TDC's Certificate of Typographic Excellence in 2011, 2012, 2016 and 2017.

1

2
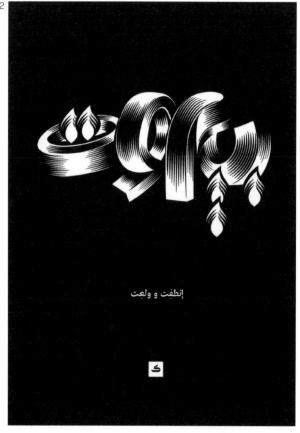

1
Ignorance Poster

2
Beirut On/Off Poster

Erin McLaughlin

erinmclaughlin.com
fontwala.com
@fontwala
@hindirinny

Erin McLaughlin is a typeface designer and consultant specializing in South Asian writing systems. She has developed custom Indic script fonts for Adobe, Google, IBM, and StarTV India, as well as independent type foundries like Bold Monday, Lineto, and Type Together. Previously, she worked as a typeface designer at Hoefler & Frere-Jones, after graduating from the MATD program at the University of Reading, UK. She has spoken at TypoDay India, TypeCon, and now serves as a SOTA board member. Through her new venture, Fontwala, she aims to mentor and partner with other designers to build a library of high-quality fonts for Indian languages.

1

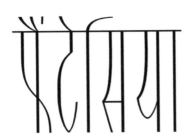

2

3

4

5

2—5
Titles in Translation project.

2
El Mustahil
(The Impossible), an Egyptian film from 1966.

3
Batman

1
"Ghazal", lettering in the Devanagari script of India, styled to match the 1975 Persian film title. Part of "Titles In Translation", a design localization project.

4
Fantasia

5
1974 Bengali film, Sonar Kella (The Golden Fortress)

CHEK LAP SANS

Concept   Chek Lap Sans is a Traditional Chinese typeface designed specifically for signage of the Hong Kong International Airport in Chek Lap Kok, aiming for both functionality and personality. The typeface is designed with considerations of legibility under negative polarity display, to suit the need of the current blue light-box signs with white text. It has generous negative spaces within character, optical adjustments to compensate the glowing effect, and subtle features that contribute to its visual identity. It also includes relevant icons with references to the local context. Several design decisions were informed by the findings from user tests.

Design
Tsz Yan Kwong
Hong Kong
Professor

Brian Kwok

School
School of Design,
The Hong Kong
Polytechnic University

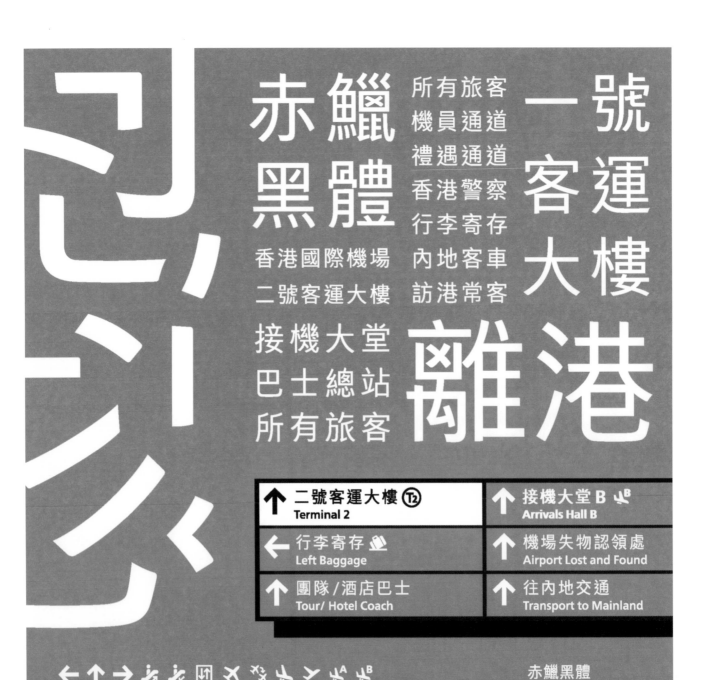

赤鱲黑體
Chek Lap Sans

接機大堂

行李寄存

外幣找換

T1 一號客運大樓 →
Terminal 1

↑ 旅客登記行段
Check-in Aisles

← 團隊 / 酒店巴士
Tour/ Hotel Coach

洗手間 →
Toilets

貴賓室 →
Lounges

歡迎蒞臨香港

離港

往市區

行李包裝服務

機場郵政局

二號客運大樓 T2

香港國際航空學校

赤鱲

黑體

所有旅客

機員通道

巴士總站

內地客車

閘口

赤鱲黑體

Chek Lap Sans

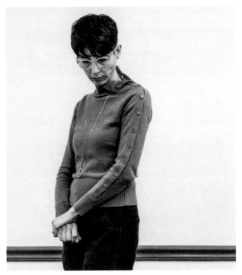

Nicole Dotin

When considering students' work, you're looking at what's directly in front of you but also hoping to get a peek into their future. Pyk is an accomplished piece of design. It manages to be quirky, energetic, and full of character without sacrificing the harmony that must be maintained for a well-functioning typeface.

With its unusual angular shapes, this is no small feat. Step back and you'll see a designer developing her voice, choosing an uncommon path. If Pyk is indicative of Erica's future, then we'd be lucky to see more.

Nicole Dotin

Pyk

Typeface Design
Erica Carras°
New York

Instructor
Hannes Famira

School
Type@Cooper
2018

URL
typographic.design

Instagram
@tinytypo

Pyk was inspired by Helmut Salden's brush lettering, and the process of uniting a running hand (italic) system of calligraphy into an upright text face gave Pyk its unconventional letter shapes.

The traditionally round **o**, **e**, **c**, and **s** instead follow a triangular model, echoing the countershape of the **n** and the bouncing upstrokes that connect the stems. This upward motion directs the eye forward and creates an even diagonal rhythm across the line of text.

To increase legibility as a typeface, Pyk has low-contrast, uniform letter widths and generous spacing. Pyk stands at the crossroads between calligraphy and type design, with a bounce in its step.

Erica Carras

Light

ABCDEFGHIJKLMNOPQRSTUVWXYZabcdefghijklm nopqrsttuvwxyz0123456789------&()[]{}|\/'"''""".,:;…!¡?¿

Medium

A Å Á B C Ç D E Ę F G H I Ì Í Î Ï Ĩ Ī Ĭ İ J K Ķ L Ľ M N O Ò Ó Ô Õ Ö Ō Ŏ Ő Ø Œ P Q R S T U Ų V W X Y Z Æ Ð Þ Ð Ħ Ł Ŀ Ŋ Ŧ a å ą æ á b c ç d ď đ þ e ə f g h ħ i j k ĸ l ľ ŀ ł m n ñ o ò ó ô õ ö ō ŏ ő ø ơ p q r s t ť ţ ŧ u ù v w x y z z ß ı ŋ œ ŋ 0 1 2 3 4 5 6 7 8 9 _ - - — ( ) [ ] { } # % ' " ' ' " " , „ ‹ › « » * † ‡ . , : ; … ! ¡ i ? ¿ ¿ ¿ ? / \ | @ & ϟ ϟ · · + − ± = < > ≤ ≥ ˊ ˋ ˆ ˇ ˘ ˜ ˉ ˙ ¨ ° , ¸ © ™ ° fi fl ff tt & tt tt ↑ ↓ ↖ ↗ ↙ ↘ → ←

Black

ABCDEFGHIJKLMNOPQRSTUVWXYZabcdef ghijklmnopqrstuvwxyz------&()[]{}*«»ϟϟ"''""".,:;…!¡?¿

Light	Medium	Black
NOT INVITED!? →Was justified So Pop-culture Mainstream & Hoodie Pockets Non algorithm Cassette tapes Brainwashing?	DOWNBEATS! @250 Vixen St. ft. lo-fi battles: Quarrelsome ‡ Judi Hooliganz + Synthesizers Punk Millenial ϟwearing pink	The UPBEATS ‡U Hooliganz Brainwashed, Heavy Metals Fin.Orchestra Go finagling!? Equipment In ϟ Discoteques*

Pyk manages to be quirky, energetic, and full of character without sacrificing the harmony that must be maintained for a well-functioning typeface.

DOWNBEATS!
@ 250 Vixen St.
ft. lo-fi battles:
Quarrelsome ϟ
Judi Hooliganz
+ Synthesizers
Punk Millenial
ϟ wearing pink

Tobias Frere-Jones

Crochet begins with the textface from a French pocketbook published in 1887. To revive this Perle-size typeface for modern uses, I learned that the solution was not a direct auto trace. The end result preserves the original face's skeleton and restores its quirky details from ink spreads, while still maintaining the warmth and elegance of a letterpressed page.

Crochet is readable and intriguing to look at, which makes it suitable for typesetting long, small (8–10pt) text. Fun little details also suggest a potential display use.

You Lu

You Lu's Crochet is a revival and remodeling of Louis XV from Fonderie Turlot of Paris. It shows a sophisticated sense of how to work with historical precedent: what to keep and what to leave behind in working with past sources.

In any revival, but especially one that uses a small size from an old source (around 5pt, from a book published in 1887), it's tempting to become ensnared in the bumps and wobbles of each shape. But Lu does a good job of looking through that noise and considering the shapes underneath.

The original Louis XV was an oddball design, pushing curves into a squarish profile so that many letters begin to resemble cobblestones. With so much similarity in the shapes, it relied on loose spacing to be legible. Lu made those blocky curves relax a bit, just enough to reset the spacing and vastly improve its usability. There was a nervous quality in the original—even cranky—but the slightly softened corners also soften the voice. Even so, the French style and formality is still there, tasting as much of the Belle Époque as the present day.

When revivals keep their focus on the big picture, they can improve on the original and still be accurate. Crochet is a promising (and successful) example of that approach.

Tobias Frere-Jones

Crochet

Typeface Design
You Lu°
Brooklyn,
New York

Instagram
@youahyou

Professor
Hannes F. Famira

School
Type@Cooper
Extended Program

ÀăBbÇcDdEêFfGgHhIiJj
KkLĿLİMmNñØoPpQqRř
ȘsTtŲůVvWwXxYỳŽz
?&ﬃß¢;""«Æœ0123456789
Crochet Typeface

ÀăBbÇcDdEêFfGgHhIiJj
KkLĿLİMmNñØoPpQqRř
ȘsTtŲůVvWwXxYỳŽz
?&ﬃß¢;""«Æœ0123456789

There was a nervous quality in the original—even cranky—but the slightly softened corners also soften the voice.

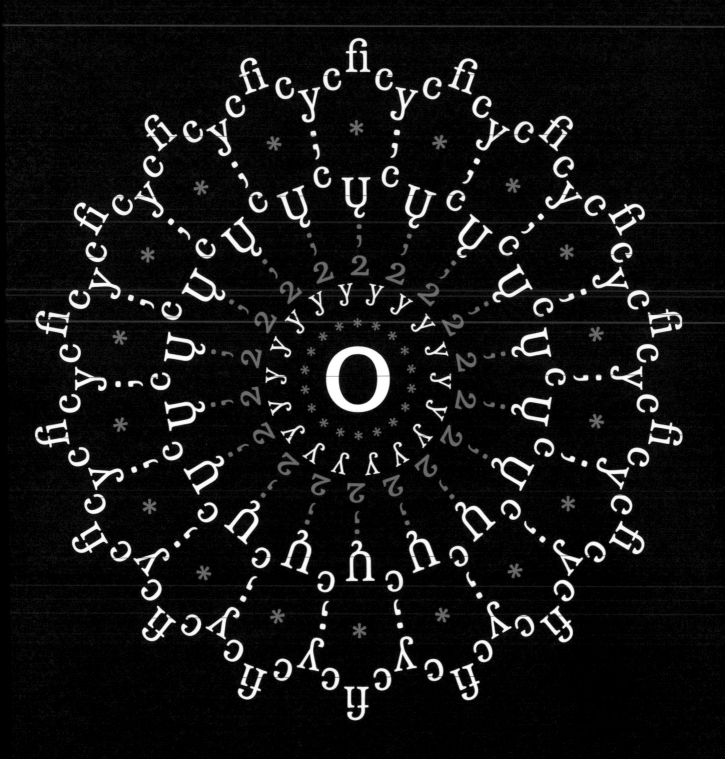

Erin McLaughlin

In a reverse-contrast typeface, the normal weight distribution is reversed. The result is that the weight becomes concentrated along the cap-height, x-height, and baseline, creating a strong horizontal visual connection. Unlike with the Latin alphabet, the weight distribution in Kanji and Kana is much more complex, and not just on the verticals.

Many strokes are diagonal or curved, so the weight distribution varies on different strokes. Simply reversing the weight distribution may not create the same visual result as in the Latin one. Instead of reversing the weight literally, my approach is to create a typeface that captures the visual essence of the Latin reverse contrast. That essence is the quirky personality and strong horizontal connection; thus, both can work together in a visually compatible way.

Tien-Min Liao

This project drew me in like a magnet. It's not often that you get to see a boisterous, reverse-contrast display typeface elegantly executed in four writing systems. Harmonizing scripts with differing calligraphic traditions is no easy feat, and a majority of the industry's recent attempts have succeeded only by reducing these differences as much as possible, via a low-contrast approach.

This project, instead, turned the challenge on its head, by tackling a high-contrast, detail-rich style that must fully consider and respect the differing structures and densities of each writing system. The Latin-based, horizontally stressed design formula had to be adapted to suit the fluid, organic forms of Hiragana; the stark, angular shapes of Katakana; and the structured, often extremely complex Kanji.

Its careful balancing of weight, the smart handling of negative space, the designer's deep understanding and respect of the structure of the letterforms, and the infusion of just the right recipe of detail and quirkiness have resulted in a masterfully executed work that type designers can look up to. It's also a project whose exciting, exuberant forms can be noticed and appreciated by anyone—no matter their level of typographic knowledge. For these reasons, I feel that this project firmly stands as one of the world's best examples of typeface design.

Erin McLaughlin

Ribaasu

Typeface Design
Tien-Min Liao
New York

URL
typeji.com

Twitter
@typeji

Latin, かな & 漢字

Google Home は Google music と Spotify に たいおうしています。

It's not often that you get to see a boisterous, reverse-contrast display typeface elegantly executed in four writing systems.

すること

York ニューヨ

ニョーニ

麗して

mography を学べる

Tokyo 東

して成長するた…

tin, カナ＆漢字

Kristyan Sarkis

Orientation was designed in 2015. It was commissioned by the graphic designer Thanh Phong Lê as a way-finding project for new student housing. Because the type would be painted onto a building, one of the constraints was to make a stencil. This fact defined the identity of the typeface and justified the opened slanted cut.

Another request was to design a geometric typeface that would fit with brutalism architecture. I enjoyed playing with legibility of signs: On their own some letters could look abstract, but when they composed a word the result became readable. Orientation was developed with other weights (Bold, Regular, and Light) and styles (Roman and Italic) and is released by Commercial Type.

Sandrine Nugue

Orientation represents everything I am interested in and excited about when it comes to type design: a clear understanding of the writing system at hand, experimenting with novel ideas, and having fun in the process.

To begin with, its striking forms are not made out of loose aesthetic tricks; this level of abstraction is the result of a deep understanding of the core elements of the letterforms and a decidedly novel approach to stenciling. The smart—and in many instances, unusual—choices Sandrine made in how to abstract the forms and where to cut the letters make Orientation read very smoothly while boasting a dramatic 3D-like texture of light and shadows (Є, N, Y).

These characteristics are delicately and seamlessly brought to all the weights and their respective italics, giving them just enough different personalities to create a more dynamic range within one consistent type family.

And last, it is quite clear that Sandrine had fun drawing these playful forms (especially M, W, K, and several others), and that adds even more charm to Orientation. Fun did not, however, get in the way of drawing clear and direct forms that do their job very well, especially in wayfinding contexts.

Orientation is the kind of typeface that makes me want to design an Arabic counterpart for it.

Kristyan Sarkis

Orientation

**Typeface Design
Sandrine Nugue
Paris**

**Twitter
@SNugue**

**Client
Thanh Phong Lê and
Bathilde Millet
Architects**

**Foundry
Commercial Type**

Bogotá to Kyoto
14.326,73 km

Orientation represents everything I am interested in and excited about when it comes to type design.

Kalmuck

THEORY

Capacity

Telúrica

FORSØK

Measure

k — Zangezi Sans Black by Daria Petrova
L — Galapagos A Regular by Felix Salut

22nd TDC Typeface Design Winners

ADOBE TELUGU

Concept Adobe Telugu is a typeface tailored specifically for usage in print while made to also render crisply on screen. Harmonizing with Robert Slimbach's Minion, which is used for the Latin portion of the character set, Valentin Brustaux's design for the Telugu script shows his own masterful touch, drawing from traditional manuscript forms and shaped for contemporary use.

Typeface Design
Valentin Brustaux (Telugu) and Robert Slimbach (Latin)

Project Manager and Production Engineer
Paul Hunt

Advisor
Fiona Ross

URL
fonts.adobe.com/foundries/adobe

Foundry
Adobe Originals

కెక్కికెక్ష్లూక్క్ష్
రైరొర్తర్ర్థింతరి
జ్జిజ్జొజ్జూజైజః
పూప్పుపిప
ఇిఇ్ఇొఇుఇ్లొ

హాహ్హాహౌహిహి
ద్దెధథధిచద్దేఢ
ఴిఴ్లుఴైఴూ
గెగిగ్గిగూగః
పపిపెపీప్హపా

యొగా

అంటే వ్యాయామ సాధనల సమాహారాల ఆధ్యాత్మిక రూపం. ఇది హిందుత్వ అధ్యాత్మిక సాధనలలో ఒక భాగం. మొక్షసాధనలో భాగమైన ధ్యానం అంతఃదృష్టి, పరమానంద ప్రాప్తి లాంటి అధ్యాత్మిక పరమైన సాధనలకు పునాది. దీనిని సాధన చేసే వాళ్ళను యోగులు అంటారు. వీరు సాధారణ సంఘ జీవితానికి దూరంగా మునులు సన్యాసులవలె అడవులలో ఆశ్రమ జీవితం గడు-పుతూ సాధన శిక్షణ లాంటివి

ధ్యానయోగం ఆధ్యాత్మిక సాధనకు మానసిక ఆరోగ్యానికి చక్కగా తోడ్పడుతుంది. హఠయోగ-ములో భాగమైన శారీరకమైన ఆసనాలు శరీరారోగ్యానికి తోడ్పడి ఔషధాల వాడకాన్ని తగ్గించి దేహధారుఢ్యాన్ని, ముఖ వర్చస్సున ఇనుమడింప చేస్తుంది. బుద్ధమతం, జైనమతం సిక్కుమతం మొదలైన ధార్మిక మతాలలోనూ, ఇతర ఆధ్యాత్మిక సాధనలలోను దీని ప్రాధాన్యత కనిపిస్తుంది.

పులి Puli   ఏనుగు Ēnugu
గాడిద Gāḍida   ఎద్దు Eddu

మౌస్ Maus   డక్ Ḍak
గాడిద Gāḍida   డాల్ఫిన్ Ḍālphin

JALI

Concept Jali is a way-finding signage typeface designed to achieve optimum legibility by combining two widely used scripts: Latin and Arabic. The concept started as a graduation project motivated by the lack of Arabic typefaces that successfully serve signages. The project was positioned for the market and redesigned with the URW foundry offering extensive help to make the type family reach its maximum potential in both the scripts. Jali literally translates to "clear." It is a low-contrast sans serif with large counters, distinguishable dots and marks, and compact ascenders and descenders to enhance legibility, especially when viewed from a distance. With its distinct humanistic voice, Jali aims to warmly welcome its readers and efficiently direct them to their destinations. Jali has an Arabic Display companion that is highly characterized to add a memorable identity. Aimed to be an attractive yet easily readable style, it borrows features from both the decorative Diwani and the conventional Naskh calligraphic styles.

Typeface Design
Mohamad Dakak
Cambridge,
United Kingdom

Reviewer
Gerry Leonidas°

Professors
Gerry Leonidas,
Fiona Ross,
and Gerard Unger

Members of Type Family
Weights and styles:
Extra Light, Light, Regular, Medium, DemiBold, Bold, Extra Bold, and Display

استلام الأمتعة
Baggage Claim

Ground Floor الطابق الأرضي

Departures المغادرون

Central Metro Station محطة المترو الرئيسية

Oman Airways • WY667 • 14:20

Permanent Galleries المعارض الدائمة

Kuala Lumpur كوالا لمبور

GLIKO MODERN

Concept Gliko Modern is a legible and economical text typeface made for editorial design. The family offers thirty fonts divided into three optical sizes: S for body text, M for medium-sized headlines, and L for large headlines and titles. The design goes back and forth between the sturdy elegance of late seventeenth- and eighteenth-century Dutch Old Style types, and the delicacy and extreme rationalization of the Didot style that came after.

Typeface Design
Rui Abreu
Lisbon

URL
r-typography.com

Twitter
@rui_abreu

Type Foundry
R-Typography

Coffee
Waltz
Reading
Bossa
Ginza

RIZADO SCRIPT

Concept   Rizado Script is a classy one-weight typeface made with "dolce vita" in mind. Its high contrast and pointy tone recall the fine nib handwriting of a meticulous and decisive person who has no free time to spare but surely knows how to enjoy life. Instead of quick and dry strokes, there is a wide, elegant, and strong-minded temper that will bring a long-lasting touch to your packaging layouts. Rizado also works well for a more ephemeral design, such as a weekend high-class cocktail promotion or a wedding invitation.

Typeface Design
Nikola Kostić
Belgrade, Serbia

URL
kostictype.com

Twitter
@kostictype

Type Foundry
Kostić Type Foundry

Rizado Script

Prosecco, Aperol & Soda Water

Aperol Spritz

Rizado Script

Prosecco, Aperol

& Soda Water

SERIF UI

Concept **The New York type family works seamlessly across user interfaces, marketing, and editorial. It supports over a hundred languages using Latin, Greek, and Cyrillic scripts. Its stylistic range covers uprights and italics, as well as weights from Regular to Black. Variation axes offer versatility and aid legibility by allowing the font weight and contrast to be crafted at every point size. This gives it the ability to perform as a traditional reading typeface at small sizes and transition to a more graphic, elegant design at larger sizes.**

Typeface Design
**Apple Design Team
Cupertino, California**

Members of the
Typeface Family
New York Text Black, New York Text Black Italic, New York Text Bold, New York Text Bold Italic, New York Text Heavy, New York Text Heavy Italic, New York Text Medium, New York Text Medium Italic, New York Text Regular, New York Text Regular Italic, New York Text Semibold, and New York Text Semibold Italic

New York Display Black, New York Display Black Italic, New York Display Bold, New York Display Bold Italic, New York Display Heavy, New York Display Heavy Italic, New York Display Medium, New York Display Medium Italic, New York Display Regular, New York Display Regular Italic, New York Display Semibold, and New York Display Semibold Italic

ABCDEFGHIJK
LMNOPQRSTU
VWXYZ**abcdef
ghijklmnopqrs
tuvwxyz**123456
7890

MINÉRALE

Concept Minérale was imagined as a geometrical exaggeration of the structure of serifs, where the central part of the vertical stems is thinned. This phenomenon is pushed to the extreme: Rather than a flared rectangle, the stem becomes two triangles joined at the tips, creating a clear, almost luminous zone at the center. Sober in its thinnest versions, Minérale becomes more exuberant in its thicker versions: The axis is tilted, resulting in a silhouette close to the "italians," with reversed contrast. All permutations are possible because all of the weights occupy the same space. Minérale also exists as a variable font.

Typeface Design
Thomas Huot-Marchand
Lyon

Design Firm
205TF

URL
205.tf

Twitter
@205Corp

Minérale ✦ Minérale italic
Thomas Huot-Marchand

France
205.tf

TF 205 ®

MINÉRALE

PLOMB

EXTRALIGHT LIGHT   MEDIUM   BOLD   BLACK

Anatase   Cassitérite   Corindon
Brookite   Chrysobéryl

MINÉRALE ITALIC

OPALE

EXTRALIGHT   LIGHT   MEDIUM   BOLD   BLACK
ITALIC   ITALIC   ITALIC   ITALIC ITALIC

Autunite   Phosphates   Monazite
Apatite   Brazilianite

ALSO AVAILABLE AS A VARIABLE FONT

NO MOLESTAR!

Concept **Fox Channel trusted us to design a custom font for its No Molestar! animation program block, which includes The Simpsons. For the rebranding we suggested the development of a sans serif system with a DNA that responded to the block's personality: irreverent, cocky, absurd. So we built up an inverted contrast display family with notable color and open counterforms. It consists of two display fonts: Condensed for high impact and Expanded to stand out. In addition, an authentic cursive Script reinforces the inverted contrast core, and a full set of icons serves as a complement to build different types of compositions.**

Typeface Design
**Yanina Arabena
and Guillermo Vizzari°
Buenos Aires**

Art Direction
Nicolás Sarsotti

VP
André Takeda

Manufacturers/
Distributors
Yani & Guille

URL
yaniguille.com

Twitter
@yaniandguille

Client
**Fox Latin American
Channel LLC**

Members of the
Typeface Family
**Condensed, Expanded,
Script, and Icons**

2019 *Buenos Aire*

No Molestar

This is the Do Not Disturb –No Molestar– type fam

A Sans Serif family t

STAND OUT

ncluding an awesome cursive italic version t

we call the Scrip

oing legible but at the same tim

LE MURMURE

Concept The Murmure font plays on a skillful mismatch between characters, creating a unique rhythm that carries our voice. This fruitful and enriching collaboration strengthens Murmure's graphic and collaborative vision to undertake singular and sensitive projects. Used as a titling font, it is paired with a text font, the Prophet typeface (from the Dinamo Foundry). Its height and the stability of its shapes lend it elegance, while details inspired by calligraphy and technique reveal all of Murmure's notions of experimentation, research, and creativity. The Murmure font is a typeface devoid of serifs that combines effectiveness, legibility, and singularity. Its highly condensed proportions draw their inspiration from magazine titling fonts and add the editorial dimension with which we wished to endow our new identity.

Typeface Design
**Julien Alirol,
Jeremy Landes,
and Paul Ressencourt
Caen, France**

Art Direction
**Julien Alirol
and Paul Ressencourt**

Typographer
Jeremy Landes

URL
murmure.me

Twitter
@agencemurmure

Agency
Murmure

Le Zozoteur

MOWHOAK

MOWHOAK

MOWHOAK

PUNTA DISPLAY

Concept   This is a contemporary high-contrast serif family characterized by extremely sharp and pointy details. Upright styles are elegant and condensed, partly drawing inspiration from the work of Claude Garamond. Italics emphasize a broad nib contrast even more, bringing warmth with their combination of tense curves and sharp details. The type family ranges from Regular to Black with corresponding italics. Unique texture, large lowercases, and compact spacing help this typeface perform well in titles, headlines, and shorter passages of text in bigger sizes.

Typeface Design
Marko Hrastovec
Zagreb, Croatia

Twitter
@markhrast

Instagram
@hotfonts

Design Firm
Hot Type

Entblößen

ATSIŲSTOSE

Tomatoroña

Hűtőszekrények

POMYKALO

forårsjævndøgn

Râge|or

GUSTELLA

Concept Gustella is a masterful design that explores the field of extreme reverse contrast in multiple variations: Solid, Striped, Inline. The design benefits from Thiemich's playful-calculated approach to design, but also the precision the digital technology allows for nowadays. So with these ingredients in the background, Gustella has the contrast "volume" turned up to the maximum, making it a juicy and multifaceted typeface with which to design.

Typeface Design
**Thomas Thiemich
Antwerp**

URL
typeby.com

Foundry
TYPE BY

Members of Type Family
**Gustella Boxed,
Gustella Inline,
Gustella Solid,
and Gustella Striped**

PILAT

Concept Pilat is a constructed grotesque developed with a large range of weight and width variations. Its base structure, commonly called a "superellipse" or "Lamé curve," could be described as a circle trapped inside a box. Though the letter-shape predates the twentieth century, it is mostly seen as an expression of the post–World War II era, a glorifying combination of craft and technology.

Typeface Design
Stéphane Elbaz
New York

Type Foundry
General Type Studio

URL
generaltypestudio.com

Twitter
@general_type

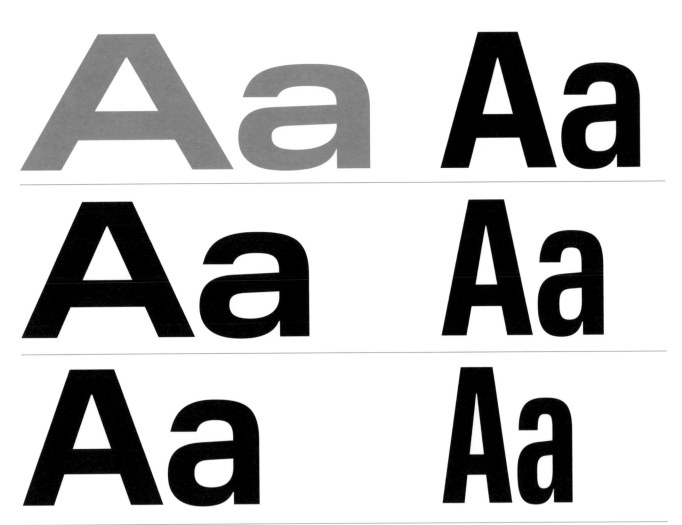

Pilat Extended Thin	Pilat Narrow Thin
Pilat Extended Light	Pilat Light
Pilat Extended Regular	Pilat Regular
Pilat Extended Book	Pilat Book
Pilat Extended Demi	Pilat Demi
Pilat Extended Bold	**Pilat Bold**
Pilat Extended Heavy	**Pilat Heavy**
Pilat Extended Black	**Pilat Black**

Pilat Wide Thin	Pilat Thin	Pilat Condensed Thin	Pilat Compressed Thin
Pilat Wide Light	Pilat Light	Pilat Light	Pilat Light
Pilat Wide Regular	Pilat Regular	Pilat Regular	Pilat Regular
Pilat Wide Book	Pilat Book	Pilat Book	Pilat Book
Pilat Wide Demi	**Pilat Demi**	Pilat Demi	Pilat Demi
Pilat Wide Bold	**Pilat Bold**	**Pilat Bold**	**Pilat Bold**
Pilat Wide Heavy	**Pilat Heavy**	**Pilat Heavy**	**Pilat Heavy**
Pilat Wide Black	**Pilat Black**	**Pilat Black**	**Pilat Black**

HOPE SANS

Concept The Hope Sans typeface is a throwback to the type styles of the 1970s, with most of the family's characters offering swash alternates that enable almost limitless combinations for designers. Designed by Charles Nix of the Monotype Studio, this versatile sans serif comes in six weights. The typeface's large counters and open spacing allow it to work effortlessly across a range of environments—including digital, print, text, headlines, editorial, advertising, and branding.

Typeface Design
Charles Nix°
Woburn, Massachusetts

Type Foundry
Monotype

URL
monotype.com

Twitter
@Monotype
@ChasNix

Members of the
Typeface Family
Hope Sans,
Hope Sans Bold,
Hope Sans Bold Italic,
Hope Sans Italic,
Hope Sans Light,
Hope Sans Light Italic,
Hope Sans Regular,
Hope Sans Semibold,
Hope Sans
Semibold Italic,

Hope Sans Thin,
Hope Sans Thin Italic,
Hope Sans Ultra Light,
and Hope Sans Ultra
Light Italic

The Vogue of the Victoria

Astronaut Breakfast Game

Throughout the Caribbean

Dad's first light

kyward!

Fly the Sapphire Service to Ceylon

Jämtland: Province of mountains, falls, forests, and endless summer nights in the middle of Sweden!

Let yourself go!

See what we saw on a Flagship Tour (in just 2 weeks!)

These three international commuters use one timetable.

You'll love Joan Davis!

It's Super Constellation 4 to 1

Cruise the skies with Affordable Luxury.

How to make the smallest problem out of travelling with little ones

Across the Pacific and to South America

Extra hands assure extra luxuries on Delta Ray Service Flights

Les Belles Vacances

V roce 1941 pracoval nejprve jako truhlář, pak byl nasazen k práci na stavbě železniční vlečky; záhy však za pomoci přátel ze Skupiny 42 získal místo číšníka.

Enjoy the Holiday!

"...and all I did was...call the Businessman's Airline"

LANDING HAS NEVER BEEN SO BITTERSWEET.

Hawaii is only 22⅓ Mainliner Hours from Chicago!

HELDANE

Concept Heldane is a contemporary serif family inspired by the renaissance works of Hendrik van den Keere, Claude Garamond, Robert Granjon, and Simon de Colines. Rather than emulating a specific font, Heldane amalgamates the best details from these sources into a cohesive whole. The classical typographic foundations of Heldane are refined with rigorous digital drawing.

Typeface Design
Kris Sowersby°
Wellington,
New Zealand

Foundry
Klim Type Foundry

Engineer
Noe Blanco
Spain

URL
klim.co.nz

Typography

Ys. Le Fevre

Gault–1561

Humanists

Lambrecht

Antiquité

FR KRAKEN SLAB

Concept FR Kraken Slab is a mild-mannered monster of a typeface with a sturdy skeleton, characteristic features, and a powerful personality. The goal was to create a contemporary design inspired by the raw and lively looks of the nineteenth-century English Antiques. It aims to encapsulate the spirit of those models and delivers more than just a digital reproduction of any particular design from that period. FR Kraken Slab, like a portrait of an old friend drawn from memory, captures and truthfully redefines the character of a well-known style.

Typeface Design
Béla Frank
Budapest

Type Foundry
Frank Fonts

URL
frankfonts.com

Twitter
@Frank_Fonts

Members of the
Typeface Family
FR Kraken Slab Bold,
Black and Heavy, Light,
Regular, Medium,
SemiBold, and Thin

ABCDEFGHIJKLM
NOPQRSTUVWXYZ
abcdefghijklmnop
qrstuvwxyz01234
56789!"£$%^&*()+,-.
ÀÁÂÃÄÅÆÇÈÉÊË
ÌÍÎÏÐÑÒÓÔÕÖØÙÚ
ÛÜÝÞßàààáâãã
äååæçèéêëìíîïð
ñòôõö÷øùúûüýýþ
ÿÿĀāāĂăăĄąąĆćĎ

FAUNE

Concept Faune explores the plurality of the animal world and the diversity of its morphologies. It is based on two magistral reference works that were produced by the French Imprimerie Nationale: Histoire Naturelle by Buffon (1749–1788) and Description de l'Égypte, commissioned by the Emperor Napoleon I (1809–1830). Three categories of animals found in these books (reptiles, birds, and mammals) formed the basis for a heteroclite typographic grammar:

A sinewy viper inspired the design of the Display Thin variant, while a stocky ram dictated the design of the Display Black and a black ibis gave rise to the very particular design of the Display Italic. These three founding members of the type family were then rendered "genetically compatible" through an interpolation process that resulted in three hybrid variants (Text Regular, Italic, and Bold), which are perfectly adapted to continuous reading at text sizes.

Typeface Design
Alice Savoie
Lyon and Paris

Kerning and Font Mastering
Roxane Gataud

Illustrations
Marine Rivoal

Design and Development of the Micro-Site
Prototypo.io

URL
frenchtype.com

Twitter
@alicesavoie

Typeface Family Micro-Site
cnap.graphismeenfrance. fr/faune

Client
Centre National des Arts Plastique & Imprimerie Nationale

SIG

Concept Sig is a revival of Rudolf Koch's typeface Wallau, which was a hybrid between blackletter and antiqua. Sig reinterprets Wallau, moving it a bit closer to antiqua and extending it to Cyrillic and Greek. Sig was designed during the first semester of the TypeMedia master course. The Latin was designed for Paul van der Laan's class, the Cyrillic for Ilya Ruderman's class, and the Greek for Peter Bil'ak's class.

Typeface Design
Ethan Cohen
New York

URL
ethancohenstudio.com

Twitter
@ethanac

Instagram
@ethancohenstudio

School
Royal Academy of Art,
The Hague (TypeMedia)

бефстроганов
Quesadillas
Бородинский хлеб
Gefilte Fish
χωριάτικη σαλάτα
Bagels & Lox
Окрошка на кефире
Anchovies
γίγαντες πλακί

SANDWICH

Concept Sandwich is a flared sans serif typeface family that emphasizes the horizontal strokes of the letterforms. It aims to subvert the conventions of thicks and thins without entirely throwing them out the window. It is a versatile family designed to be used both in small contexts such as a guitar pick or liner notes and in display contexts such as an album cover.

Typeface Design
**Varissara Mew Ophaswongse
San Francisco**

URL
typecooperwest2018. com/mew

Instructors
James Edmondson, Frank Grießhammer, and Tânia Raposo

School
Type@Cooper West

Members of the Typeface Family
**Hoagie,
Lettuce Italic,
Lettuce Regular,
Sandwich Bold,
Sandwich Italic,
and Sandwich Regular**

Hoagie   **Hoagie**

Sandwich   **Sandwich**

Sandwich   Sandwich

Sandwich   *Sandwich*

Sandwich   Sandwich

Sandwich   Sandwich

Sandwich   *Sandwich*

Lettuce   Lettuce

Lettuce   *Lettuce*